Nabokov and the Russian Provisional Government

Photograph of V. D. Nabokov taken on
February 17, 1922. Courtesy of V. V. Nabokov.

V. D. NABOKOV
and the Russian Provisional
Government, 1917

Edited by
Virgil D. Medlin and Steven L. Parsons

Introduction by Robert P. Browder

New Haven and London, Yale University Press, 1976

Published with assistance from the
foundation established in memory
of William McKean Brown.

Library of Congress catalog card number: 75-18177
International standard book number: 0-300-01820-7

Designed by John O. C. McCrillis
and set in Times Roman type.
Printed in the United States of America by
The Vail-Ballou Press, Inc., Binghamton, N.Y.

Published in Great Britain, Europe, and Africa by
Yale University Press, Ltd., London.
Distributed in Latin America by Kaiman & Polon,
Inc., New York City; in Australasia by Book
& Film Services, Artamon, N.S.W., Australia;
in India by UBS Publishers' Distributors Pvt.,
Ltd., Delhi; in Japan by John Weatherhill, Inc., Tokyo.

Contents

Frontispiece: Photograph of V. D. Nabokov   ii

Editorial Note   vii

Introduction, Robert P. Browder   1

V. D. Nabokov in 1917, Baron B. E. Nol'de   13

1   The Provisional Government, V. D. Nabokov   33

2   The Bolshevik Coup D'État, V. D. Nabokov   143

Index   179

Editorial Note

Over a decade ago Kenneth I. Dailey, our friend, colleague, and former teacher, suggested that we undertake an English-language edition of V. D. Nabokov's memoir, "Vremennoe Pravitel'stvo" ("The Provisional Government"). We began with a preliminary draft translation supplied to Dailey by a Russian princess, but quickly discarded it as too abridged and free in its rendering of the Russian into English. Pressed as we were by other commitments, the Nabokov translation became a highly intermittent project. Throughout it all Professor Dailey encouraged us to continue the translation, read our drafts, and, as the author of a lengthy, unpublished study of the Provisional Government, gave us criticisms and invaluable aid. As the manuscript neared completion, Vladimir V. Nabokov offered us his services. He read the entire manuscript, made a flood of corrections, and offered numerous helpful suggestions with all phases of the preparation and publication of this edition. His continued encouragement over the past three years supported us through a period of time when a chain of complications arose and hindered the project.

We are also deeply indebted to Robert P. Browder, who not only interrupted his busy schedule to supply the introduction, but also offered many helpful suggestions throughout the manuscript. Herbert Marshall gave us the benefit of his expertise in rendering into English some of the more difficult Russian passages. We also wish to express our appreciation to Dragan Milivojevich, Ben May, and Gloria Parker, who have helped in the preparation of this book in one way or another. Finally, we wish to thank Vladimir Gessen (Hessen), heir of the publisher of the Russian-language original, for his endorsement of this edition.

We have prefaced Nabokov's "The Provisional Government"

with a short sketch of Nabokov in 1917 by his close associate, Baron Boris Emmanuilovich Nol'de (1876–1948), an eminent historian, educator, and jurist. Baron Nol'de served as chief legal adviser to the Imperial Ministry of Foreign Affairs prior to 1917, and in 1917 served as undersecretary of state for foreign affairs and as a member of the Juridical Council. The Nabokov and Nol'de works derive from the liberal, Russian-language, emigré historical journal, *Archives of the Russian Revolution,* published in Berlin between 1921 and 1937.

The Julian or Old Style (O.S.) calendar (which was thirteen days behind the Western Gregorian, or New Style, calendar in 1917) is preserved throughout for dating events, in order to conform to Nabokov's usage of it. Occasionally Nabokov used both calendars so, October 25/November 7, thereby indicating both the Julian and the Gregorian dates; we have retained this usage in the text and have occasionally used it in editorial notes. The Library of Congress system of transliteration from Russian, minus ligatures and diacritical marks, has been used throughout the book. Names, however, which are commonly written otherwise, remain unchanged here, for example, Trotsky, not Trotskii.

We assume all responsibility for any errors in translation or editing that remain in the work.

V. D. M.
S. L. P.

Oklahoma City
January 7, 1975

Introduction

Vladimir Dmitrievich Nabokov's memoir of the Russian Provisional Government in 1917 is a primary document of major historical importance. Its immense value to students of the period may be ascribed to a number of factors. Although not published until 1921, the manuscript was completed while the author's recollections were fresh in his mind. For the most part he made no effort to recount or analyze events beyond his immediate knowledge. His position as Head of Chancellery of the government for half of its brief existence provided him with a unique observation post. In that capacity he was privy to, but not a participant in, its decision-making, a role he found frustrating but which enabled him to make a more lasting contribution to the history of the revolution than many ministers whose names and deeds have faded into obscurity. He also served on the Juridical Council, which advised the ministry on legal matters, on the special council for drafting the electoral laws to the Constituent Assembly, and on the subsequent Electoral Commission. He was in the Pre-parliament and, throughout, an influential member of the Executive Committee of the Kadet Party. But these fortunate circumstances would not have been so effectively employed without the talents, temperament, and character of Nabokov himself.

Significantly, all shades of later political writing on the revolution by participants and historians reflect confidence in the integrity and judiciousness of his account. Leon Trotsky pronounced it "truthful" and utilized it extensively in his monumental history of the revolution. A. F. Kerensky, who received rather acid treatment by the author, relied upon it in many of his publications. Less surprisingly, the Kadet leader P. N. Miliukov, who himself does not emerge unscathed from its pages, referred to the article as "an indispensable aid in acquainting oneself with the members and earliest activities of the first government of the revolution.'' Many other examples might be cited from emigré commentators and non-Russian historians. Amongst the diatribes, apologies, justifications, and partisan narratives of that chaotic time, his clear, cool, though certainly not uncritical, report is exceptional for the fairness and care with which it delineates events and assesses the actors in the great drama of 1917. Everyone who has had occasion to use this graphic and informative chronicle is in Nabokov's debt.

V. D. Nabokov was born on July 20, 1870, near Tsarskoe Selo on one of the country estates belonging to his family, which had been long distinguished for military and civil service to the state. The founder of the line was a fourteenth-century Russianized Tartar prince, Nabok Murza. His descendents held lands near Moscow and served the grand princes and tsars in various capacities as their fatherland grew from principality to world power, thus linking them to many of the great events in their nation's history. Nabokov's father was minister of justice under both Alexander II and Alexander III, a troubled time of changing political currents from reform to oppressive reaction, during which he tried to steer a course that would salvage some of the advances of his first master from the atavism of his second. The author's mother was the daughter of Baron Ferdinand Nichlaus Viktor von Korff, of German origin, whose family was prominent in the Russian army and bureaucracy. Among Nabokov's three brothers and five sisters one is deserving of note here—Konstantin, who ended his professional diplomatic career as chargé d'affaires in London representing the Provisional Government, which he came to deplore, to an increasingly disenchanted and uninformed ally.

After private tutoring at home, Nabokov made an enviable record at the gymnasium and entered the University of St. Petersburg, where he graduated in law in 1891. Following further study at Halle in Germany, he returned to Russia, married Elena Ivanovna Rukavishnikova, and accepted the post, which he held until 1904, of lecturer in criminal law at the Imperial School of Jurisprudence in St. Petersburg. It was during this period that his later well-developed political views became evident. An article condemning the Kishinev pogrom of 1903 led to the deprivation of his court rank. He indicated his indifference to this action by advertising his court uniform for sale in the daily papers.

In 1904–05 Nabokov was deeply involved in the liberation movement. One of the four sessions of the famous Zemstvo Congress was held in his home in early November 1904. It will be recalled that this congress drafted and presented to the government demands which were a milestone on the road to the October Manifesto: freedom of speech, press, and assembly, as well as public participation in legislation. By July 1905, with the revolution deepening, Nabokov was urging the opposition "to defend the natural rights by all peaceful means, not excluding disobedience to the orders of the authority which violates these rights," a harbinger of imminent events.

Following the October Manifesto and its promise of a legislative assembly, Nabokov became quite naturally a member of the newly formed Constitutional Democratic (Kadet) Party, which was to be the dominant voice of political opposition in prerevolutionary Russia. He served from the beginning on its Central Committee. In 1906 he was elected to the First Duma. There he quickly established himself as one of its most promising young leaders and as a brilliant speaker. When the Duma decided to reply to the tsar's welcoming remarks with an Address to the Throne in the English manner, it was Nabokov who carried the debate, according to one observer, with "exceptional ability." The shocked response of the government was a parliamentary scolding from the chairman of the Council of Ministers, I. L. Goremykin. In the silence that followed, Nabokov suddenly rushed to the podium and challenged the government with the stirring words, "Let the executive power bow before the legislative," which excited loud applause. He moved a vote of censure. After a devastating debate the motion carried. Of course, the ministers did not resign, but the young Kadet spokesman had firmly and publicly placed himself in the forefront of the opposition.

Nabokov's rising political reputation was clearly reflected in the unofficial discussions that were concurrently taking place between

P. N. Miliukov, the leader of his party, and General D. F. Trepov, commandant of the Palace Guard and confidant of the tsar, concerning the possibility of establishing a ministry of confidence drawn largely from the Kadet plurality in the Duma. On the cabinet list that was drawn up, but of course never implemented, V. D. Nabokov, along with V. D. Kuzmin-Karavaev, was proposed for the position of minister of justice.

Early in July, despairing of a pliant assembly, the government dissolved the First Duma after less than three months of existence. A number of angry deputies crossed the border to Finland and, in the little town of Vyborg, protested their dismissal with a manifesto calling upon the populace to refuse to pay taxes or submit to military conscription until the Duma was reconvened. The gesture was fruitless: the revolutionary tide had ebbed. But the signators were eventually tried, barred from political activity, and in some cases sentenced to terms in jail. Nabokov was among the latter, belatedly serving three months in 1908.

His parliamentary career was ended, but much earlier he had begun work as a journalist, for which he was perhaps to be better known and remembered by his contemporaries. In 1898, with I. V. Gessen and A. I. Kaminka, he had established the juridical periodical *Pravo,* where his Kishinev article appeared. In 1906, together with his *Pravo* associates, Miliukov and others, he became a founder, publisher, and editor of the Kadet daily newspaper *Rech'* (*Speech*), which quickly achieved a wide though select circulation among liberal intellectuals in the provinces as well as the capital. Nabokov's articles, some editorials (though Miliukov was responsible for most of the political leaders), and news reports were read throughout Russia. As a publicist he won particular acclaim for his coverage of the sensational Beilis case in Kiev from 1911 to 1913. The government, in an effort to distract attention from the growing opposition and not so subtly to encourage pogroms, had accused a Jewish youth of the ritual murder of a Christian boy. Despite the efforts of the prosecution, Beilis was acquitted, but the series of illegalities that marked the proceedings aroused a vociferous reaction from all shades of enlightened opinion. Among the most outspoken commentators was Nabokov in the pages of *Rech'*, where his indignant articles earned him a fine of one hundred rubles.

During these years his juridical publications, principally on criminology, continued to appear in *Pravo* and elsewhere. From 1905 to 1915 he was president of the Russian branch of the International Criminology Association. Clearly, this amalgam of political, journalistic, and professional activity identified him as one of the leading public men in the prewar period, when he and his kind strove desperately to loosen the bonds of absolutism and stay the tide of revolution by advancing political and social reform within the narrow limits afforded by the regime.

With the outbreak of hostilities he was mobilized, serving first at the front and later at Staff Headquarters in St. Petersburg. Because of his military status, he largely refrained from the political activity which burgeoned in the capital after the spring of 1915, when the ineptitudes and blindness of the tsarist government ended the short-lived patriotic truce between the opposition and the regime. But neither his journalistic reputation nor his legal and political prominence was forgotten. In early 1916 he was invited by the British government, along with several other Russian journalists, to make a goodwill tour of England and examine her war effort. His experiences there, where he and his colleagues were exposed to British life and leaders from royalty to literary figures, were recounted in *Iz voiuiushchei Anglii* [*A Report from England at War*] (1916).

At home his political allies in the Fourth Duma, galvanized by the Galician defeat and the deficiencies they highlighted in the general conduct of the war, joined with other central parties in the summer of 1915 to form the Progressive Bloc, which drew up a common platform of reform. Chief among its demands was the establishment of a ministry "enjoying the confidence of the people" that would work with the Duma in taking the necessary civil and military steps to bolster the war effort. For the most part, the bloc was unsuccessful and the nation continued its descent into the abyss. But from that time forward there circulated in Duma circles ministerial lists for comment in anticipation of the day the tsar might accede to their pressure. By April 1916, having undergone several revisions, the list showed V. D. Nabokov again as an alternate choice for the portfolio of justice, this time with V. D. Maklakov. It is remarkable how closely this cabinet paralleled that of the First Provisional Government. Obvious exceptions were Nabokov and Maklakov, who were replaced by Kerensky, the ubiquitous and unexpected star of the February Days.

The same reasons of military obligation that restrained Nabokov from wartime political activity enforced his role as an observer of the February demonstrations and uprising until his legal talents were enlisted in preparing the manifesto of Grand Duke Mikhail. From that point until his flight to the Crimea in November, his activities in 1917 are delineated in detail in the memoir.

During the following winter and spring he lived in relative seclusion with his family in the Crimea, where he began his memoir while that unfortunate area was tugged back and forth between the Bolsheviks and the German invaders. In June and July he spent more than a month in Kiev where, along with Miliukov, he entered into brief, tentative, and abortive conversations with the Germans, seeking support to rid Russia of Bolshevik rule. Later, in Simferopol, he again entertained the possibility of some sort of accommodation with the German occupiers. The discussions broke down primarily on the inevitable question of Russia's future territorial integrity. These attempts at pragmatic collaboration most certainly damaged his and especially Miliukov's reputation.

On his return to the Crimea, he served briefly as minister of justice in the regional White government, then in March 1919, left for London via Greece. In England he joined Miliukov in editing an English-language weekly, *The New Russia,* which reported news from the homeland, supported anti-Bolshevik intervention, and continued the struggle for the restoration of a liberal Russia. However, the differences between the two Kadet leaders, some of which are foreshadowed in the memoir, soon intensified, reflecting a growing split in the party concerning the direction of its policies in exile. Miliukov transferred the base of his operations to Paris; Nabokov joined those of like mind in Berlin.

Miliukov advocated cooperation to the left, specifically with the Socialist Revolutionaries, to broaden the movement for greater flexibility and strength. Nabokov could not accept this stratagem, seeing in the socialist admixture a betrayal of liberal principles. Meanwhile, his other colleagues on *Pravo* and *Rech'*, Gessen (Hessen) and Kaminka, now in Berlin and sharing his views, had entered into negotiations with a German publishing firm to finance a newspaper that would reflect their opinions and program. In the fall of 1920, they invited Nabokov to Berlin to serve as editor of the daily *Rul'* (*Rudder*). The enterprise was remarkably successful, its circulation and influence rivaled only later by A. F. Kerensky's *Dni* (*Days*), which followed an equally independent Socialist Revolutionary line. The free-wheeling editorial policy of *Rul'*, more eloquently critical of the flaws in Soviet and in other emigré programs and action than dogmatic in advancing its own, attracted an audience far beyond its ideological sympathizers. Although the faction it represented found itself more and more outside the ebb and flow of emigré alliances and alignments, the organ itself, ironically, continued to enjoy wide readership and respect.

The year 1921 and the spring of 1922 marked a turning point in Soviet domestic and foreign policy, which in turn had a decided influence upon emigré politics, especially in Berlin. At home Lenin introduced the New Economic Policy, a temporary retreat to partial capitalism and greater social and intellectual freedom. Abroad, the Soviet Union, its hopes of immediate world revolution fading and desperately in need of security and foreign trade to preserve the regime, sought diplomatic and economic support from the West. The first major breakthrough was the Anglo-Soviet Trade Agreement of March 1921. The second was to be the Rapallo treaty of April 1922, with Germany, a fellow international pariah and promising diplomatic partner. This new direction in Soviet policy perturbed the entire emigré community and threw it into further disarray. The reactionary wing of the monarchist movement became especially distraught and enraged, seeking scapegoats and imagining enemies among its fellow exiles. Miliukov, a symbol of the revolution and now advocating openings to the left, stood irrationally high on their list.

The rift between the Paris and the Berlin factions of the Kadets was not so deep as to prohibit communication and the exchange of ideas between their spokesmen. Accordingly, it was not surprising that when Miliukov came to address a large audience in the Philharmonia Hall in the German capital on the night of March 28, 1922, his former associates and still personal friends, albeit political antagonists—Nabokov and Kaminka—should serve as hosts. Interrupting his long lecture to greet old comrades in the audience, Miliukov stepped off the platform, to be met by the cry "For the tsar's family and for Russia!" and a volley of revolver shots. A member of the audience pulled him to the floor, while Nabokov and Kaminka rushed forward to struggle with the gunman. At that moment the would-be assassin's companion fired indiscriminately into the panic-stricken house. Kaminka was wounded, Nabokov killed instantly. The two assailants, former tsarist army officers, were tried by a German court and sentenced to prison terms. Both were released early and ended their infamous careers as assistants to the notorious Alfred Rosenberg under the Nazi regime.

The assassination had a traumatic effect upon the emigration. The monarchist movement in particular was weakened and badly discredited. To all who had known V. D. Nabokov or his work, it was a tragic end to a life whose course and conduct in Russia and in emigration had won universal respect and confidence.

It is a great temptation to comment extensively on the memoir and to present detailed interpretations and criticism. But to do so would intrude on the reader's own use and appreciation of the text. In any case, a careful analysis of a document of this length, written with such economy that almost every sentence is sharply descriptive or soberly judgmental, would overwhelm the original. Each reader must therefore seek and assess its substance for himself. But some remarks may be appropriate and helpful.

The style is lucid, sparse, and straightforward, dry but somehow compelling. According to his distinguished son, Vladimir V. Nabokov, whose delightful *Speak, Memory* includes a vivid and affectionate filial tribute, Nabokov possessed a fine and ready sense of humor that he obviously did not indulge in this or his other writings. Nor is his exceptionally broad knowledge and great admiration for the literature of Russia and the West particularly evident beyond the occasional use of foreign phrases that were, after all, part of the vocabulary of most educated Russians of his class. His style does, however, reflect his long journalistic experience and legal training. Apparently, Nabokov had the enviable ability, refined by years of meeting reportorial deadlines, to put his observations and interpretations clearly and directly on paper in an even flow with little revision. One has the impression, verified by his son, that he thought through rather carefully beforehand what he wanted to say, clarified his memory on certain points, and then described and evaluated events with the facility of a professional journalist and the prudence of a jurist. In his style one also detects the influence of the English, whose prose as well as mode he greatly admired—not the elegance of the essayist, perhaps, but the absence of emotionalism and flights of fancy. It might even be said, daringly for today, that his composition and approach identify him—in the behavioral, not the class use of the designation—as a gentleman, both in his self-restraint and in his obvious dislike of those who lacked it.

This is not to suggest that Nabokov was less than candid. In fact, one of the most valuable contributions of his memoir is his perceptive, sometimes brutally frank, but scrupulous appraisal of his associates' strengths and weaknesses. It is not surprising that he reacted negatively to some, though certainly not all, of the Soviet types he encountered. But his frank assessment of his long-time Kadet colleagues, especially his close collaborator, leader, and friend, Miliukov, is impressive. On the other hand, while inherently repelled by Kerensky's temperamental outbursts, impetuous decision-making, and vanity, he manifestly strove to recognize fairly his revolutionary zeal, genuine humanity, and patriotism.

Another facet of his commentary is more troublesome: the apparent evidences of anti-Semitism. At first glance, certain of his characterizations seem to bear that stain. Yet many of his closest collaborators were Jewish, and his scathing attacks on the Kishinev pogrom and the Beilis prosecution were highlights of his journalistic career. A resolution of this dilemma is offered by his son: "My father felt so infinitely superior to any accusation of antisemitism (its official brand, or even the more disgusting household variety) that out of a kind of self-confidence and contempt for showcase philosemitism he used to make it a point—and go out of his way to make it—of being as plainspoken about Jew and Gentile as were his Jewish colleagues (such as Joseph Hessen and Grigory Landau) or the Christian but impeccably unprejudiced Milyukov.'' Surely this interpretation goes far toward reconciling latter-day attitudes with the somewhat academic rationale of a man of intellect, goodwill, and rigorous probity of an earlier era. All in all, Nabokov's assessment of personalities is an admirable example of plainspokenness tempered by compassion in circumstances that tempted most commentators to excesses.

The same approach is evident in Nabokov's evaluation of the fast-flowing events of those hectic months. Witness, for example, his arguments and conclusion on the question of the monarchy. Nabokov is sometimes classified as a right-wing Kadet, though his various positions during his political career at home and abroad do not, in fact, fall so neatly into that category. "Centerist" or "moderate" would be more accurate designations. Certainly, however, he was a constitutional monarchist. In the memoir, he deplores the loss of the dynasty in the February Days as a stabilizing factor in the new order, even as he helps to draft Mikhail's renunciation of the throne. Yet, after a closely reasoned discussion of the prevailing situation, he concludes that however desirable the preservation of the monarchy might have been to provide continuity and a symbol of state power, the conditions to support such an outcome were clearly not present.

Again, note his unorthodox comments and judgments on such fundamental questions as the real causes of the revolution, the health of the army, the formation of the first coalition, the June offensive, the continuance of military operations, negotiated peace, and the work of the council for drafting the electoral laws to the Constituent Assembly. Considering that he was a Kadet and a leading member of its Central Committee holding strong political convictions, he frequently demonstrated refreshing flexibility. Unlike so many of his compatriots, he had the ability to stand back a bit from the turmoil and to see with unusual detachment the tragedy being played out before him. With signal insight, he perceived the futility of dogmatism as factionalism progressed with alarming intemperance. These qualities no doubt reduced his effectiveness as a politician in a revolutionary setting, but they greatly enhance his contribution as a chronicler of an epoch.

Nabokov's background and proclivities, however, are by no means completely disguised. Some he reveals, others are implicit in his account. He was a nationalist, an intellectual, a landowner, at home in military as well as political circles, a libertarian but not an equalitarian. Above all, he was a jurist, greatly concerned with legitimacy and legality at a time when both were hard to discern and out of fashion. As a consequence, his greatest weakness is the lack of any real comprehension of the motivations, aspirations, and urgency of the masses. Like most members of his party, he believed that positive social and economic action must await the establishment of a stable and accountable government and the winning of the war. Thus, while describing and evaluating the leaders, affairs of state, and politics, he frequently underestimated elemental forces at work in the revolution.

Of Nabokov's activities and writings, this memoir will no doubt survive as his personal monument. His political work was for a defeated cause, though of course it is always impossible to predict with accuracy the future course of Russia or any other nation. Likewise, his learned legal publications investigated a system that vanished with the advent of the Soviets. However brilliant, his journalistic writing was the product of the moment and will be infrequently consulted. But no student of the Russian Revolution will be able to ignore Nabokov's description of the tortured men and cataclysmic events of 1917.

Robert Paul Browder

The University of Arizona

V. D. Nabokov in 1917

BY BARON B. E. NOL'DE

Allow me to share with you my reminiscences about V. D. Nabokov in 1917.* I do not think that my decision to speak about this period of his life needs a lengthy justification. I have my own personal reasons for choosing this period, for during these months I met with Nabokov regularly every day. But this is not the point. Nor is it that during the turbulent months through which Russia then lived, Nabokov played an important role or guided events. He did not—much to the detriment of Russia's welfare. I will go so far as to say that, for Nabokov's personal destiny as a statesman and a politician, the year 1917 was an important phase of inner development and growth. Observing him over a span of two decades, I was continually struck by Nabokov's ability always to remain true to himself. This characteristic of his intellectual and moral personality was confirmed by all who knew him intimately and who loved and understood him. He had a rare sense of logic in his approach to life, strengthened by remarkable qualities of self-control and emotional balance.

Regardless of all this, the year 1917 was for Nabokov, as well as for all Russians in general, from the least to the greatest, a year that cost an expenditure of intellectual and moral energy unequaled in any other year in the lives of our generation. Certainly, no other Russian generation of Russians has had to experience what we have experienced since the beginning of the twentieth century and are

---

* Read in a memorial session of the Juridical Society in Paris dedicated to the memory of V. D. Nabokov, May 24, 1922. [Nol'de's note]

experiencing still. In this expenditure of every last drop of strength, in this stream of alternating happiness and despair, hopes and disappointments, victories and defeats, triumphs and humiliations, the caliber of each one of us, his ability to think and act, his enthusiasm and his common sense, were tested more than in any other period in the development of the Russian people and Russian society.[1] For this reason, when I speak of Nabokov in 1917, I speak about him at a time when the greatest trials were imposed on his intellectual and moral strength, during the months of his most intensive work and most intensive deliberations concerning the fate of the country, of its past, present, and future.

Nabokov, as all of the political group to which he belonged, could not be blamed for the events which caused the fall of the old Russian regime. But from the first moment that the inevitability of the collapse became clear, he and other members of his political circle became clearly conscious of their responsibility for the evolution of the political inheritance. The historical verdict on the successors of tsarist power has not yet been handed down, and no one could then foretell it, precisely as Tsar Boris [Godunov] did not know that his successors would be Grishka Otrep'ev and the "Brigand" of Tushino.[2] Yet the presumptive heir was at hand. This was the upper circle of the Russian intelligentsia, independent and unconnected with the bureaucratic apparatus. The feeling of responsibility of its leaders for the fate of the state, though paralyzed in some by doctrinairism and civic unpreparedness, and in others by personal ambition, was especially strong in Nabokov.

When recalling that day, March 3, the first revolutionary day, I would sum up the whole of Nabokov's attitude as his awareness of the responsibility attending his association with the new state order which was only just beginning to crystallize. He was not concerned with an abstract scheme of revolution. He had inherited a thoroughly specific knowledge of the mechanism of the Russian

1. "Russian society" was the socially and politically conscious upper circle of the Russian intelligentsia, "independent and unconnected with the bureaucratic apparatus."
2. A reference to the First and Second False Dmitriis during Muscovy's Time of Troubles (1598–1613).

state from ancestors in the service of the state. He struggled from the beginning of the century for its reconstitution, but he knew that, under the pretext of reconstruction, it was impossible to arrest its motion, and that its demolished parts must be replaced with new ones, without losing a single moment. The Vyborg proclamation deprived him of electoral rights, and at the outset of the war he was called into military service as an ensign in the reserve, at the time serving in the offices of General Staff. From the beginning of the [First World] War he had not participated in any way in political life, but he was immediately remembered, as a matter of course, in the very first revolutionary days. Without hesitating a moment, without weighing the offer made to him on the scales of personal ambition or his personal political career, he became the so-called Head of the Chancellery of the "Council of Ministers" [3] (or the "Provisional Government," as it came to be termed a few days later, since the new authority did not know at first whether it was a newly composed Council of Ministers or the center of Russian supreme power).

I found Nabokov on the evening of March 3 in one of the rooms of the Tauride Palace,[4] amidst incredible chaos and confusion, endeavoring, with his peculiar, methodical way and sense of order, to carry out, in the performance of the duties of his new post, the first functions of the new regime: the publication of *Vestnik [Vremennago] Pravitel'stva* [5] and the promulgation of the initial acts of the new regime. I shall never forget the circumstances of that evening. It seemed that the entire rebellious Petersburg [6] garrison had poured from the streets into the Tauride Palace, mixing with another throng

3. The Council of Ministers consisted of ministers appointed by the tsar who were responsible only to him, not to the chairman of the council.

4. The Tauride Palace was the site of State Duma sessions. During the first months of the revolution the Petrograd Soviet met there (and initially the Provisional Government).

5. The official daily newspaper of the Provisional Government, 1917.

6. At the outbreak of World War I, St. Petersburg became Petrograd, thereby severing the city's Western ties by relinquishing its Germanized name. Many Russians continued to call the city Petersburg out of habit. Socialists and liberals, however, generally labeled the act as chauvinistic and deliberately referred to the city as Petersburg. In 1924 Petrograd became Leningrad.

of people in civilian clothes, partly known and partly unknown to me, who were trying to rally around the two centers crystallizing at the moment—a new Council of Ministers, and, repeating the precedent of 1905, a Soviet of Workers' Deputies.[7] While the three of us—Nabokov, Miliukov,[8] and myself—were pondering how to entitle the promulgation of Grand Duke Mikhail's [9] abdication of the throne, which had been signed several hours earlier, we were interrupted by telegrams about sailors executing admirals and officers in Sveaborg and Kronstadt.

I will not interrupt the train of personal reminiscences. It brings me to the first half of that highly memorable day, to Nabokov, inspired by the same sense of responsibility for the ship of state on the stormy waves of those days, to his participation in the establishment of the new government.

M. I. Tereshchenko,[10] a young man whom I had never seen before and who turned out to be the minister of finance, entered the room where we sat preparing the promulgation of the manifesto of the grand duke. He asked me to go with him to the session of the new ministers, in order to determine how to publish the very first law of the new regime. With difficulty, we pushed our way into

7. The 1905 Soviet (council), entirely proletarian in its makeup, emerged from an oversized strike committee and suffered from a lack of direction. The 1917 Soviet was organized by a group of socialist intelligentsia who led a large body of workers' and soldiers' representatives, elected from factories and military units. See Oskar Anweiler, *The Soviets: The Russian Workers, Peasants, and Soldiers Councils 1905–1921* (New York, 1974).

8. Paul Nikolaevich Miliukov (1859–1943), prominent historian; leader, Constitutional Democratic (Kadet) Party; deputy, Third and Fourth State Dumas; political editor, *Rech'* (*Speech*), Petrograd, 1906–18; minister of foreign affairs, March–May 1917; emigrated 1919; coeditor, *The New Russia,* London, 1919–20; editor, *Posledniia Novosti* (*The Latest News*), Paris, 1921–40; author of works cited in editorial notes.

9. Grand Duke Mikhail Aleksandrovich (1878–1918), only brother of Nicholas II; executed by the Bolsheviks.

10. Mikhail Ivanovich Tereshchenko (1888–1958), sugar manufacturer; chairman, Kiev Regional War Industries Committee, 1915–17; minister of finance, March–May, minister of foreign affairs, May–October, 1917; emigrated after Bolshevik coup.

another room where several ministers were sitting—of whom I remember Shingarev, Godnev, V. L'vov, and Nekrasov.[11] Tereshchenko explained that it was necessary today to increase the rights of issue of the State Bank, as the existing currency would not be sufficient in the immediate future. Shingarev and Godnev said that, in their opinion, the law should be promulgated in accordance with Article 87 of the Fundamental Laws. Let me remind you that the article in question permitted the Supreme Power, His Majesty the Emperor, to promulgate decrees with full legal force when the State Duma was not in session, subsequently submitting them for approval by the State Duma and State Council.[12] After everything that had happened, this legal scheme was certainly fantastic, but no one could think of another. The council waited for some advice from me, an authority on government. I had to tell them something which none of them presently knew because of the prevailing confusion—that three hours before, Grand Duke Mikhail had signed a manifesto in which "plenary powers" were proclaimed for the

11. Andrei Ivanovich Shingarev (1869–1918), physician; Zemstvo leader; Kadet party leader; deputy, Second, Third, Fourth State Dumas; minister of finance, March–May, minister of agriculture, May–July, 1917; murdered by Bolshevik sailors while under arrest, January 1918.

Ivan Vasil'evich Godnev (1856–?), physician; Octobrist deputy, Third, Fourth State Dumas; state controller, March–July 1917.

Vladimir Nikolaevich L'vov (1872–1930s), Octobrist deputy, Third, Fourth State Dumas; ober-procurator general of the Holy Synod, March–July 1917; emigrated after the Bolshevik coup; returned 1922; not related to Prince George L'vov, minister-president, 1917.

Nikolai Vissarionovich Nekrasov (1879–1940?), professor, Tomsk Technological Institute, Kadet deputy, Third State Duma; vice-chairman, Fourth State Duma; member, Provisional Committee of the State Duma, 1917; minister of transport, March–July, minister of finance and deputy minister-president, July–August, 1917; governor-general of Finland, September 1917; later served Soviets.

12. The tsar promised a State Duma (legislature) during the course of the 1905 revolution, and four Dumas were elected between 1906 and 1917. These bodies, though in theory popularly elected, were increasingly restricted in franchise at each election and never had more than an advisory, or pseudoparliamentary, role.

The State Council (*Gosudarstvenny Sovet*) was from 1906 on the upper chamber of the Russian legislative body. The tsar appointed half of its members; half were elected on the basis of an extremely restricted franchise.

Provisional Government until the convocation of the Constituent Assembly.[13] Therefore the Provisional Government itself should promulgate laws without any reference to Article 87. This seemed at first to surprise everyone, but it was difficult to dispute, and the legal authority of the Provisional Government was recognized. In the midst of chaos, some kind of support was found for the establishment of a new legality.

Nabokov was the principal participant in the creation of that basis of authority. In his reminiscences about the Provisional Government published in the first volume of *Arkhiv Russkoi Revoliutsii,* Nabokov has related how we wrote the act of abdication from power of the grand duke. This event is so important in Russian history that I hope you will not object if, in addition to his reminiscences, I furnish mine. After lunch on March 3, I was in my office on Palace Square. The telephone rang and I heard Nabokov's voice, as always even and unhurried, saying: "Leave everything, take the first volume of the Code of Laws and come right away to Millionnaia, number so-and-so, to Princess Putiatin's apartment."[14] Ten minutes later I was ushered into a room with a child's school desk that belonged to the owner's daughter. There I found Nabokov and V. V. Shul'gin.[15] Shul'gin in a few hurried

13. The Constituent Assembly was the body that was to have established self-rule in Russia. The idea for the convocation dates from the nineteenth century and its implementation became possible in 1917, at which time elections set for delegates took place only after the Bolshevik coup. Of the 703 delegates elected by 36,265,560 voters, 75 percent cast their ballot for parties other than the Bolsheviks. The assembly's first and only meeting occurred on January 5/6, 1918 (O.S.), and was broken up by Bolshevik-led sailors and Lettish sharpshooters who had been liberally plied with vodka. See O. H. Radkey, *The Election to the Russian Constituent Assembly of 1917* (Cambridge, Mass., 1950), and M. V. Vishniak, *Vserossiiskoe uchreditel'noe sobranie (The All-Russian Constituent Assembly)* (Paris, 1932).

14. Grand Duke Mikhail transferred his headquarters to the Putiatin flat on February 28 (O.S.) and remained there for negotiations. The flat was convenient, and continued residence in the Winter Palace would have placed his life in danger. Prince M. S. Putiatin was at Tsarskoe Selo, where he helped to draw up the act making Russia a constitutional monarchy.

15. Vasilli Vital'evich Shul'gin (1878–?), lawyer; nationalist member, Second, Third State Dumas; leader, Progressive (Independent) Nationalist bloc, Fourth State

words described his trip to Pskov, the signing by Emperor Nicholas of the abdication from the throne, and the decisive refusal on the same morning of the grand duke to accept the throne. Nabokov added that a manifesto concerning this should be prepared for the grand duke and that there was a draft available, composed by Nekrasov. The draft was quite inadequate and obviously unsuitable. We started rewriting immediately.

The first form of our draft—the three of us pondering every word as well as the Nekrasov draft—was phrased as a manifesto beginning with the words: "We, by God's mercy, Mikhail I, Emperor and Autocrat of all the Russias. . . ." The only thing said in Nekrasov's draft was that the grand duke refused to accept the throne and that he left the decision about the form of the government up to the Constituent Assembly. What would happen before the Constituent Assembly was convened, who would draw up the electoral laws, etc.—all of this he did not consider. It was completely obvious to Nabokov that under such conditions the only power at hand—the Provisional Government—would be suspended in mid-air. By mutual consent we inserted in our draft a statement about the plenary powers of the Provisional Government. Nabokov, sitting at the small school desk, copied the draft in his beautiful handwriting and took it to the grand duke in the next room.

The grand duke, after some time had elapsed, came to inform us of his observations and objections. He did not wish the manifesto to mention him as a monarch who had accepted the throne and asked that we insert the phrase that he was calling for God's blessing and that he was beseeching Russian citizens to obey the authority of the Provisional Government—in our draft we had "commanding." The necessary alterations were made, the manifesto was once more copied by Nabokov, and after making, I believe, a few minor changes, the grand duke approved it. Prince G. E. L'vov, Rod-

---

Duma; editor, *Kievlianin* (*Kievian*), 1917–19; member, Provisional Committee of the State Duma, 1917; active in White movement during Civil War; emigrated 1920; captured by Soviet armed forces, 1944; returned to Russia, serving ten years in prison; released 1956; produced Soviet film on the year 1917, 1965; author, *Dni* (*Days*), Belgrade, 1925.

zianko, and Kerensky [16] arrived at this time. The grand duke, sitting at the same small desk, signed the manifesto, stood up and embraced Prince L'vov and wished him every good fortune. The grand duke acted with irreproachable tact and nobility, and everyone was permeated with the consciousness of the enormous importance of what had occurred. Kerensky stood up and said, addressing the grand duke, "Believe me, Your Imperial Highness, that we will carry the precious vessel of your authority to the Constituent Assembly without spilling a single drop."

The act of March 3 was in essence the only constitution during the period of existence of the Provisional Government. It was possible to live with it until the Constituent Assembly—carrying out, of course, in practice Nabokov's formula of "plenary powers."

The old Russian administrative tradition had established the post of Head of the Chancellery of the Council of Ministers (i.e. the Provisional Government) as an important component of the machinery of governmental power. Having accepted this tradition, Nabokov tried to do everything that was possible to transform the Provisional Government, as they called themselves, from an extremely haphazard collection of people, looking in different directions and united only by the flow of the revolutionary tide, into a real power. This task, however, could not be completed under the

16. Prince George Evgen'evich L'vov (1861–1925), Kadet deputy, First State Duma; president, All-Russian Union of Zemstvos and Towns, 1915–17; minister-president, March 2–July 2, 1917; emigrated to Paris; see his memoirs, *Posledniia Novosti,* nos. 186, 190, 192, 194 (November–December, 1920).

Mikhail Vladimirovich Rodzianko (1859–1924), wealthy landowner; Zemstvo leader; Octobrist deputy, Third State Duma; president, Fourth State Duma, 1911–17; chairman, Provisional Committee of the State Duma, 1917; after Bolshevik coup supported General A. I. Denikin's army; emigrated to Yugoslavia, 1920. See his memoir in *Arkhiv Russkoi Revoliutsii (Archives of the Russian Revolution),* 6 : 5–80.

Alexander Fedorovich Kerensky (1881–1970), lawyer; Trudovik leader, Fourth State Duma; member, Provisional Committee of the State Duma, 1917; minister of justice, March–May, minister of war and navy, May–August, minister-president, July–October, Supreme Commander, September–October 25, 1917; emigrated; editor, *Golos Rossii (The Voice of Russia),* Berlin; *Dni,* Berlin, Paris; *Novaia Rossiia (New Russia),* Paris; died in New York City where he had lived since 1940; author: *The Catastrophe* (New York, 1927); *The Crucifixion of Liberty* (New York, 1934); *Russia and History's Turning Point* (New York, 1965).

circumstances of that moment. The atmosphere of the Tauride Palace on March 3, 1917 was carried over into the chamber of Mariinskii Palace, where the government moved in the first days of its existence. Nabokov was exhausting all his energy, all his sense of order, to dispel that atmosphere, but as early as the first month he bitterly complained about the hopelessness of his endeavors.

I remember the evening when we, together with Kokoshkin,[17] were called to Mariinskii Palace for consultation regarding the preparations for summoning the Constituent Assembly. Nabokov explained to us when we arrived that it was impossible to determine positively the opening hour of the session. It turned out, as a matter of fact, that only at some time between midnight and 1 A.M. did a sufficient number of ministers gather for the session to open. We were asked to wait until the conversation with the representatives of the Soviet of Workers' and Soldiers' Deputies terminated. Steklov,[18] for two hours in succession, kept pulling out of his pocket telegrams and letters from the front, every statement, enveloped in revolutionary jargon, caviling about the "bonapartism" of General A., about the counter-revolutionary activities of Chief Surgeon B., about the dealings with the Germans on the part of Colonel V. (this material, too, was in the pockets of the current editor of the Moscow *Izvestiia*),[19] etc. Sitting across from Nabokov, I saw what suffering this scene caused him. The sense of responsibility for the important task that Russian society had taken upon itself did not leave him for a moment. He did what he could to keep the carriage on a straight road, but the circumstances were such that the carriage was being pulled inevitably into a quagmire.

17. Fedor Fedorovich Kokoshkin (1871–1918), law professor, Moscow University; Kadet deputy, First State Duma; state controller, July–August 1917; imprisoned by Bolsheviks; murdered by drunken sailors while he was convalescing at Mariinskii Hospital, January 1918.

18. Iurii Mikhailovich Steklov [Nakhamkes] (1873–1941), historian; Social Democrat; exiled several times; cofounder, Borba Publishing House; member, Executive Committee, Petrograd Soviet, 1917; editor, *Izvestiia* (*News*), March, then after October 25, 1917; member, Presidium, All-Russian Central Executive Committee (VTsIK), 1918; author, *God bor'by za sotsial'nuiu revoliutsiiu* (*The Year of Struggle for the Socialist Revolution*), (Petrograd, 1919).

19. The organ of the Moscow Soviet of Workers' and Soldiers' Deputies, 1917.

Nabokov thought it proper that the members of the Provisional Government politically close to him remain in it until the end. No one knew at that time whether a member of the Provisional Government could legally submit his resignation at all, and the line followed by Nabokov—to remain until the end within the government—corresponded to the original concept of the organization of the provisional authority. Consequently, in view of this, he personally remained to administer affairs after Miliukov's resignation, an action that revealed the first deep crisis of power and was brought about by the joint efforts of Kerensky and Albert Thomas.[20] After this first crisis, however, to continue the duty of administering the Provisional Government's affairs was by then an act of inner discipline and self-denial, the uselessness of which was becoming clearer and clearer with each day. Nabokov resigned and was named a Senator of the recently revived First Department.[21]

He returned to independent journalism and independent political work. It was now necessary to proclaim aloud all he had been telling his friends, to make it the subject of his political sermon—to do this once more, in the name of that same sense of common responsibility of Russian society for everything that had happened, for all the evenings with Steklov, for all the torrents of words, for all the inaction of authority.

I have before me Nabokov's article of May 25, 1917 entitled "Practical Lessons." Published in the [*Vestnik*] of the Party of People's Freedom,[22] it is doubly interesting, as it indicates the direc-

20. Albert Thomas (1878–1932), French politician; Socialist member, Chamber of Deputies; 1910–21; minister of munitions, minister plenipotentiary to Russia, 1917; director, International Labour Office, League of Nations, 1921.

21. Peter the Great created the Senate in 1711 to serve, at least theoretically, as the chief administrative organ under the tsar. By the end of Catherine II's reign (1796), the Senate, the Imperial Council, and the Procurator-Generalship made up the agencies of central government. Alexander I (1801–25) retained the Senate, abolished the other two, and created the Council of State and the Committee of Ministers. After 1864 the Senate functioned primarily as the Supreme Court of Appeals. The tsar appointed its members.

22. The Party of People's Freedom, commonly called the Constitutional Democratic party, or Kadet (from the pronunciation of the initials, "kah" and "deh"), was founded in October 1905 as the result of the fusion of the Union of Liberation and the Zemstvo Constitutionalists. The Kadets were considered left-wing liberals;

tion in which Nabokov wanted to lead his party. It is permeated with profound pessimism. He wrote: "The miraculous swiftness of the *coup d'état,* the kind of magical ease with which it toppled at once and totally, the rot-riddled facade of the old order—the genuine enthusiasm that seized everyone, led to the unanimous recognition of the new order by the whole country and by Western Europe, the countless expressions of confidence and readiness to support the Provisional Government—all this promised success and prosperity, durability, and fruitfulness for the existing Republic." "What happened?" Nabokov asked himself. "No matter in what area of state life we look, nowhere arise iridescent images, but only ominous indications of decay and destruction. The general atmosphere commences to resemble more and more the old, prerevolutionary one. As then, conscientious people who realized what was taking place around them, anxiously asked themselves and each other—What lies ahead? Where is the way out?—so now, too, there is no other question. With the exception of the politically unconscious masses and the groups of anarchically inclined conscious elements, there is no one now who does not experience this painful anxiety." And here is his conclusion: "A viewpoint exists in France that the Great French Revolution should be accepted completely, *en bloc.* This view is understandable and valid. It is possible that future Russian historians will agree in one hundred years to accept the Russian Revolution *en bloc.* However, we contemporaries—we are participants and cannot now rise to the height of historical perspective. There is for us in this living process of transformation that which

---

the Octobrists, right-wing. The Kadets dominated the First State Duma, but disenfranchisement of a number of these deputies and of voters reduced their numbers in the Second, Third, and Fourth Dumas. During World War I they participated in the Progressive bloc of Duma deputies and were important in the War Industries Committees. After March 1917, they were initially dominant in government throughout Russia, but with the radicalization of the revolution, they quickly waned in official positions. After emigration, the Kadets organized into groups in Paris and Berlin. See William G. Rosenberg's admirable study, *Liberals in the Russian Revolution* (Princeton, N.J., 1974).

Vestnik Partii Narodnoi Svobody (Herald of the Party of People's Freedom), Petrograd, May 1917–August 1918, was the official organ of the Kadet Central Committee.

we oppose and which we will continue to oppose. And when we struggle against the excesses and the abuses, against the intentional and unintentional sins of the revolution, we are strengthened by one thought: we are strengthened by the conviction that in this struggle we stand for its great, fruitful, and genuine principles."

Nabokov was one of the first who possessed the courage to say publicly what I cite now. He was, of course, not alone in this diagnosis, even in that early month in the existence of the Provisional Government. Nevertheless, all around, a hastily put together official optimism prevailed in the evaluation of everything that took place, and along with it a tendency—very strongly represented in the nonsocialistic intelligentsia by Nekrasov—to base all calculations, as it was phrased then, on the seizure of the revolutionary wave so as to construct influence and power on its crest. Nabokov was too well-balanced and sober to be lulled by the trite revolutionary optimism and too honest to accept Nekrasov's Machiavellianism.

This question—"What lies ahead? And where is the way out?"—this patriotic anxiety for the future, determined all further activity for Nabokov in the summer and fall of 1917.

Everyone remembers the way this question was posed. It consisted of two parts—the foreign situation and the domestic one. The consciousness of the connection between the war and the revolution, the necessity of choosing between "a struggle to a victorious conclusion" and the organization of a normal state life in new forms, was far from commonly accepted in these months. On the contrary, it appeared then to be rather a sinful, forbidden political heresy. Miliukov's concept reigned: the revolution was accomplished in order to conclude the war successfully—this was one of the most naïve self-deceptions of this epoch, rich in all kinds of fictions. Looking back now with the calmness that the passage of time provides, I must say that among the socialists who were then playing the principal roles, Dan, Gots, Skobelev [23]—even

23. Fedor Il'ich Dan [Gurvich] (1871–1947), physician; member, League of Struggle for Liberation of the Working Class; later, Social Democrat; arrested and exiled several times; permanent member, Menshevik Central Committee; Right Menshevik, 1905– ; member, Executive Committee, Petrograd Soviet, 1917; staff,

Kerensky and A. Ia. Gal'pern (who replaced Nabokov in the role of guardian of order in the Provisional Government and was likewise hopelessly depressed by the muddle in the minds of its members)— the awareness of the impossibility of waging war and at the same time channeling the revolution was much more acute than among the official Kadet leaders. The socialists, however, were seldom able to express their political views intelligently and knew only the clichés of their Internationale [24] affiliates, a commodity which did not have international currency and which had little response in Western European countries, Allied and enemy.

When Nabokov, Adzhemov, Vinaver,[25] and I tried to prove for the first time, in the midst of a meeting of the Kadet Central Committee at No. 8 French Quay, that it was necessary to turn from the

Narkomzdrav, 1919–20; emigrated 1922; editorial board member, *Sotsialisticheskii Vestnik (The Socialist Herald),* New York, 1922–47; author, "K istorii poslednikh dnei Vremennogo Pravitel'stva," *Letopis' Revoliutsii ("On the History of the Last Days of the Provisional Government," Chronicle of the Revolution),* 1 (1923) : 161–76.

Abram Rafailovich Gots [or Gotz] (1882–1937), member, Central Committee, Socialist Revolutionary party; deputy chairman, Socialist Revolutionary All-Russian Central Executive Committee; member, Committee for the Salvation of the Fatherland and the Revolution, 1917; imprisoned, pardoned, 1920–23; active in agriculture in Siberia; arrested and perished in Stalin purges. Soviet sources claim he became an agricultural worker in 1937 and died in 1940.

Matvei Ivanovich Skobelev (1880–1939), son of a merchant; Social Democrat, 1903– ; Social Democratic party organizer and propagandist, Baku; coworker with Trotsky, Vienna *Pravda (Truth),* 1907–12; Menshevik deputy, Fourth State Duma; deputy chairman, Petrograd Soviet, 1917; minister of labor, May–September, 1917; emigrated 1920; member, Communist Party of the Soviet Union, 1922– ; president, Foreign Trade Section, Moscow, 1925–26; disappeared 1929; presumably perished in the purges, 1930s, posthumously rehabilitated, 1950s.

24. The Second International Workingmen's Association (1889–1914).

25. Moisei Sergeevich Adzhemov (1878–?), Armenian; physician and lawyer; Kadet deputy, Second, Third, Fourth State Dumas; member, Kadet Party Central Committee; commissar in the Ministry of Justice, Provisional Committee of the State Duma, 1917; member, Council of the Republic, 1917.

Maksim Moiseevich Vinaver (1863–1926), active Jewish leader, publicist, and lawyer; founding member, Kadet party; Kadet deputy, First State Duma; member, Kadet Party Central Committee; minister of foreign affairs, Crimean Provisional Government, 1918; emigrated; published *Zveno (The Link);* contributor, *Posledniia Novosti,* Paris.

line of our classical imperialism, we were confronted with the most tenacious resistance. Miliukov, with the frigid precision so characteristic of him, argued that the aims of the war should be attained and that it was impossible to talk about peace as long as Yugoslavia was not created, etc. General Alekseev,[26] leaning at the time toward the Kadets and listed on our party rolls for the elections to the Constituent Assembly, developed the thought that the army might be meliorated, but only if we could find the Archimedean point at which to place the lever that would raise it. Our group kept asking where this point lay, but we did not receive an answer. K. N. Sokolov [27]—who was then the most eloquent herald of the truths of genuine Kadet foreign policy—kept demolishing our arguments with the kind of speech, both brilliant and commonplace, that was peculiar to him.

After our sessions, in which Nabokov participated as the cautious leader of the whole party who took into account the opinions of all its divisions, we composed a draft for the Pre-parliment,[28] then gathering, outlining the rules of procedure and cautiously mentioning peace as a mutual decision of the Allies. But we—and especially myself, who worked with a diminished sense of party responsibility—lost the debate by an enormous majority of votes. I will not recount the other session which took place about that time at the house of Prince G. N. Trubetskoi,[29] when the question about the continuation of the war was posed still more decisively and sharply. Nabokov relates it in his reminiscences, and I shall not repeat it. However, I should add that I remember this meeting just as vividly

26. General Mikhail Vasil'evich Alekseev (1857–1918), chief-of-staff, 1915–17; Supreme Commander, March–May 1917; chief-of-staff to A. F. Kerensky, September 1917; founder, Volunteer Army, 1918.

27. K. N. Sokolov, right Kadet; member, Kadet Party Central Committee; member, Council of the Republic, 1917.

28. The Pre-parliament or "Provisional Council of the Russian Republic" was a temporary legislative body that opened on October 7 and remained in session until the Bolshevik takeover. Total membership consisted of 313 deputies presided over by the Socialist Revolutionary, N. Avksent'ev.

29. Prince Grigorii Nikolaevich Trubetskoi, conservative liberal; served in the Foreign Ministry under the tsar; member, General Alekseev's council during the Civil War.

as Nabokov did. As a matter of fact, neither earlier nor later did Nabokov, Konovalov,[30] and others, so clearly and simply formulate the dilemma forced by events upon Russia, a reasonable peace or Lenin's inevitable triumph.

Nabokov was extremely interested at that time in questions of foreign policy. His appointment as ambassador to London was mentioned at M. I. Tereshchenko's initiative, where, as it is known, the Provisional Government did not find time to assign its representative. Of course, one could not have made a finer selection among the current governmental and society leaders for the post of Russian ambassador in London than Nabokov. He had all the prerequisites—a profound intellectual culture and *homme du monde's* education, a superb political schooling, a magnificant knowledge of language, self-discipline and persistence, flexibility, and resourcefulness. The plan to send Nabokov to London was, nevertheless, not realized—I do not remember now for what reason. He remained in Petersburg to fight for the second part of his answer to the question, ''What lies ahead, and where is the way out?''

This was indeed the arena of internal political relations in revolutionary Russia. We saw his understanding of the tasks whose time had come. In the enormous chaos to which the entire Russian nation was reduced, it was necessary to ascertain and to affirm ''the great and genuine principles of the Russian Revolution.''

Nabokov wrote down these principles in the abdication act of Grand Duke Mikhail: a strong government leading the country to the Constituent Assembly. This manifesto ended: ''Therefore calling on God's blessing, I am beseeching all citizens of the Russian State to obey the Provisional Government, which was created by the initiative of the State Duma and which is vested with all plenary powers, until the summoning, as soon as possible, on the basis of a universal, direct, equal, and secret ballot, of the Constituent As-

30. Aleksandr Ivanovich Konovalov (1875–1948), industrialist; member, Progressive bloc, Fourth State Duma; deputy chairman, Central War Industries Committee; member, Provisional Committee of the State Duma, 1917; Kadet, 1917; minister of trade and industry, March–May, September–October, 1917; deputy minister-president, September–October 1917; emigrated and died in New York City.

sembly, which by its decision regarding the form of government will express the will of the people.''

Was this concept wrong or not? I cannot make a lengthy judgment here. The stake on Russian democracy was definitely lost. Did it not follow from this that another goal should be set and that, in general, another goal *could* be set? I am deeply convinced that, having devoted all his strength to achieving the triumph of this political concept, Nabokov was not wrong in thinking that the ideas of constitutional authority and the universal, direct ballot which humanity inherited from the two French revolutions could play in Russia an enormous organizational role, just as it had countless times in other countries. It was necessary, however, that the country be led to the Constituent Assembly by a strong authority capable of building the state through the will of the people, and not destroying it.

Nabokov dedicated himself with the greatest interest and enormous attention to the forthcoming task of governmental organization. If the epoch of the short existence of the Provisional Government gave birth to legislative acts utterly remarkable in their intrinsic value—buried together with the Provisional Government in its destruction—then this is due to the merit, primarily, of two individuals, Nabokov and Kokoshkin. In the Juridical Council [31] attached to the Provisional Government, and in the Commission for Drafting the Electoral Law for the Constituent Assembly, both of them stood in the first rank. The Juridical Council was a small board of jurists who rapidly came to terms, and the work in it was easy and pleasant. However, the Commission for Drafting the Electoral Law for the Constituent Assembly was a large gathering, almost a parliament, and those like Nabokov, who took an active part in it, came to face the greatest difficulties. I well remember Nabokov as the president of the Editing Commission of the conference, discussing electoral regulations for the front. I believe that the relevant section of the statute on elections will forever remain a unique precedent of its kind in the history of suffrage. The general elec-

---

31. The Juridical Council consisted of six members plus a chairman and the Head of the Chancellery of the Provisional Government. It dealt with questions of public law concerning the establishment of a new state order.

tions in their most current and most exact applications were supposed to take place in the trenches, face to face with heavy German
artillery. How much persistence, tenacity, and tact had to be put
into this work in order not to turn elections at the front into a
simple pretext for desertion! With difficulty the maximalism of left-
wing colleagues was repulsed, as some of them had still not succeeded in learning statecraft by that time.

Finally the work was completed and the elections were set. The
conditions, however, in which they were supposed to have taken
place, had utterly deteriorated. If in May, 1917, when Nabokov
wrote his appeal not to take the Russian Revolution en bloc, one
still might have entertained some illusions, by the fall months—
when the Collected Statutes began gradually to include various
parts of the statute on elections to the Constituent Assembly—all
authority had been totally vitiated.

One kept repairing it and touching it up in every possible way
during those months. Nabokov—after relinquishing the post of
Head of the Chancellery of the Provisional Government—quickly
took one of the first places among the leadership of the Kadet party,
participating in all the endless episodes of the interparty negotiations "about the construction of authority," as it was then phrased.
He felt utterly hopeless. The people in Russia at that time were
governed by words, not by will. Verbal psychosis generated everywhere an irreparable lack of willpower. Kerensky's gesturing was
all that remained of the "plenary powers." Nabokov exhibited the
strictest honesty and goodwill in all attempts to come to some
agreement with the leftists and to help in this miserable situation.
Even to intimates, I am convinced, he did not admit what in the last
months of the Provisional Government was to him the internal
death sentence of the February revolution. He enjoyed, I know, the
confidence of the leftists, and he kept defending publicly and within
the party the so-called principle of coalition.

A last hope and last chance remained—the Constituent Assembly. Nabokov was nominated and elected. He actively conducted his pre-electoral campaign and spoke constantly in meetings
in St. Petersburg and St. Petersburg province. Work of a different
kind also went on. After the termination of the Conference for

Drafting the Electoral Law to the Constituent Assembly, the so-called All-Russian Commission for Elections to the Constituent Assembly continued to act as its successor in the management of elections and the elucidation of the electoral law. V. D. Nabokov was its deputy president. You remember that the elections to the Constituent Assembly took place after the Bolshevik coup d'état. The commission continued to meet, and to note every day, the way in which every legal basis for the elections was being destroyed. In the capacity of deputy president of the commission, Nabokov signed the proclamation on behalf of the commission on November 8, 1917, ending with the words: "The gravest responsibility regarding the country shall fall upon all who dare encroach on the regularity of the Constituent Assembly elections, on which the entire country is now pinning its hopes." These words were the finale of the whole organizational work of the epoch of the Provisional Government, on the eve of the final defeat of the organizational formula of the February revolution. After several days, a platoon of soldiers entered the Conference of the All-Russian Commission with Lenin's personally signed order for the arrest of the "defensist [32] Kadet-members" of the commission. V. D. Nabokov and the rest of us were taken to Smol'nyi.[33]

In the arguments of recent years about the Russian Revolution, I have never found an understanding of the profound tragedy of all that happened at that time. One discussed who was guilty and guilty of what. Some sought in its fate lessons and warnings for the future, while others maintained that it was necessary to return to its precepts. Above all these arguments there stands, for me, one fact beyond all dispute: the vast majority of Russian society, everything that was best in it, was united in an attempt to build Russian democracy by some means or other, in this or that form, as participants or as the opposition, with faith or disbelief. I have attempted

32. "Defensism" referred to those persons who supported a united war effort to protect national interests from the Germans.

33. Smol'nyi, a well-known finishing school for girls (1808–1917), became the headquarters of the Petrograd Soviet of Workers' and Soldiers' Deputies on August 4, 1917 (O.S.). It also became the headquarters of the Bolsheviks subsequent to their assumption of the direction of the Petrograd Soviet in September 1917.

to remind you of what Nabokov contributed to that effort. All his intellect and all his will, all his culture and self-restrained but profound, basic enthusiasm, were dedicated to affairs of state during this period of Russian historical development. Together with others, Nabokov suffered defeat. Yet is it possible to forget that this was the defeat of everything really precious in the nation?— "The fateful, native land" as one of Blok's [34] poems states it? Yes, this and the other combined: fateful and native. To its fate was brought Nabokov's sacrifice; but he gave himself to his country.

34. Alexander Blok (1880–1921), lyric poet; secretary, Murav'ev Commission, 1917; author, "Poslednie dni starogo rezhima" ("Last Days of the Old Regime") *Arkhiv Russkoi Revoliutsii,* 4 : 5–54.

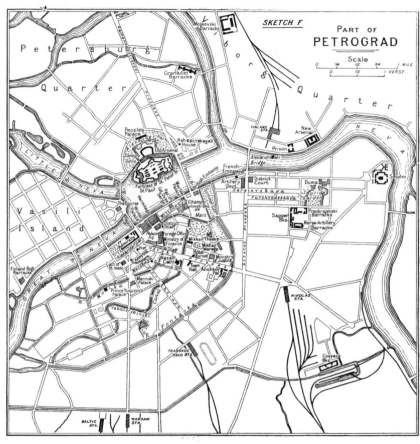

Street map of Petrograd in 1917. From Sir Alfred Knox, *With the Russian Army, 1914–1917,* vol. 2 (New York: E. P. Dutton and Company, 1921).

1

The Provisional Government

BY V. D. NABOKOV

Exactly a year ago,* during these very days, 20–22 April, events occurred in Petersburg whose entire significance for the fate of the war and the fate of our fatherland could not *then* be fully comprehended and evaluated. *Now* it can be clearly seen that it was precisely in those turbulent days that for a moment the hideous, ferocious face of anarchy showed itself for the first time after the triumph of the revolution. Once more in the name of party intrigue and demagogic lusts, the Acheron [1] arose and with criminal levity unconsciously abetted treacherous political designs, then presented an ultimatum to the Provisional Government, and got from it fatal concessions and renunciations on two basic questions—foreign policy and the organization of power. In those days the first brilliant and victorious phase of the revolution was concluded, and though still vague, the path which led Russia to collapse and disgrace was becoming discernible.

This does not mean, of course, that all was satisfactory during the course of the first two months, when the new free Russia was

* Written 21 April 1918. [Asterisked footnotes are Nabokov's.]
1. The swift River of Woe in the Hades of Grecian and Latin mythology. The reference here is to the words of the Latin poet, *flectere si nequeo superos Acheronta movebo* ("if I cannot budge the gods, I shall move Acheron"). The term *Acheron* was an everyday expression of the Russian intelligentsia which signified the revolutionary masses, and was used before 1917 in order to avoid the attention of censors.

being organized on the ruins of the autocracy (actually obsolete from 17 October 1905 [2] but eleven years later still intact, attempting to preserve its importance). On the contrary, from the first days of the "bloodless revolution" [3] an attentive and objective observer could have discovered the symptoms of the approaching decomposition. Now, ex post facto, when one looks through the newspapers of that time, those symptoms seem so certain and so obvious! But then, those persons who took upon their shoulders the unquestionably difficult task of governing Russia, particularly at the beginning, seemed to have been under certain illusions. They wanted to believe in final success; without this faith where would they have found the moral strength?

Their faith was first clearly shaken during those ominous April days [4] when on the city squares "revolutionary Petrograd" raised the vital question of Russia's foreign policy aims, and when for the first time slogans appeared on red banners calling for the overthrow of the Provisional Government or its individual members.

From that moment began the martyrdom of the Provisional Government. It can be established that Guchkov's [5] resignation and the

2. A reference to Tsar Nicholas II's Imperial Manifesto of that date, which proclaimed civil liberties, broadened the franchise for elections to the Duma (a "parliament" previously conceded that year), and announced that no law would be valid without the consent of the Duma.

3. The victims of the revolution included 169 killed, 996 wounded, and 279 sick and hospitalized. For further information, see R. P. Browder and A. F. Kerensky, eds., *The Russian Provisional Government, 1917,* 3 vols. (Stanford, Calif., 1961), 1 : 140, hereafter cited as B. & K.

4. The "April Crisis" was precipitated by Foreign Minister Miliukov's note to the Allies of April 18 (O.S.) and led to the formation of a coalition government of liberals and socialists. I. G. Tseretelli wrote a detailed account of the crisis: "Reminiscences of the February Revolution: The April Crisis," *The Russian Review* 14 (1955) : 93–108, 184–200, 301–21; 15 (1956) : 93–108. For Miliukov's own version, see his *Political Memoirs, 1905–1917* (Ann Arbor, Mich., 1967), as well as his *Istoriia vtoroi russkoi revoliutsii* (*History of the Second Russian Revolution*) (Sofia, 1921–23), pt. 1, pp. 92–117. See also B. & K., 3 : 1236–85.

5. Aleksandr Ivanovich Guchkov (1862–1936), son of wealthy Moscow industrialist; Moscow University graduate; veteran, Boer War; cofounder and leader, Octobrist party; president, Third State Duma; president, Central War Industries Committee; twice head, Russian Red Cross; first minister of war and navy, 1917; emigrated to Berlin in 1918, then to Paris. See his memoirs in *Posledniia Novosti,* Paris, nos. 5654, 5661, 5663, 5668 (September–October, 1936).

sacrifice of Miliukov to the demands of the Executive Committee of the Petersburg Soviet of Workers' and Soldiers' Deputies dealt the Provisional Government the first blow, from which it never recovered. Strictly speaking, the next six months with their periodic upheavals and crises, with the vain attempts to create a strong coalitionary power, with the fantastic conferences in Malachite Hall and in Moscow's Bolshoi Theater—these six months were one continuous process of dying. True, there was one short moment in the beginning of July when the government's authority again seemed to recover: this was after the suppression of the first Bolshevik uprising. But the Provisional Government was unable to take advantage of this moment, and the favorable conditions evaporated unexploited. They were never repeated. The ease with which Lenin and Trotsky succeeded in overthrowing Kerensky's last coalition government revealed its internal impotence. The degree of this impotence surprised even well-informed people at the time.

From the first days after the [February] coup [6] I was quite intimate with the Provisional Government. In the course of the first two months (during the first crisis) I occupied the post of Head of the Chancellery and consequently found myself in one way or another rather closely associated with it. Unfortunately, at the time I kept neither a diary nor any systematic records. Busy from early morning till late at night, I could hardly manage to accomplish the work that fell to me. Thus I have virtually no documentary evidence relating to this period. I have long hesitated to try to write down what has been preserved in my memory, wondering if it was worthwhile to take up my pen after the passage of so many months. The difficulty of this task is made greater by the conditions in which I now find myself, living in this "god-forsaken corner" of the Crimea, which has been completely cut off from the rest of Russia for a whole month and has just been occupied by the Germans. There is nothing at hand to aid my memory except piles of

6. Nabokov carefully distinguishes between *coup d'état* (*pereverot*) and *revolution* (*revoliutsiia*). For him, February/March and October/November 1917 were coups, not revolutions. What happened in March was an overthrow followed by revolution, during the course of which occurred a second coup on November 7. The distinction is observed throughout the translation.

Rech' [7] which I. I. Petrunkevich [8] fortunately kept and has put at my disposal. True, this is a very valuable aid, but it cannot, of course, reflect the movement of that inner political life behind the scenes which, as is always the case, directed and entirely determined the course of external life.

In the course of those two months in which I occupied the post as Head of the Chancellery of the Provisional Government, I attended its closed sessions almost every day where I was the only person who was not officially a member of the government. I shall refer later in more detail to the question of my position and the reason which led me during my brief period of work to put up with a situation that made me a mere witness to, and not a participant in, the political "creativity" of the Provisional Government. Now I want only to establish at this time that, to my knowledge, no trace remains of all these conferences. I could take no notes during the debates because of their strictly confidential character. This, of course, would have elicited a protest, above all from Kerensky, since he was always very suspicious and jealous of anything in which he could detect an encroachment on the "supreme prerogatives" of the Provisional Government. I had no time to write anything ex post facto. I do not think one of the ministers had the opportunity to make any notes after the meetings. So it is understandable that now, a year later, there is not the slightest possibility of my recounting systematically what happened at those conferences.

I have nevertheless decided to record these notes. However

7. *Rech'*, 1906–18, was the Petrograd daily and central news organ of the Constitutional Democratic party. Its chief editors were I. V. Gessen, Paul N. Miliukov, V. D. Nabokov, and A. I. Kaminka. After the Bolshevik coup it appeared under the names of *Nasha Rech'*, *Svobodnaia Rech'*, *Vek*, *Novaia Rech'*, and *Nash Vek*. See Thomas Riha, "Riech': A Portrait of a Russian Newspaper," *Slavic Review* 22 (December 1963) : 663–82.

8. Ivan Il'ich Petrunkevich (1844–1928), prominent early Zemstvo leader; cofounder, Union of Liberation and Kadet party; Kadet deputy, First State Duma, which resulted in his imprisonment; emigrated 1920. See his memoirs in *Arkhiv Russkoi Revoliutsii* (Berlin, 1934), vol. 21 and Fedor Rodichev's essay in *Slavonic and East European Review* 7 (1929) : 316–26; and Charles Timberlake's essay in his *Essays on Russian Liberalism* (Columbia, Mo., 1972), pp. 18–41.

meager the material at the disposal of my memory, I feel that it would be regrettable if this material were totally lost. I consider it extremely important that all those who in any way took part in the work of the Provisional Government follow my example. A future historian will collect and evaluate all the evidence. It may vary greatly in worth, but none of it will be without value if the writer endeavors to satisfy two absolute requirements: not to permit any conscious falsehood (though no one is immune from errors), and to be completely sincere to the end.

This introduction seemed necessary since it clarifies the very character of my memoirs and my own relationship to them. I shall now begin my narrative.

As soon as the war broke out I immediately received—on 21 July 1914—a notice informing me that as a reserve officer I was assigned to the 318th Novgorodskii Infantry Detachment and was required to report to the mobilization point of this detachment in Staraia Russa. I do not intend to give a detailed account here of my experiences, first in Staraia Russa, then in Vyborg where the detachment was quartered until May 1915, and afterwards in the little town of Gainash on the shores of the Gulf of Riga, halfway between Pernov and Riga. At first I was aide-de-camp of the detachment; then in Gainash, where three detachments were consolidated into one regiment (called the 434th Tikhvinskii Infantry Regiment), I became regimental aide-de-camp, and in this first year of the war witnessed the preparatory work at the rear, a process that was probably more or less the same in all of Russia. I think that my observations on this period are not entirely without interest, but for the time being I am postponing the writing of this material and everything that relates to my service in the Asiatic Section of the General Staff, to which I was transferred from Gainash in September 1915, quite unexpectedly as far as I was concerned and without any action on my part. I remained there right up to the very coup, which came when I was temporarily responsible for the clerical services of that institution. If I speak of my war service here, it is only to show that from July 1914 to March 1917 I took no part whatsoever in politics. Even when I returned to Petersburg, I did not resume my journalistic work on the newspaper *Rech'* * or my work with the Central Committee of the Party of the People's Freedom. I could not return openly to either because of my position as an officer serving with the General Staff. I had no desire to do so covertly—besides, there would have been no real sense in any such secret participation. Nevertheless, it is important for a clear understanding of much that follows that I state this circumstance.

From the beginning of the war until the very revolution I was cut off from politics, and in particular from party life, and only followed it on the outside as a sideline observer. It was quite unaware of the complicated relationships that had developed during those years within the Duma and within the core of our Central Committee. I hardly knew Kerensky—my acquaintance with him was purely superficial—when we met we exchanged greetings and trivial small talk. I could judge his political physiognomy only by his speeches in the Duma, and of these my opinion had never been high. Of course, because of my propinquity with the editorship of *Rech'* and my personal relationship with Miliukov, Gessen, Shingarev, Rodichev,[9] and others, I neither could, nor indeed wanted to, lose my connection, or rather contact, with the party and with politics; nor did I lose it. Nevertheless, my isolation was the reason that, after the coup and in the beginning of my renewed political activity, I was not immediately able to decipher the tangled webb of both personal and party relationships which ensnared, and

---

* If one does not count a series of sketches that appeared as a result of my trip to England in February 1916 and subsequently were published as a separate book under the title *From England at War*.

9. Iosif Vladimirovich Gessen [Hessen] (1866–1943), jurist, publicist; cofounder, Kadet party; editor, *Rech'*, 1906–18; emigrated; editor, *Rul'* (*The Rudder*), Berlin, 1920–31; *Arkhiv Russkoi Revoliutsii,* Berlin, 1921–37. See his *V dvukh vekakh* (*In Two Epochs*) (Berlin, 1937).

Fedor Izmailovich Rodichev (1856–1933), jurist; Zemstvo leader; Kadet deputy, First, Second, Third, Fourth State Dumas; member, Kadet Party Central Committee; minister state secretary for Finland, March 1917; emigrated after Bolshevik coup. See his articles in *Slavonic and East European Review* (June, December, 1923) and in *Poledniia Novosti,* Paris, Sept. 19, 1931; May 5, 1934; April 22, 1932. See also Bernard Pares and Peter Struve's essays in *Slavonic and East European Review* (July 1933) and (January 1934) plus Kermit McKenzie's essay in Charles Timberlake, ed., *Essays in Russian Liberalism,* pp. 42–61.

partly fettered, the work of the Provisional Government. There was much I did not know, and therefore much I did not understand. This had an effect on the role I played, as will be seen later.

I will now proceed to the extrinsic facts in their chronological sequence.

On 23 February my wife was due to return from Raahe, in Finland, where she had gone with our [eldest] son in mid-January and where she had stayed several days after his return, convalescing from bronchitis. I drove to the station to meet her and vividly recollect how on our way home I was telling her and Colonel Miatlev (to whom we gave a lift in our car to his house in St. Isaac's Square) that Petersburg was very restless—a workers' movement, strikes, great crowds in the streets—that the authorities were nervous and apparently irresolute, and that it appeared that the troops, and in particular the Cossacks, could not be counted upon. On Friday the 24th and Saturday the 25th I went to work as usual. On Sunday the 26th the Nevskii [Prospekt] had the appearance of a military camp; it was cordoned off. That evening I was at I. V. Gessen's, where friends and acquaintances usually gathered on Sundays. This time, I remember, I found only Guber (Arzub'ev) [10] there, and he soon left. We exchanged impressions. What was happening seemed to us rather ominous. The circumstances that power—the highest—was deposited at such a critical time with persons like Prince Golitsyn, Protopopov, and General Khabalov [11] could not but fill us with the gravest concern. Nevertheless, that evening of the 26th we hardly thought that the following two or three days would bring colossal and decisive events of universal historical significance.

Returning home by the Malaia Koniushennaia, I could not take

10. P. Guber [Arzub'ev], coworker of A. V. Peshekhonov in the Commissariat of the Petrograd side after March 1917.

11. Prince Nikolai Dmitrievich Golitsyn (1850–1925), chairman, council of Ministers, December 1916–March 1917.

Aleksandr Dmitrievich Protopopov (1866–1918), Octobrist deputy, Third State Duma; deputy-chairman, Fourth State Duma; acting minister, then minister of the interior, 1916; shot by the Bolsheviks.

General Sergei Semenovich Khabalov (1858–1924), commander, Petrograd Military District, 1916–March 1917.

the usual way—straight to the Nevskii and the Morskaia—because I would not have been allowed to cross the Nevskii. I took a side street to the Bol'shaia Koniushennaia, then I went through Volynkin Lane to the Moika, over the Pevcheskii Bridge, across Palace Square which was completely deserted, gloomy, and vast, and past the Nevskii along Admiralty Prospekt. Passing the office of the municipal governor, I could not help noticing the large number of automobiles (ten or twelve) parked in front. I got back about 1 A.M., filled with alarm and somber forebodings.

On Monday morning the 27th, I left for work at 10 A.M. as always. The Asiatic Section of the General Staff was housed then in the building of the former Chief Administration of Cossack Troops, on the Karavannaia across from the Simeonovskii Bridge. Walking along the Karavannaia and coming to a public garden, I was stopped by a gentleman of familiar face (who he was I neither remembered then, nor have I been able to since), and he told me that there was shooting in the Kirochnaia and that a military unit was mutinying. I recollect that he mentioned the Preobrazhenskii Regiment.[12] When I got to the Asiatic Section I received no new information. Routine work got under way, but it somehow proceeded sluggishly that day. Nevertheless, we (my colleagues and I) stayed the usual time, until 3 o'clock, when I went home along the Nevskii, which, though still accessible to traffic at the time, was crowded with masses of people.

By evening, as far as could be seen from the windows, and particularly from the side windows of an oriel which overlooked the street and afforded a view as far as the Hotel "Astoria" [13] in one direction and Konnogvardskii Lane in the other, the Morskaia had become totally deserted. Armored cars began to pass by, rifle shots and machine-gun volleys could be heard, soldiers and sailors ran by keeping close to the walls. Occasionally single shots grew to volleys. Sometimes, but only momentarily, everything became quiet. The telephone continued to work, and during the day, I recollect, a number of friends related information about what was happening.

12. One of the Household Guards.

13. The Hotel Astoria on St. Isaac's Square was commonly known in 1917 as the Hotel Militaire, as most foreign military attachés resided there.

We went to bed at our usual time. On the morning of the 28th of February very heavy firing began again in the square and also in that part of the Morskaia which runs from the Lutheran Church to the Potseluev Bridge. It was dangerous to venture out, partly because of the shooting and partly because officers were beginning to have their epaulets torn off their shoulders. Rumors were already circulating among the population about soldiers attacking officers. At about 11 A.M. (perhaps even earlier) a large throng of soldiers and sailors passed beneath the windows of our house on their way to the Nevskii. They were walking along disorderly and out of formation; no officers were with them. This crowd was apparently being fired on, either from the Astoria or from the Ministry of Agriculture, but this has never been definitely established; even the fact of the shooting has never been established, so it may have been invented later. However it was, this throng, influenced either by the shots (if there were any), or for some other reason, began to demolish the Astoria. "Refugees" from the hotel began to turn up at our place: my sister with her husband Admiral Kolomeitsov,[14] then a whole family with small children brought along by some English officers we knew, then another family of distantly related Nabokovs. All these were somehow accommodated in our house.

All day Tuesday the 28th and Wednesday, 1 March, I never left the house. There was much bustling about in settling in the unexpected and involuntary guests, but the greater part of the day was spent in a kind of stupor and anxious waiting. Precise news was scarce. All that was known was that the State Duma appeared to be the focal point, and toward evening, the 1st of March, it was being said that the whole Petersburg garrison, and also several units which had arrived from the suburbs, had joined the rebels.

As early as the morning of 2 March officers could appear freely in the streets, and I decided to go to the Asiatic Section to clarify the situation. Upon arrival I found on the first landing a large crowd of officials, officers, and clerks. I quickly passed through to our office proper, but presently I was asked to come and say a few words concerning current events. I went to join the gathering. They met

14. Admiral Nikolai Nikolaevich Kolomeitsov was a hero of the Russo-Japanese War.

me with applause. We all passed into the big hall; I climbed upon a table and made a short speech. I do not remember my exact words, but the general idea was that despotism and lawlessness had been overthrown, that liberty had conquered, that it was now the duty of the entire country to fortify this liberty, and that to do this tireless work and enormous discipline were necessary. In answer to individual questions I said that, thus far, I myself knew little of what had occurred, but that I intended to go to the State Duma during the day and, of course, find out the details, and that tomorrow we could gather again. With that we ended the meeting, and the staff dispersed in lively conversation. I did not stay long at the Asiatic Section, inasmuch as neither its chief, General Manakin, nor his immediate assistant, General Davletshin,[15] were present, and as it was impossible, of course, to think of any work that day. Returning home, I had lunch, and at 2 o'clock went out again, intending to go to the State Duma.

At the corner of the Nevskii and the Morskaia I immediately ran into all the General Staff personnel, proceeding to the State Duma to declare their allegiance to the Provisional Government, whose formation had just become known. I joined them, and we went along the Nevskii, Liteinaia, Sergievskaia, Potemkinskaia, and Shpalernaia. The streets were full of people. Agitated, excited faces were visible everywhere and already red flags were flying. Just as we were passing the Anichkov Palace, an elderly, well-dressed man of intelligent countenance noticed me and, stepping off the pavement (I was walking on the outside), ran up to me, grabbed me by the hand, shook it and thanked me ''for all that you have done,'' adding with tremendous energy and decisiveness: ''Only do not leave us any Romanovs,[16] we have no use for them.'' On the Po-

15. Major-General Abdel-Azis Aziovich Davletshin was later a member of the Turkestan Committee in 1917, which the Provisional Government set up to administer the Turkestan Krai, the Transcaspian and Semirichensk provinces, as well as Khiva and Bukhara.

16. By 1917 the Romanovs consisted of several branches: Pavlovich, Constantinovich, Nikolaevich, Mikhailovich, etc. Technically, the male line that began with Michael in 1613 ended with Peter II (1730) and the Holstein Gottorp (related to the Romanovs through Peter the Great's daughter) took over with Peter III (1762), though the tsars continued to call themselves Romanovs.

temkinskaia we met a fairly large group of policemen under guard, apparently from the Chevalier Guard Regiment's riding-school, where they had been locked up at the beginning of the uprising.

During the forty or fifty minutes when we were walking to the State Duma I experienced a sense of spiritual elation such as I have not since known. It seemed to me that something great and sacred had occurred, that the people had cast off their chains, that despotism had collapsed. . . . I did not then properly assess the fact that essentiallly what had occurred was a military revolt which had spontaneously broken out in consequence of conditions created by three years of war, and that in this soil lay the seeds of future anarchy and catastrophe. . . . If such thoughts even appeared, I dispelled them.

When we approached the Shpalernaia it proved to be completely blocked by troops leading the way to the Duma. Our progress was halted several times and we had to wait quite a while. Automobiles were continuously edging along, hardly able to get through the throng. The square in front of the Duma building was so crowded that there was no room to move. In the alley leading to the entrance considerable shouting and a great deal of pushing was occurring; at the entrance gates some Jewish-looking young men were interrogating those who were passing through; from time to time shouts of "hurrah!" were audible. For a minute I despaired of getting to the Duma entrance, and I lost contact with my companions. At last, by elbowing and pushing through, I got to the entrance steps.

At that moment V. N. L'vov climbed onto a platform in front of the doors, or possibly upon the seat of an open [touring] car (I did not have a good view) and made a short speech to the military units gathered in the square. His voice was scarcely audible, and his speech produced no impression. When he had finished and stepped to the doors of the Duma, the crowd surged that way too, and the crush became even heavier. I do not remember how I came to be in the vestibule. The interior of the Tauride Palace immediately struck one with its unusual appearance. Soldiers, soldiers, and more soldiers, with tired, dull faces, seldom gay or smiling faces; everywhere were signs of an improvised camp, rubbish, straw; the air was thick like some kind of a dense fog, there was a smell of soldiers' boots, cloth, sweat; from somewhere we could hear the hysterical voices of orators addressing a meeting in the Catherine Hall—everywhere crowding and bustling confusion.

Already leaflets listing the members of the Provisional Government were being circulated. I remember how astonished I was upon learning that Kerensky had been appointed minister of justice. (At the time I did not understand the significance of this fact and had expected that Maklakov [17] would be appointed to the post). Just as unexpected was the appointment of M. I. Tereshchenko. I came across a journalist I knew, and at my request he showed me the way to the rooms where Miliukov, Shingarev, and others of my friends were situated. We went along some corridors, through small rooms, seeing everywhere a multitude of familiar faces. We bumped into Prince G. E. L'vov on the way. I was struck by his somber, despondent appearance and the tired expression in his eyes.

In the room farthest back I found Miliukov bending over some papers with pen in hand. As it turned out, he was revising the text of a speech he had just made, the speech in which he had declared himself for the preservation of the monarchy (assuming that Nicholas II would abdicate or be deposed). Anna Sergeevna, his wife, was sitting next to him. Miliukov could not speak a word: he had lost his voice, having apparently strained it speaking all night at soldiers' meetings. Shingarev and Nekrasov had similar hoarse, toneless voices. The rooms were full of all kinds of persons. For some reason a highly dismayed Prince General S. K. Belosel'skii was there, anticipating Guchkov, so he said. After a time

17. Vasilii Alekseevich Maklakov (1870–1957), lawyer; cofounder, Kadet party; Kadet deputy, Second, Third, Fourth State Dumas; member, Kadet Party Central Committee; ambassador to France, 1917; president, Russian Emigrants' Committee (France), after 1917. See his *Iz Vospominanii (From My Recollections)* (New York, 1954) and Michael Karpovich's essay in E. J. Simmons, ed., *Continuity and Change in Russian and Soviet Thought* (Cambridge, Mass., 1955), pp. 129–43; also, the essay by David A. Davies in Charles Timberlake's *Essays in Russian Liberalism,* pp. 78–89; and R. P. Browder's article in *Texas Quarterly* 1, no. 4 (Winter 1958): 157–64.

Kerensky, accompanied by Count Aleksei Orlov-Davydov [18] (the hero of the Poiré case), appeared from somewhere, excited, agitated, hysterical. It seems he had come directly from a session of the Executive Committee of the Soviet of Workers' and Soldiers' Deputies, at which he had announced his acceptance of the portfolio of the minister of justice and had received a sanction in the form of his reelection as a member of the Presidium [19] of the committee. While Miliukov seemed calm and completely composed, Kerensky, on the contrary, struck one with his loss of emotional balance. I remember one strange gesture of his. He wore, as he always did (that is, before he took upon himself the role of the ''hostage of democracy'' in the Provisional Government),[20] a jacket, a starched collar with upturned corners. He grabbed these corners and ripped them off, achieving a deliberately proletarian look . . . instead of that of a dandy. While I was there he nearly fainted, and Orlov-Davydov gave him something to inhale or to drink, which I do not remember.

In the neighboring room some military conference was proceeding. From a distance I recognized Generals Mikhnevich and Aver'ianov.[21]

Apparently, at the time it was already being told—with disapproving skepticism—that Guchkov and Shul'gin had left for Pskov.

There was nothing for me to do at the Duma. It was impossible

18. Count Aleksei A. Orlov-Davydov (1871–?), Progressive bloc, Fourth State Duma; prominent in Masonic movement; one of the richest landowners in Russia; maintained close relationship with Kerensky and Grand Duke Nikolai Mikhailovich.

19. The Presidium consisted of the chairman and the two deputy-chairmen of the Petrograd Soviet. For Kerensky's speech, see B. & K., 1: 128–29.

20. In the first Provisional Government Kerensky referred to himself as ''the hostage of democracy,'' because he was the lone ministerial liaison between the nonsocialist ministers of the government and the socialist ''revolutionary democracy'' of the Petrograd Soviet of which he was deputy chairman. Actually, Kerensky often headed a majority in the cabinet against a minority led by Miliukov, and thus the phrase was not entirely apt. Kerensky really considered himself above party in 1917, and a rallying point.

21. Aver'ianov, commandant of the Military Region of the Caucasus after May 15.

to carry on any sort of systematic conversation with people who were deathly tired. Having spent some time there and having absorbed the frantic and crazed atmosphere, I made my way toward the exit. Along the way, in one of the small rooms, I met P. B. Struve [22] who, if I am not mistaken, had been at the Duma almost constantly since Tuesday. His mood was extremely skeptical. We talked about the unusual complexity and difficulty of the present situation. Then I went home.

On the morning of the following day, 3 March, I went to the Asiatic Section at the usual time. At the corner of the Morskaia and the Voznesenskii I met M. A. Stakhovich,[23] who reported to me, as though it were an accomplished fact, about the abdication of Nicholas II (for himself and for his son) and of the succession to the throne of Mikhail Aleksandrovich. This was corroborated by M. P. Kaufman [24] (the former minister of education) whom I met not far from the Karavannaia. Arriving at work, I again found great excitement, with crowds on the stairs and in the big conference hall, and was asked again to give some kind of clarification of the present situation. I agreed. In the hall the entire staff gathered, and the highly respected General Agapov, chief of the Cossack Section of the General Staff, also came. In my speech I imparted what information I had (in truth, extremely meager) and said that the fact of the tsar's abdication must also resolve the problem for all who

22. Peter Bernardovich Struve (1870–1944), economist; most prominent Legal Marxist of 1890s; author, Social Democratic Manifesto; later, member, Kadet Party Central Committee; Kadet deputy, Second State Duma; minister, Denikin and Wrangel governments after the Bolshevik coup; in emigration he associated with monarchists and edited *Russkaia mysl'* (*Russian Thought*) in Prague, and *Vorozhedenie* (*The Renaissance*), Paris. See Richard Pipes, *Peter Struve: Liberal on the Left, 1870–1905* (Cambridge, Mass., 1970) and Peter B. Struve et al., *Food Supply in Russia during the World War* (New Haven, Conn., 1930), and his *Razmyshleniia o russkoi revoliutsii* (*Reflections on the Russian Revolution*) (Sofia, 1921).

23. Mikhail Aleksandrovich Stakhovich (1861–?), Octobrist deputy, First, Second State Dumas; elected member, State Council, 1907, 1912; governor-general of Finland, March–September 1917.

24. M. P. Kaufman was minister of education in the Imperial Government after the 1905 Revolution; he opposed all reform.

stood by the principle of true loyalty *quand-même;* and then, dwelling on the impending task, I developed the thoughts I had expressed the day before concerning the necessity to make every effort in our power in our work for absolute discipline. Others, including General Agapov, spoke after me. The general mood was very firm and positive, with no noticeable dissent. I even remember that Agapov raised a few urgent practical questions which, as he explained, demanded immediate solution if regular work were not to cease and the normal course of affairs to be disrupted.

After spending a short time with my colleagues, I decided to visit the chief of the Asiatic Section, General Manakin, who had not left his house on account of sickness. (I think he had asked me over the telephone to drop by his house). It was gloriously sunny, frosty weather. I had hardly arrived at General Manakin's and begun speaking with him when my wife telephoned and told me that I had been requested by Prince L'vov to report at once to No. 12 Millionnaia, where Grand Duke Mikhail Aleksandrovich was in Princess Putiatin's apartment. I immediately took leave of General Manakin and hurried to that address, on foot of course, as neither cabs nor trams were available. The Nevskii presented an unusual picture: not a single cab or automobile was about, no police, and throngs of people occupied the expanse of the street. In front of the entrance to Anichkov Palace, people were burning the emblematic eagles [25] that had been taken down from the signs of the court-appointed purveyors.

I must have arrived at the Millionnaia around 3 o'clock. A sentry from the Preobrazhenskii Regiment was standing on the steps of residence No. 12. An officer came out to meet me, I gave my name, he went away to get his instructions and, returning at once, invited me upstairs.

Removing my wraps in the hall, I first went into a big sitting-room. (It was here, I discovered, that a conference had taken place that morning between Mikhail Aleksandrovich, members of the Provisional Government, and members of the Provisional Commit-

25. The emblem of the House of Romanov was adopted in the 1490s from the double-headed eagle of Byzantium.

tee [26] of the State Duma, ending with the grand duke's decision to decline the "legacy" which had been thrust upon him.) Prince L'vov and Shul'gin sat in the neighboring room, apparently the boudoir of the hostess. Prince L'vov explained the reason I had been invited. He told me that even in the Provisional Government opinions differed concerning the question of whether or not Mikhail Aleksandrovich should accept the throne. Miliukov and Guchkov were definitely and categorically in favor of acceptance and were making this question the *punctum saliens* on which their participation in the cabinet would depend. Others opposed acceptance. The grand duke had listened to all of them and had requested time to consider the matter in private (I assume that he consulted his secretary Matveev,[27] whom he greatly trusted and who advised him to respond negatively.) After a time he returned to the room where the conference was in process and declared that under the present circumstances he was far from convinced that his acceptance of the throne would be for the good of the fatherland, that it might not serve the cause of unity but rather of disunity, that he did not wish to be the unwilling cause of possible bloodshed, and that, therefore, he deemed it impossible to accept the throne and referred the definitive decision of the question to the Constituent Assembly.

At this time Prince L'vov added that, as a result of this decision, Miliukov and Guchkov were withdrawing from membership in the Provisional Government: "If Guchkov leaves, it does not matter; after all, as it happens (*sic*) the Army can't stand him; the troops simply hate him. But it is necessary to persuade Miliukov to stay without fail. That is the duty of you and your friends to help us." In response to my question of why I had been asked to come, Prince L'vov said that it was necessary to prepare Mikhail Aleksandrovich's act of abdication. The draft of the act had been outlined by Nekrasov, but the effort was incomplete and not entirely

26. The Provisional Committee of the State Duma was a group of deputies who decided to meet unofficially in the Tauride Palace, despite the tsar's order proroguing the State Duma. From this Provisional Committee emerged the Provisional Government. See B. & K., 1 : 45–47.

27. For A. S. Matveev's account, see *Vorozhdenie,* Paris, 24 (1952) : 141–45, or the excerpts in English in B. & K., 1 : 106–09.

satisfactory, and, since everyone was dreadfully tired and in no condition to think straight, not having slept all night, they requested that I undertake the task. Then he gave me Nekrasov's draft, which I still have among my papers, together with the final version of the text.

At this point I would like to pause momentarily in my narrative to consider the question of Mikhail Aleksandrovich's abdication.

Subsequently, I returned many a time in thought to that moment. Now, at the end of April 1918, as I write these lines in the Crimea, conquered by the Germans (''temporarily occupied'' as they say), having experienced all the bitter disappointments, all the horrors, all the humiliation, and all the shame of that nightmare year of revolution; standing before the ruins of a broken, dismembered, defiled Russia; having experienced all the abominations of the Bolshevik orgy; and having realized the infathomable incompetence of those forces to whose lot the creation of a new Russia has fallen, I ask myself whether there would not have been a better chance of a satisfactory outcome if Mikhail Aleksandrovich had accepted the crown from the tsar's hands.

It must be said that, of all possible ''monarchical'' solutions, this would have been the worst. Above all, it contained an incurable intrinsic flaw. Our Fundamental Laws did not envisage the possibility of the abdication of a ruling emperor and had not established any rules concerning succession to the throne in this case. But of course, no laws can erase the fact of the abdication, lessen its meaning, or thwart it. It is specifically this fact to which certain juridical consequences must be related. Since, where the Fundamental Laws are mute, abdication means precisely the same thing as death, then clearly the consequences must be the same—that is, the throne passes to the lawful heir. One can ony abdicate in one's own name. An abdicating emperor has no right to deprive one of the throne who has a right to it by law, whether that person be an adult or a minor. The Russian throne is not the emperor's private property nor his patrimony (*votchina*) to appropriate according to his own free will. Nor is it possible for this to be based on the supposed agreement of the heir, since this heir was not yet thirteen years of age. In any case, even if this agreement were categorically expressed, it would be subject to dispute, and in the present case the question did not even arise. Therefore, the transfer of the throne to Mikhail was an unlawful act. Mikhail had no lawful title to it whatsoever. The only legal recourse would have been to adhere to the succession that would have been followed had Nicholas II died. His heir would have been made emperor and Mikhail would have been regent. If the decision undertaken by Nicholas II had not turned out to be such a surprise to Guchkov and Shul'gin, they might have drawn his attention to the inadmissibility of the decision that Mikhail accept a crown to which he had no right while the lawful heir to the throne was still alive.

I mention this aspect of the question because it is more than a matter of juridical quibbling. Doubtless, it significantly weakened the position of the supporters of the preservation of the monarchy. No doubt it also influenced Mikhail's reasoning. I do not know whether the question was discussed from this perspective at the morning conference, but undoubtedly Nicholas II himself had done the most (although hardly consciously) to complicate and confuse the situation which had arisen. True, he was governed—according to the wording of the act of abdication—by his feelings as a loving father who did not wish to be separated from his son. But however honorable these feelings may be, they certainly cannot justify the terms of the act.

Mikhail's acceptance of the throne would therefore have been *ab initio vitiosum,* as the jurists say, defective from the very beginning. But let us suppose that this, so to speak, formal side of the matter were to be ignored. What, essentially, would have been the situation?

On a priori grounds one can present very strong argumentation that in the event of acceptance the consequences would have been favorable. First of all, it would have preserved the continuity of the apparatus of power and its structure. The basis of Russia's state system would have been preserved, and all the essentials would have been there to guarantee that the monarchy would be of a constitutional character. Those conditions under which Mikhail ascended the throne would have facilitated this, as would his personal integrity and indisputable nobility of character, a character devoid, moreover, of a lust for power and of despotic inclinations. The fatal question of the calling of the Constituent Assembly in wartime would have been eliminated. What could have been established would have been a true constitutional government, founded firmly on the law, providing the framework for the new constitution—not a Provisional Government nominally endowed with dictatorial power though in practice forced to struggle for and consolidate this power. The great shock to the national psyche caused by the collapse of the throne would have been avoided. In short, the coup would have been kept within certain limits and perhaps the international position of Russia would have been saved. There would also have been a chance to preserve the army.

But all this, unfortunately, is only one aspect of the matter. For this aspect to be decisive, there would have to have been present a number of conditions that simply were not there. Having accepted the throne from Nicholas's hands, Mikhail would at once have aligned against himself those forces which emerged in the very first days of the revolution and which wanted to control the situation through close contact with the troops of the Petersburg garrison. By that time (3 March) the minds of these rebellious troops had already been poisoned. They offered no real support. The consolidation of Mikhail's position would undoubtedly have demanded decisive actions—not stopping short of bloodshed, the arrest of the Executive Committee of the Soviet of Workers' and Soldiers' Deputies, and in the event of resistance, the proclamation of a state of siege. Everything would probably have been reduced to appropriate limits within a week. But for that week it would have been essential to have at one's disposal actual forces upon which one could count and rely completely and unconditionally. No such forces existed.

Moreover, Mikhail was by nature a man who was ill-suited, or even completely unsuitable, for the difficult, responsible, and dangerous role he would have had to play. He possessed neither popularity in the eyes of the masses, nor the reputation of being an intellectually renowned person. True, his name was not tarnished; he had not been involved in the dark perpetrations in the scandalous

Rasputin [28] chronicle—for a time he had even seemed to be in opposition to him—but this, of course, was not sufficient to enable him to take the helm of the ship of state with a firm, confident hand. I cannot imagine what elements would have supported him for the sake of higher interests and not for their own sake. The Kadets, who three weeks later raised the republican flag (I shall deal with this in more detail in its appropriate place), could have given such support. As for the bureaucracy, the nobility, the court circles? These were certainly not organized; they were completely perplexed and did not present a fighting force. Finally, we must take into account the general mood that prevailed in Petersburg in those days: a revolutionary intoxication, an unconscious maximalism which had turned the most sober heads. In such an atmosphere the monarchical tradition—which was, moreover, devoid of profound spiritual strength—could not be an effective force for unity and solidarity.

I am formulating my conclusion, at which I arrived long ago, in the following manner: if Mikhail's acceptance of the throne had been possible, it would have been beneficial, or at least would have given hope for a favorable outcome. But unfortunately the aggregate conditions were such that an acceptance of the throne was impossible. In common language, "nothing would have come of it." And from the beginning Mikhail must necessarily have felt this. If "we all hope to be Napoleons," [29] he had the least inclina-

28. Grigorii Efimovich Rasputin [Novykh] (1872–1916) was an illiterate Siberian peasant who was considered by those who met him to have hypnotic and clairvoyant faculties. His seemingly incredible ability to stop the bleeding of the young tsarevich gained him, from 1905 on, the closest access to the Imperial Family. His life was scandalous (thus the name Rasputin, or debauchee), and during the First World War his influence and machinations in affairs of state caused greater and greater disaffection for the court. Conservative forces assassinated him in December 1916 in the hope that his removal would stave off an open assault on the dynasty. See M. V. Rodzianko, *The Reign of Rasputin* (London, 1927); Bernard Pares, *The Fall of the Russian Monarchy* (London, 1939); René Fülop-Miller, *Rasputin—The Holy Devil* (New York, 1929): and Prince Yussupoff, *Rasputin: His Malignant Influence and his Assassination* (London, 1927).

29. References to Napoleonic and French revolutionary history were common in 1917. Sergei Eisenstein, in his film *October,* depicts A. F. Kerensky as a Napoleonic figure. During the 1930s Trotsky labeled Stalin a bonapartist.

tion to do so. It is interesting to note that he particularly stressed his resentment at his brother's "thrusting" the throne on him without even asking his consent. And it would be still more interesting to know how he would have reacted if Nicholas had previously asked for his agreement.

I resume my interrupted narrative.

It goes without saying that under the circumstances I did not have to ponder whether the decision was right or wrong. One thing was clear to me: it was necessary to retain Miliukov in the makeup of the Provisional Government; and then, with regard to the urgent matter for which I had been summoned, a clear, definitive, and accurate formulation of the grand duke's abdication had to be determined. As to the first matter, I promised Prince L'vov that I would utilize all the strength and influence I might have with Miliukov, intending to meet him that evening in the Tauride Palace. Regarding the act of abdication, I immediately requested the collaboration of that astute and exacting specialist in state law, Baron B. E. Nol'de. With Prince L'vov's agreement I telephoned him; he happened to be nearby in the Ministry of Foreign Affairs and arrived within a quarter of an hour. We were situated in a room belonging to Princess Putiatin's daughter. V. V. Shul'gin joined us there. The three of us drew up the text of the abdication, Nekrasov's draft undergoing considerable change.

To conclude my account of the drafting of the text, I shall simply say that after we had completed our work, I transcribed the text and presented it through Matveev to the grand duke. The changes he offered, which were accepted, consisted of the addition of a reference to God (absent from the original) and, in the address to the population, for the words drafted by us, "I command," were substituted the word "I beseech." As a result of these changes I had to transcribe the historical document once more. It was now about six in the evening; M. V. Rodzianko arrived. The grand duke came in and in front of us signed the document. He appeared rather embarrassed and somewhat disconcerted. I have no doubt that he was under a heavy strain, but he retained complete self-composure; to tell the truth, I believe he did not fully realize the importance and

significance of the step he was taking. Before we adjourned, he and
M. V. Rodzianko embraced and kissed and Rodzianko called him a
most noble man.

To determine the correct form of the act of abdication we at first
had to settle a number of questions before the juridical ones. First
was the question regarding the external form of the act. Should we
consider that, at the time of its formulation, Mikhail Aleksandrovich was already emperor and his act was the same type of
document as the act of abdication signed by Nicholas II? But then,
in the event of an affirmative answer, Mikhail's abdication could
elicit the same doubts in relation to the rights of other members of
the Imperial Family as those which essentially arose out of Nicholas II's abdication. In addition, this would sanction Nicholas II's
erroneous assumption that he had the right to make Mikhail emperor. We therefore concluded that the situation had to be interpreted thus: Mikhail declined to accept supreme power—this, in
fact, was what the legally valid content of the act had to convey.
But in the prevailing circumstances it seemed necessary not to be
limited by the negative aspect of the act, but to use his statement in
order solemnly to secure, in the eyes of that portion of the population for which it might have serious moral meaning, the plenary
powers of the Provisional Government and its preeminent connection with the State Duma. This was achieved by the words, ''to the
Provisional Government which has arisen on the initiative of the
State Duma and which is invested with plenary powers.'' Shul'gin
supplied the first part of the formula; I, the other.

Again, from the juridical point of view, the objection could be
raised that Mikhail Aleksandrovich, by not assuming supreme
power, could not issue any compulsory and binding instructions
concerning the limits and substance of the Provisional Government's authority. But, I repeat, in this case we did not view the
center of gravity to be the juridical force of the formula but only its
moral and political meaning. It must be noted that the act of renunciation of the throne signed by Mikhail was the *only act* which
defined the limits of the Provisional Government's authority and simultaneously resolved the question concerning the forms of its operation—and in particular, and principally, the question concerning

subsequent activity of the legislative institution. As is known, in its first declaration the Provisional Government termed itself a ''cabinet,'' and the formulation of this cabinet was considered ''a more stable structure of executive authority.'' Obviously, during the formulation of this declaration it was still unclear what features the provisional state regime would take. From the moment of the act of renunciation it was assumed that plenary legislative powers also belonged to the Provisional Government. Yet on the previous day the question had been raised within the Provisional Government (in the words of B. E. Nol'de) of the publication of laws and the undertaking of financial measures according to Article 87 of the Fundamental Laws.

It may seem strange that I have dealt with the contents of the act of renunciation in such detail. It may be said that this act did not make any big impression on the population, that it was soon forgotten and overshadowed by events. Perhaps this is so. Nevertheless, from a more general historical viewpoint, the act of 3 March had without doubt very great significance, was in fact a historical act, and its significance could still become evident in the future. For us at that very moment in the first days of the revolution—when it was still completely unknown how the rest of Russia and the foreign Allied powers would react to the coup, the formation of the Provisional Government, and the entirely new situation—every word seemed enormously important. And it seems to me that we were right.

I have already referred to the fact that our work lasted until evening. When we left it was already dark. If my memory serves me correctly, I did not return home but drove straight to the State Duma to meet with Miliukov, to show him the draft of the act which I had with me, and to arrange for its publication in the press. But first of all, of course, I had to fulfill the promise I had given to Prince G. E. L'vov to make every effort to dissuade Miliukov from withdrawing from the membership of the Provisional Government.

I, of course, had not the slightest doubt that if Miliukov stood by his decision, serious and possibly even disastrous complications would result. This was not to speak of the impression of discord [that would arise] from this very step, of the consequences for the

[Kadet] party, which would be thrown immediately into disarray, and of the grievously difficult position of the Kadet ministers who remained. With Miliukov's resignation, the Provisional Government would be losing its strongest intellectual force and the only person who could direct foreign policy and who was known to Europe. Essentially, his exit would have been a veritable catastrophe.

Arriving at the Tauride Palace, I immediately found Miliukov. That same day Vinaver had already talked to him about the resignation and had also tried to persuade him to change his decision. I read him the text of Mikhail's statement. He was satisfied with this text, and I think it served as the final impetus that induced him to stay in the membership of the Provisional Government. Who influenced Guchkov in the same way, and when, I do not know.

Anna Sergeevna was with Miliukov as before. From her I learned the tragic news of the massacre in Helsingfors [30] and the terrible situation at the front. She seemed totally crushed by these events. I was badly shaken by them. Somber and mournful notes burst immediately upon the joyful triumph, boding nothing good. I must note here that the conviction was promptly stated that German agitation was responsible for these massacres.

To what extent the Germans had a hand in our revolution is a question which, I suppose, will never receive a full and exhaustive answer.[31] In this connection I recall one very sharp episode which occurred about two weeks later, during one of the closed sessions of the Provisional Government. Miliukov was speaking and remarked, in what context I do not remember, that it was no secret

30. The Helsingfors massacre in the first days of the March coup refers to the flare-up of a number of sailors at that naval base, which resulted in the death of Vice-Admiral A. I. Nepenin (b. 1871) and several other officers. See B. & K., 2 : 862.

31. George Katkov has written extensively about this subject in his book *Russia, 1917: The February Revolution* (New York, 1967). See also Z. A. B. Zeman, *Germany and the Revolution in Russia, 1915–18* (London, 1958); S. P. Mel'gunov, *Zolotoi nemetskii kliuch k bol'shevistskoi revoliutsii* (*The Golden German Key to the Bolshevik Revolution*) (Paris, 1951); and Georges Bonnin, "Les Bolchéviques et l'argent allemand pendant la première guerre mondiale," *Révue historique* (January–March 1965), pp. 101–26.

that German money had played a role in a number of factors that
contributed to the overthrow. I stipulate that I do not recollect his
exact words, but the sense was precisely that, and it was expressed
quite categorically. The session was taking place late at night in the
Mariinskii Palace. Miliukov was sitting at a table. Kerensky, as
usual, was impatiently and irritably pacing the hall from one end to
the other. The moment Miliukov spoke these words, Kerensky was
in a far corner of the room. He suddenly stopped and shouted
"How's that? What did you say? Repeat it!" and approached his
seat at the table with quick steps. Miliukov calmly and, so to
speak, emphatically, repeated the phrase. Kerensky became as if
possessed. He grabbed his briefcase, slammed it on the table, and
yelled, "After this, as Mr. Miliukov has dared to slander the sacred
cause of the Great Russian Revolution in my presence, I do not
wish to stay here another minute." With these words, he turned
around and flew out of the hall like a shot. Tereshchenko and some
other minister ran after him, but returned and reported that they
were not successful in detaining him and that he had gone to his
residence (in the Ministry of Justice where he was then living).

I remember that Miliukov preserved his complete composure,
and when I said to him, "What a disguisting and ridiculous sally!"
he replied, "Yes, that's Kerensky's usual style. In the Duma, too,
he often used to pull stunts like that, picking out some phrase used
by a political opponent, then twisting it and using it as a weapon."
Pointedly, none of the remaining ministers said one word about
what had elicited Kerensky's indignation, but they all thought he
should be immediately pacified and dissuaded—explaining that Miliukov's words were not a general appraisal of the revolution.
Someone (Tereshchenko, I think) said that Prince L'vov ought to
go to Kerensky. The others agreed with this (Miliukov remained
quiet, this whole incident was, of course, deeply distasteful to
him). Prince L'vov readily agreed to go and "have a talk" with
Kerensky. The whole incident had no consequence but it left a
painful impression. Frankly, was there ever a closed session which
did not leave such an impression? But about this—later.

That same evening (3 March) in the Tauride Palace, Miliukov informed me that they were counting on me for an important new

post and asked whether I would agree to accept an appointment as governor-general of Finland.[32] I immediately and decisively refused. Apart from any considerations of a personal nature—particularly the fact that I would have to leave Petersburg—my refusal derived from my awareness that I was completely unsuited to administer Finnish affairs. I had never had any special interest in them, I had no contacts or even close acquaintances in Finland, and I was badly oriented about political and party inclinations there.

Refusing any kind of administrative post, I offered my services in the capacity of ''Head of the Chancellery of the Provisional Government,'' an office equivalent to the former Head of the Chancellery of the Council of Ministers. I considered that this post, outwardly a secondary one, would acquire special importance under the conditions of a new provisional state regime, whose functions still remained so vague and undefined. Fundamentally, here we were now faced with the task of creating firm, external limits to government activity, of giving the governmental process a correct and regular form, and also of resolving a whole number of questions in which none of the ministers was interested. But apart from that (while still not realizing the atmosphere in which I would find myself), because I was tightly linked by party relationships with a number of ministers, I expected to be given a consultative vote at the sessions of the Provisional Government. I shall subsequently return to the question of that position which was created for me and which led me, during the first crisis connected with the resignation of Miliukov and Guchkov, to reveal decisively my desire to resign the post of administrative affairs.

Miliukov could only agree with the arguments I presented. We discussed possible candidates for the post of governor-general of Finland. At that time my old friend M. A. Stakhovich had not yet been mentioned, and I do not know who proposed his candidacy, but it was a choice which proved to be entirely successful in many respects, if not in all. I do not remember whether it was that same evening or the next morning that my appointment as Head of the Chancellery was confirmed. At any rate, on Saturday, 4 March, I

32. Finland was part of the Russian Empire from 1809 to 1917.

was attending the evening sessions of the Provisional Government that were being held in the large hall of the Council of the Minister of Internal Affairs in the ministry building in Aleksandrovskii Theater Square.

In the first days of the existence of the Provisional Government (Thursday the 2nd and Friday, 3 March) it was impossible, of course, to speak about organized clerical work. But some sort of chancellery had to be improvised at once, and this job was entrusted to Ia. N. Glinka, who had supervised the State Duma's clerical section. He utilized the staff of the Duma's chancellery. It is necessary to say that the notes of the first and extremely important session of the Provisional Government, in which it established the fundamental principles of its power and policy, were quite unsatisfactory and even unintelligible. When I acquainted myself with the notes, I was rather puzzled and told Miliukov about it. Reading the record, he appraised it more sharply than I. Then it was agreed that he would take the record and reconstruct from memory the proceedings and decisions of the first session, after which the Provisional Government would sign it, having corrected the record in full session. Pavel Nikolaevich actually took the record with him, but in his two months as minister of foreign affairs he apparently did not find the necessary spare time to do the job. However often I reminded him of it, he always gave me an embarrassed smile and promised to work on it in the next few days, but even so he never fulfilled his promise. So the record was never used, and it seems he did not return it. This explains why the printed minutes of the sessions of the Provisional Government begin with no. 2.[33]

Here I will briefly speak about how I organized the Provisional Government's chancellery. First to be resolved was the question of my assistant, the person on whom would fall the largest portion of the preparatory chancellery work. Obviously this could only be a person whom I could trust completely and categorically and who at the same time was not a stranger to the chancellery of the Council of Ministers, which had to be transformed into the chancellery of

33. Apparently the record of session no. 3 of March 4, 1917 is the first set of minutes for a meeting available, even though Nabokov notes no. 2 as the first printed. See B. & K., 1 : 161.

the Provisional Government. It goes without saying that the first of these demands was not satisfied by the current assistant (or deputy) to the Head of the Chancellery of the Council of Ministers (I. N. Lodyzhenskii), A. S. Putilov, whom I did not know personally and who, moreover, was not popular among his colleagues. My choice fell on A. M. Onu.[34] I had known him since 1894, had served in the state chancellery with him for five years (from 1894 to 1899, when I retired), and I had absolute confidence in his loyalty and his preparedness to devote his efforts to his work. On the other hand, I considered him to have sound administrative experience, occupying as he had the post of assistant to the state-secretary of the State Council, so he would not be a *homo novus* in the chancellery.

I did not anticipate any prejudice with regard to myself in the chancellery (where I met some of my former students from the School of Jurisprudence, Messrs. Kirshbaum and Freigang). But at the same time I could not have expected, in the two months I worked with the chancellery, to establish exceptionally cordial relations. It is necessary to attest here that the vast majority of the staff proved fully equal to the task, which demanded of them a quite exceptional capacity for work, conscientiousness, and "discretion." I retain the very best memories of our work together and of our parting, when I received from them a very warmly worded address.

Regarding A. M. Onu, I was not disappointed either with his devotion and preparation for the work or with the splendid qualities of his mind and heart. I must add that our personal relations always were and have remained the best, and that my feelings for him could only be those of warm gratitude and profound respect. On Saturday I informed him by telephone of my intentions regarding him and obtained his agreement. I was still faced with formulating my own position. Obviously, my appointment as Head of the Chancellery of the Provisional Government was henceforth incompatible with my commission as an ensign. For this reason, as early as the evening of Saturday the 4th, A. I. Guchkov signed an order placing me on the retired list. On Monday the 6th I assumed control of the chancellery in the Mariinskii Palace. A. S. Putilov, who visited me

34. See Onu's article "The Provisional Government of Russia in 1917," *Contemporary Review* (October 1933), pp. 446–54.

that morning, introduced the staff to me. He made a welcoming speech, and I replied with a short speech. Then I. N. Lodyzhenskii arrived, and we had a fairly long chat in what had formerly been his study. Everything was conducted in a most proper manner and as well as could be expected. But it was in respect to Lodyzhenskii and Putilov that I first encountered the problem of providing for retiring officials who had attained relatively high rank, a problem that was later to cause the Provisional Government considerable trouble. Since I neither intend nor am able to follow chronological order in these notes, I will deal with this problem now, since it has come to mind.

As is known, during the first days and even weeks of the revolution, a favorite topic in the press and in many public speeches—apart from the "bloodless" character of the revolution, which in its further course and development caused so many rivers of blood—was the tremendous speed and ease with which the new structure was acknowledged by all forces that had appeared to be the most reliable and faithful bulwarks of the old order. Among these were the bureaucracy—the all-Russian, and in particular the Petersburg branch. I recall that as early as 1905, at the First Congress of Zemstvo and Municipal Officials [35] after the October 17 Manifesto (held in Moscow, in Mme. Morozov's house in Vozdvizhenka), the question was raised concerning the radical replacement of the entire local administration (mainly governors, of course). The view was put forward that one could not expect from servants of absolutism either the willingness or the ability to serve the new order—that they would be hostile to it and would adopt an attitude which in present-day revolutionary jargon is called "sabotage."

35. The Congress of Zemstvo and Municipal Officials convened on November 7, 1905 in Moscow and was the last such congress, as political parties replaced them. Zemstvos were created in 1864 as the result of the 1861 emancipation of the serfs. All classes participated as electors and as delegates, though the property qualifications and indirect elections favored the gentry. Elections occurred first for district zemstvos, which in turn elected delegates for the provincial zemstvos. Though the activities of the zemstvos were greatly restricted, nevertheless the institution developed some sense of local self-government. For a discussion of the zemstvos in 1917, see Tikhon J. Polner et al., *Russian Local Government during the War and the Union of Zemstvos* (New Haven, Conn., 1930).

At the time I came out against this assumption. I indicated that we scarcely had an adequate number of ideologically trained workers available, capable of filling jobs immediately in the complex government machinery; on the other hand, I jokingly quoted the well-known phrase of Kukol'niks,[36] "If His Majesty so orders, I can be an obstetrician." I demonstrated that one should not expect from local administrators (the majority of them, of course) such a firmness of conviction, a depth of devotion to ancient principles, and an obstinacy as would resist a powerful *mot d'ordre* [watchword] from above—assuming, of course, the *mot d'ordre* to be sincere and "authentic." I. I. Petrunkevich opposed me at that time. Unfortunately, I was not present to hear the opposing speech in which he, successfully and wittily using my own quotation, revealed amid general laughter that he would not like to be a woman in childbirth attended by "an obstetrician by Royal Command," and that in such a case the mother's fate would be the fate of Russia.

Notwithstanding the wittiness of this objection, it did not convince me. Now the main argument advanced for not accepting the old administrators was not their lack of technical training, but their personal attitude and sentiments (have we very many technically trained people anyway?)—and it was only with this respite that my quotation made any sense. I wanted to say, and I think now, that the vast majority of the bureaucracy are far from infected with the aspiration to be *"plus royaliste que le roi"* [more royal than the king], that they would be ready to acknowledge a fait accompli, would subordinate themselves to a new order, and would not engage in "sabotage." Of course, both at the center and localities in 1905, as now in 1917, there were individuals unacceptable in principle and in practice to a new regime because of their previous activities and clearly defined political physiognomies. These few were subjected to dismissal.

The Provisional Government, as we know, acted differently. One of its first, and most unfortunate, acts was Prince L'vov's famous telegram of 5 March, which was intentionally circulated to all

36. Nestor Vasili'evich Kukol'nik (1809–68), author of ultrapatriotic dramas.

chairmen of provincial zemstvo boards: ''Attaching the greatest importance—for the purposes of establishing order within the country and a successful defense of the state—to the guarantee of an uninterpreted functioning of all the governmental and public institutions, the Provisional Government has deemed it necessary to remove temporarily governors and vice-governors from the execution of their functions.'' Under the same order, the governing of the provinces was temporarily entrusted to the chairmen of the provincial zemstvo boards, acting as provincial commissars of the Provisional Government. Not to speak of the fact that in quite a number of provinces, where the chairman of the board had been appointed by the old government, this order simply meant the utterly groundless and unnecessary replacement of some officials by others far from better; even in provinces with well-structured zemstvo systems it led—in many cases—to sheer absurdity. Not infrequently the chairman of the board was a protégé of the reactionary majority, while the governor was a completely acceptable person without any reactionary tinge. Very soon—almost at once, in fact—the Provisional Government was convinced that the move under consideration was extremely rash and frivolous. But what could it do? In this case, as in many others, it had to consider not essentials but actual practical interests—with the demand for revolutionary phrases, revolutionary demagogy, and the assumed inclinations of the masses. Thus, it was due to these considerations that the police force was condemned, and a few months later its members (as well as those of the gendarmerie) naturally joined the ranks of the worst maximalist brigands (''fish search where it is deeper, men, where it is better'').

The result of such a policy was the mass dismissal—and retirement, voluntary or forced—of whole ranks of high officials, military as well as civilian. The liquidation of a series of institutions and, of course, the natural cessation of work (for example, in the State Council) brought the same result. So now there arose the question—what was to happen to this vast army of people who found themselves to be, according to their own statements, ''on the rocks''? An insignificant minority of these people deserved no attention and aroused no sympathy—there were, of course, among them people who were completely secure materially. But the overwhelming majority represented people who for years had conscientiously toiled away in the bureaucracy, and in some cases had reached old age and had large families to support—people who all their lives were formerly complete strangers to politics but had worked honestly and diligently. Among the members of the State Council were such men as N. S. Taganstev, A. F. Koni,[37] and other less well-known but completely respectable and irreproachable people.

The present masters of the situation, the Bolsheviks (whose hour, incidentally, has already struck),* have, of course, never been concerned with such questions, and the very possibility would be treated with outright derision by the Lenins and Trotskys. They are completely indifferent to the fate of individuals. "When you chop down a forest, chips must fly"—this is a convenient answer to everything. They do not have, and never have had, to deal with the above-mentioned difficulties because, of course, no one could be so naïve as to turn to them expecting a fair and humane attitude. With perfect equanimity they threw out the whole Senate and the whole magistracy; and the tragic, hopeless situation of people who, after working all their lives, now find themselves old and—in the literal sense of the word—without a crust of bread, does not trouble them in the least.

The Provisional Government was in a different situation. Not possessing Jacobin fearlessness, which is frequently combined with Jacobin unscrupulousness, we found it to be extremely difficult to resolve the general problem concerning the fate of members of institutions that were liquidated and frequent questions of the fate of individuals. I shall select as one of the most striking illustrations the matter of the members who had been appointed to the State Council. Among them were men who had not rendered any service

* It was possible to think this in April 1918.

37. Nikolai Stepanovich Tagantsev (1843–1923), law professor, St. Petersburg University; senator, 1887; member, State Council from 1906.

Anatolii Fedorovich Koni (1844–1927), eminent jurist and writer; trial judge in the Vera Zasulich case, 1878; head, Criminal Cassation Department; member, State Council from 1907; law professor, Leningrad University.

to the country and had been appointed for reasons of Black Hundred [38] politics in order to form a reactionary majority; but, as I have already mentioned, there were also civil servants such as Koni and Tagantsev, as well as a number of people for whom the State Council was the apex of long and untarnished service in the ranks of the administrations or the magistracy. By law, when members of the State Council were appointed they received remunerations that were in each case personally determined by the Supreme Authority. Similarly, various pensions paid to members of the State Council were not determined by law on a general basis. Very soon after the coup, in the very first weeks, when it was clear beyond all doubt that the State Council, as an institution, was doomed to complete inactivity until the establishment of the Constituent Assembly (the assembly itself, of course, could not preserve it in any form, let alone in its present one), the State Council's most conscientious and tactful members felt the awkwardness of their position and the moral impossibility of receiving a large remuneration while doing nothing, and they raised the question as to whether they should not resign. In doing so, they had in mind (as I know for certain from my personal conversations with some of them) considerations of a dual nature.

The Provisional Government did not initially abolish the State Council as an institution. Therefore, appointed members who did not consider it possible to continue enjoying the advantages of their position would have to submit their resignations—that is, they would have to take the initiative themselves. If some submitted their resignations and others did not, then clearly an absurdity would arise: men whose primary concern was to keep their salary

38. The Black Hundred was a highly nationalistic and anti-Semitic organization that appointed itself to defend autocracy, orthodoxy, and nationalism against Jews, liberals, students, and foreign elements. It carried out pogroms from the beginning of the twentieth century and after the October Manifesto of 1905 organized the Union of Russian People, among whose leaders figured V. M. Purishkevich and A. I. Dubrovin; the former also organized the fanatical Union of Michael the Archangel. Included in its membership were highly placed officials, gentry, and clergy; supposedly, it had the funding and approval of the Imperial Court. In 1917 the Black Hundred worked for the restoration of the dynasty, and constant reference to their counterrevolutionary activities appeared in the press.

and position would remain, while the best men would be retired. Moreover, I heard fears expressed (the sincerity of which I had no reason to doubt, considering the sources from which they came) that resignations submitted by a number of people simultaneously, or one directly after another, might give the impression that some sort of demonstration was being made against the Provisional Government by men of authority—but this, of course, never was their intention.

Last, not least, loomed the question of their personal financial fate, which was causing anxiety to all those who lived solely on their salaries and who could not rely either on receiving another post or on private earnings. There were, of course, quite a number of such people, and they all were asking whether they would be assigned pensions and in what amount. At the very beginning the Provisional Government assigned pensions of 7,000 to 10,000 rubles in two cases (I think they were for V. N. Kokovtsov [39] and A. S. Taneev, but here I may be mistaken). This fact was immediately pounced upon and discussed in mass meetings outside Kshesinskaia's [40] house (which was the headquarters of bolshevism from the very first days): "The Provisional Government is giving pensions of thousands of rubles and wasting national wealth on servants of the old tsarist regime." Socialist newspapers repeated this accusation. I particularly remember a scurrilous little article in *Novaia Zhizn'* [41] written by Mr. Goikhbart (unfortunately one of the collaborators of *Pravo*).

All of this clamor made a strong impression on the Provisional Government. When the question of the members of the State Council was finally raised in all its aspects (since fierce complaints in the press and in meetings had appeared in relation to the fact that

39. Count V. N. Kokovtsov (1853–1943), a tsarist government official from 1873; assistant minister of finance, 1896–1902; minister of finance, 1904–11; chairman, Council of Ministers, 1911–14.

40. Mathilda Kshesinskaia was a Polish ballerina who was intimate with Nicholas II in the years before his marriage.

41. *Novaia Zhizn'* (*New Life*) was the news organ of the Social Democrat Internationalists. Founded by Maxim Gorky, it was published from April 1917 to June 1918. Critical of both the Provisional Government and the Bolsheviks; it is not to be confused with first legal organ of the Bolsheviks in 1905.

members of the State Council continued to receive remuneration), the government spent two entire sessions discussing it without being able to come to any definitive solution. Some members of the State Council were, as they had wished, appointed to the Senate, and accordingly received senatorial salaries. But the fate of others—in my time—remained undecided. Whether any kind of general measures were subsequently adopted, I do not know. In relation to this, I recall an episode that made an extremely sad impression on me. N. S. Tagantsev, who had been my friend for twenty years, telephoned me and asked me to visit him. It turned out that he personally wanted to give me a resignation written in his own hand and an application for a pension. (He was afterwards appointed to the First Department of the Senate and became chairman of the department, in which I also served—but more of this later). Handing me the document, he could not restrain his emotion and said with a sob: ''Yes, my dear fellow, it is very hard. After all, I have been waiting all my life for the realization of a new regime. I am the son of a peasant who, to give me an education, registered as a merchant of the third guild—and everything I have achieved has been solely by my own toil. I am obligated to no one. And now I find myself not wanted by anyone, returning to my primitive state.''

Another episode should be related here. Its protagonist was a little-respected man—Lipskii, the deputy, and at the time the right-hand man of the governor-general of Finland—and he had the reputation of being one of [the late N. I.] Bobrikov's rabid adherents. The revolution threw him overboard and, I remember, he was even arrested at the outset and deported from Finland. His political physiognomy was such that it was impossible to consider granting him any sort of salary. He and I were acquainted because he had been working in the state chancellery at the end of the nineties. Now he began visiting me. He told me that his situation was completely hopeless. His wife was to undergo a major operation, he had to get her into a sanatorium, he had no place of his own in Petersburg—''friends have given us a nook''—and his search for private employment had been in vain. He implored me to help him and lend my support in getting him assigned a senator's salary (he was a senator). What could I say to him? I understood that the matter was hopeless, but as a human being I could see that the man would simply perish. Among my shortcomings as a politician I must list that characteristic of mine which inhibits my saying in such cases, "Serves him right!" In times of revolution a politician has to be cruel and ruthless. It is difficult for someone who is organically incapable of this!

I return to my narrative.

On Saturday, 4 March, N. V. Nekrasov asked N. I. Lazarevskii and myself to meet him at the Ministry of Transportation to carry out an assignment given by the Provisional Government. It concerned the drafting of the Provisional Government's first appeal to the entire country, setting forth the meaning of the historical events which had occurred and the *profession de foi* [profession of faith] of the Provisional Government, as well as defining its political program more clearly and in greater detail than in the first declaration accompanying the very formation of the Provisional Government.[42] At about 2 o'clock we met N. I. [Lazarevskii] and together proceeded to the ministry. There we encountered feverish activity, employees bustling about and many people sitting, standing, and walking around. With some difficulty we located Nekrasov who was chairing some conference. We had to wait a while—the meeting finished in our presence—and Nekrasov took us through an inner corridor, out of the ministry building, to a minister's apartment. There, in the minister's study, we found A. A. Dobrovol'skii,[43] a member of the State Duma who was also, by his wish (and, of course, with general consent), to participate in our work. Nekrasov explained to us the program and task of the appeal and then left us. We set to work immediately and continued until 6 or 7 o'clock in the evening. The task went quickly and resulted in a draft which is still among my papers but which never came to light. Nekrasov presented the draft to the Provisional Government the next day; but, as I learned later, some of its details met with objec-

42. For the declarations, see B. & K., 1 : 135–36, 157–58.

43. A. A. Dobrovol'skii, landowner; Kadet deputy, Fourth State Duma; member, Kadet Central Committee; not to be confused with the justice minister of the same last name.

tions. A. A. Manuilov [44] proposed to give it to F. F. Kokoshkin for revision (who had arrived that morning from Moscow). This proposal was accepted. M. M. Vinaver somehow found himself involved in the capacity of Kokoshkin's collaborator, and Kokoshkin left him the job of rewriting the text of the appeal; this text, as Kokoshkin told me later, written entirely by Vinaver, was presented to the Provisional Government by him, Kokoshkin, and was sanctioned without amendment. At the end of the month, Vinaver published in *Rech'* a sort of manifesto, ''To the Jewish People,'' which also began with the same words, ''A great event has occurred.''

On the evening of the same day, the first session of the Provisional Government in which I took part—or rather, at which I was present—was held in the conference hall of the Ministry of the Interior. The second and third sessions, on 5 and 6 March, also took place there. From the 7th of March the sessions were transferred to the Mariinskii Palace and were held there all the time I was Head of the Chancellery and afterwards, until the premiership of Kerensky moved to the Winter Palace [45] (in mid-July) and transferred the sessions to the Malachite Hall.

These first sessions had—quite understandably!—a chaotic character. Much time was taken up by all sorts of trifles. I recollect that at practically the first session, on Saturday, Kerensky announced that he was choosing N. N. Shnitnikov as one of his deputies, and I recall that this unimportant fact made a great and extremely negative impression on me at the time. Here, for the first time, one of the basic features of that ominous man appeared to me: his absolute incapacity to understand and correctly appraise people. Shnitnikov is a well-known personality. The man is kind and thoroughly decent, but at the same time he has a narrowly conceived attitude on every question. He never enjoyed the least authority, as is well known, neither within the legal profession, the Municipal Duma,

44. Aleksandr Apollonovich Manuilov (1861–1929), economist; editor, *Russkiia Vedomosti* (*The Russian Gazette*); Kadet; rector, Moscow University, 1905–11; member, State Council, 1907–11; minister of education, March–July 1917; economic consultant to Soviet government, 1921; member, State Banking Board, 1924.

45. The principle residence of the Imperial Family.

nor in any other sphere. And this was the man Kerensky intended to place beside himself at the head of the entire judicial department! Obviously he would achieve only one thing by doing this: the complete discrediting of himself and his colleague. I remember that it took quite a bit of effort to dissuade Kerensky. It should be noted, however, that his decisions, as well as being sudden and impetuous, were always marked by much disorder and changeability. This appeared subsequently in a number of cases of which I shall speak in due time.

In the first few days, the question of the abdicating emperor's fate remained completely uncertain. As is well known, immediately after his abdication Nicholas II left for Stavka.[46] At first the Provisional Government regarded this circumstance somewhat indifferently. Neither on Saturday, Sunday, nor Monday, at the sessions I attended, did anyone speak of the necessity to adopt any particular measure on this subject. It is possible, of course, that this question was already being discussed at private sittings. In any case, it was a complete surprise to me when, on Tuesday 7 March, I was called to Prince L'vov's office in the Ministry of the Interior where I found, besides members of the Provisional Government, the State Duma deputies Vershinin, Gribunin, and, it seems, Kalinin.[47] They disclosed that the Provisional Government had decided to imprison Nicholas II and transfer him to Tsarskoe Selo.[48] It had also been decided to imprison the empress Aleksandra Feodorovna.[49] I was entrusted to edit an appropriate telegram addressed to General Alekseev, who was at the time the Supreme Commander's chief of staff. This was the Provisional Government's first decree countersigned by me and published over my signature.

46. Stavka, or General Staff Headquarters, was located at Mogilev in 1917.

47. V. M. Vershinin, S. F. Gribunin, and S. A. Kalinin were commissars of the Provisional Committee of the State Duma who were delegated to escort Nicholas II from Mogilev to Tsarskoe Selo. See their report in B. & K., 1 : 180–81. A. A. Bublikov (1875–?), commissar for railways, also accompanied them.

48. Tsarskoe Selo (Village of the Tsar) was located fifteen miles from Petrograd and was the residence of a palace complex of the Imperial Family; it was renamed Detskoe Selo in 1917, and Pushkin in 1937.

49. Aleksandra Feodorovna (1872–1918), a German princess and grand-daughter of Queen Victoria, was the consort of Nicholas II; she was murdered with her family at Ekaterinburg by local Bolshevik authorities.

Under the circumstances, the question of what to do with Nicholas II doubtless presented very great difficulties. In more normal conditions, no one would have objected to his leaving Russia for England, and our Allied relationship would have guaranteed against any conspiratorial attempts to restore Nicholas II to the throne. Perhaps, if the government had immediately, on 3 or 4 March, shown more resourcefulness and a better management of affairs, it would have been successful in obtaining England's consent concerning Nicholas's arrival there, and he would have been immediately deported. I do not know whether any steps were taken in this direction at the time. I think not. The depature to Stavka complicated matters, having elicited the great irritation of the Executive Committee of the Soviet of Workers' and Soldiers' Deputies and resulting in corresponding propaganda, which in turn prompted the above-mentioned demonstrative act on the part of the Provisional Government.

In fact, neither formal nor concrete grounds existed for depriving Nicholas II of his freedom. His abdication could not be considered, formally, as having been forced from him. To make him answerable for certain acts committed by him in his capacity as emperor would have been absurd and contrary to the axioms of state law. Under such conditions the government, of course, had the right to take measures to render Nicholas II harmless, and it could come to an agreement with him about a definite place of residence and secure the protection of his person. Departing to England would probably have also been the most desirable solution for Nicholas himself. Meanwhile, his warrant for arrest tied a knot that to the present day has not yet been unraveled. *

But that's not all. I am personally convinced that "kicking a man when he is down"—the arrest of the former emperor—played its role and had a most profound influence in kindling rebellious passions. It imparted to the "abdication" the character of a "dethronement," since no reasons whatsoever were given for the arrest. Furthermore, Nicholas II's presence in Tsarskoe Selo, a few steps from

* Written in May–June 1918. A more recent (16/29 July 1918) footnote reads: "On 16 June in Ekaterinburg this knot was finally cut by "Comrade" Beloborodov. [A. G. Beloborodov was chairman of the Oral Oblast' Soviet, whose jurisdiction included Ekaterinburg, the scene of the execution of the Imperial Family.]

the capital and from rebellious Kronstadt,[50] continually worried and alarmed the Provisional Government—not because of a possible restoration but, on the contrary, because of the danger of mob rule or bloody reprisal. At times, under the influence of increasing seditious propaganda, such possibilities acquired a particularly threatening character.

Anyhow, after Nicholas II's arrival in Tsarskoe Selo, all further avenues of action were in fact shut off; for the immediate future it became quite impossible to send the former emperor abroad. Considerably later, when Kerensky had become premier, it was decided to transfer all of the tsar's family to Tobol'sk,[51] and this measure was undertaken in much secrecy—so much it seems, that not even all members of the Provisional Government were informed of it.

On the evening of 7 March, as I have already mentioned, the Provisional Government met in the Mariinskii Palace for the first time. In the first weeks sessions were scheduled twice daily, at 4 and 9 o'clock. Actually, afternoon sessions (like the evening ones) opened with considerable delay and continued until 8 o'clock. Evening sessions always ended late at night. The second half of the latter were usually closed, that is, the chancellery staff left—I alone remained.

This is an appropriate place to discuss the outward course of events at sessions of the Provisional Government to which I was a witness during the course of the first two months of the revolution.

As I have said, the sessions invariably opened with great delay. I waited for their commencement while occupying myself with this or that task in my office or receiving the numerous daily visitors. I was told when a sufficient number of ministers were present to open a session. Prince L'vov, I. V. Godnev (state controller), and A. A. Manuilov were more punctual than the others. Sometimes sessions opened with a small quorum of ministers who had urgent matters of minor significance. These matters were reported by them and were promptly settled. We were not immediately successful in establishing a definite agenda, and the chancellery was not in-

50. The sailors of Kronstadt were in the forefront of radicalizing the revolution in 1917. See B. & K., 1 : 182–88, about English asylum for the tsar and Tsarskoe Selo.

51. In western Siberia. See B. & K., 1 : 189–90 for a discussion of the decision.

formed beforehand of matters subject to report. At the first sessions, which were highly chaotic, the ministers made their reports and one or another decision was recorded very roughly. I managed to arrange that, as a general rule, every presentation submitted to the Provisional Government conclude with a draft resolution, which of course could be subject to changes dependent on the course and the outcome of the discussions.

As for the deliberations at the sessions, it was at once decided not to record them officially, and also not to note differences in voting, not to enter dissenting opinions in the minutes, and so on. The original point was a desire to avoid anything that might destroy the unity of the government and its responsibility as a whole for every decision adopted. The keeping of detailed minutes for every session, moreover, would have presented a number of fundamental and insurmountable difficulties. The members of the Provisional Government, especially in the beginning, tended to view the presence of the chancellery personnel at the sessions with a certain suspicion and distrust. A detailed recording of everything said would have elicited protests and demands for verification, and finally, what with the mass of questions considered at every session, not one record of the proceedings would have been finished.

It must be said, incidentally, that with rare exceptions the deliberations at open sessions did not present much interest. The ministers always came to the sessions completely exhausted. The work of each of them, of course, exceeded normal human capacities. Often, very special questions, unfamiliar to the majority, were examined in these sessions, and the ministers would often be half dozing, barely listening to the reports. The animated and impassioned speeches began only at closed sessions and in sessions with the ''Contact Commission'' [52] of the Executive Committee of the Soviet of Workers' and Soldiers' Deputies.

Here my position was particularly distressing, and I at once felt that my role was essentially different from the part I had imagined when I took up the comparatively secondary post of Head of the Chancellery. The problem was as follows.

52. The Contact, or Liaison, Commission was established to provide a formal setting for meetings between the Petrograd Soviet leaders and the ministers of the Provisional Government. See B. & K., 3 : 1211–13.

In the Provisional Government were personal and political friends of mine, casual acquaintances, and finally, people I now met for the first time. Among the first group were Miliukov, Shingarev, Nekrasov, Manuilov, and, to a certain extent, Prince L'vov. The second group included Kerensky, Guchkov, and Tereshchenko. The third category included Konovalov, V. N. L'vov, and I. V. Godnev. I knew M. I. Tereshchenko better than the others of the second group; however, this acquaintance was purely social. I had an impression of him as being a brilliant young man, very pleasant in manner, a music lover and theater-goer, an official with special duties under Teliakovskii. The jump to the Ministry of Finance in the Provisional Government had, of course, been a very great one, and I had difficulty in reconciling Tereshchenko's new role with my old impression of him. But at the same time I had no basis for expecting his attitude toward me to be other than completely friendly.

I had known Guchkov since the days of the general zemstvo congresses in 1905. He showed me from the outset complete trust and courtesy. I must say the same of the three men in the third group. I had no doubt at all that, if Kerensky had not been a member of the government, I would have felt completely free in the milieu of the Provisional Government and would not have constrained myself to remain silent and to play the role of passive listener and observer, which finally became quite unbearable for me.

In this connection, I would like to put together here my impressions both of Kerensky and the others. I do not intend to give exhaustive characterizations, for which I do not have sufficient material anyway. But, after all, I met with each of these people daily in the course of two months; I saw them at very important and responsible moments. I was able to observe them closely, and so I assume that even my fragmentary impressions are not devoid of some interest and may in time, when my notes are used in some form or other, become part of the general mass of historical material about the Russian Revolution of 1917 and its actors.

A tout seigneur tout honneur.[53] I shall begin with Kerensky.

53. "Honor to whom honor is due."

Seven months have passed since I last saw Kerensky, but I have no difficulty whatever in recalling his appearance. I first became acquainted with him eight years ago. Our encounters were always fleeting and accidental—on the Nevskii, at some service for the dead, etc. I was told (before his election to the State Duma) that the man was gifted but not of the highest caliber. He was a bit dandified in his outward appearance, had the clean-shaven face of an actor, a constant way of squinting his eyes, and an unpleasant smile that continually bared his upper teeth. In combination this was not very attractive. In any case, not only was there nothing, either in him personally or in what one was apt to hear about him, that would lead anyone to guess what his future role would be, but in general there were no features that caught one's attention. He was just one of many political defense lawyers, and far from the first rank. The greater public began to know him only from the time of his speeches in the State Duma. There, on account of party conditions,[54] he proved to be in the first ranks. He was, in any case, a head above the drab companions around him in the Duma. Also he was not a bad speaker, occasionally even a brilliant one, and there were any number of opportunities for important speeches. Thus it was natural that after four years he should have become familiar and notable.

But for all that, he never possessed really great, generally acknowledged success. It would never have occurred to anyone to consider him as a speaker on a level with Maklakov or Rodichev, or to compare his authority as a parliamentarian with that of Miliukov or Shingarev. His party in the Fourth Duma was insignificant and had little influence. His position concerning the war question was, basically, purely Zimmerwaldist.[55] All this far from facilitated

54. Kerensky's faction was the Trudovik (Toilers), formed in 1906, of which there were 104 deputies in the Second State Duma and ten in the Fourth State Duma, 1912–17. They were unaligned, populist-oriented socialists.

55. "Zimmerwaldist" refers to a group of socialists who met at that Swiss town (Zimmerwald) in September 1915 and again at Kienthal, Switzerland, in April 1916, to express their opposition to World War I. A minority Left Zimmerwaldist group, in which Lenin was active, proposed the adoption of a manifesto urging soldiers to turn their guns on their capitalist governments rather than on each other. Zimmerwaldists rejected Lenin's proposal and instead called for an immediate armi-

the formation of any sort of aura about his name. He especially felt this, because his pride and conceit were enormous and abnormal; naturally, there became very firmly rooted in him feelings toward his main political opponents, with which it was rather difficult to reconcile the desire for sincere and wholehearted collaboration. I can attest that Miliukov was his bête noire in the fullest sense of the word. He never missed an occasion to refer to him with spite, irony, sometimes with real hate. Despite his abnormal and hypertrophic vanity, he could not but realize that there was a huge difference between himself and Miliukov.

Miliukov was incommensurate with his colleagues in the Cabinet as an intellectual force, a man with vast, almost inexhaustible, knowledge and breadth of mind. I will attempt further on to define what were, in my opinion, his insufficiencies as a politician. But he had one enormous advantage: his position with regard to the fundamental question—the decision on which the entire course of the revolution depended—this was the question concerning the war. His position was perfectly clear, well-defined, and consistent, whereas the position of "the hostage of democracy" was ambiguous, reticent, and essentially false. Miliukov did not have the slightest trace of pettiness or vanity, and his personal feelings and attitudes were reflected in his political behavior to the most insignificant degree. His conduct was never determined by them. It was quite the reverse with Kerensky; he was made up of personal impulses.

It is even difficult to imagine how the dizzying height to which he was carried in the first weeks and months of the revolution reacted on Kerensky's psyche. Yet in his soul he must have realized that all this admiration, all the idolization, was nothing but crowd psychosis, that he, Kerensky, had neither the merits nor the intellectual or moral qualities that would justify such hysterical and ecstatic attitudes. But no doubt from the first days his soul was "bruised" by the role which history specified for him, a fortuitous

---

stice and "peace without annexations." For a thorough discussion with scholarly documentation, see O. H. Gankin and H. H. Fisher, *The Bolsheviks and the World War* (Stanford, Calif., 1940).

little man, and in which he was destined to fail so ingloriously, without a trace. . . .

I have just said that the idolization of Kerensky was a sign of some psychosis in Russian public opinion. This may be too mildly stated. In fact, it was impossible not to ask oneself what was the political baggage of this man whom it had been decided to acknowledge as the ''hero of the revolution,'' what did he have to his credit? From this point of view, it is curious, now that ''petals have fallen, the lights have gone out'' [to quote a minor poet], to reread the newspaper accounts of Kerensky's *faits et gestes,* his speeches, his interviews during the eight-month period. . . . If he actually was the hero of the first months of the revolution, then this fact alone produces a sufficiently serious condemnation of the revolution.

Kerensky's abnormal vanity, which I have mentioned, was coupled with another unpleasant trait: this acting of his, a love of posing and also for any form of ostentation and pomp. Such acting, I recall, was even displayed in the narrow circle of the Provisional Government, where it would have seemed that it was especially useless and absurd because everyone knew each other and no one could be deceived by anyone. One episode of this posing has been related previously: the clash when Miliukov mentioned the part played by German money in the Russian Revolution.

Those who attended the so-called State Conference [56] in the Moscow Bolshoi Theater in August 1917 have naturally not forgotten Kerensky's speeches: the first, which opened the conference, and the last, which closed it. He made a depressing and repulsive impression on those who saw or heard him for the first time. What he said was not the calm, weighty speech of a statesman, nothing

56. The Moscow State Conference met from August 12 to 15 (O.S.), and was attended by some 2,400 representatives of social, economic, and political classes and organizations (excepting the Bolsheviks), as well as the armed forces. Kerensky, who headed the government at the time, hoped that the conference would promote unity and bring about a democratic resurgence before the convocation of the Constituent Assembly. The reaction to the calling of the conference, the speeches made, and the press reaction to the worth of the meeting, are available in B. & K., 3 : 1451–1526.

but the hysterical cry of a psychopath suffering from the mania of grandeur. One felt the tense, strained desire to leave a mark, to impress. In the second—the concluding—speech, he apparently completely lost control of himself and spouted such nonsense that it had to be carefully stricken from the stenographic record. Even to the very end he completely failed to understand the situation. Four or five days before the Bolshevik uprising in October, at one of our meetings in the Winter Palace, I asked him outright if he considered a Bolshevik uprising possible—a subject about which everyone was talking at the time.

"I would be prepared to offer prayers to produce this uprising," he replied.

"And are you sure that you will be able to cope with it?"

"I have greater forces than necessary. They will be utterly crushed."

In this whole sad story of Kerensky in power the only page which might possibly give a milder judgment of him is his role in the course of our last offensive (on 18 June).[57] In my speech at the Moscow Conference I possibly exaggerated this role. But there is no doubt that in this instance Kerensky exhibited an honest patriotic enthusiasm, a flash which came—alas!—too late.

Kerensky's relationship to the Executive Committee of the Soviet of Workers' and Soldiers' Deputies was extremely curious. He sincerely thought that the Provisional Government possessed supreme power and that the Executive Committee had no right to meddle in its affairs. Steklov-Nakhamkes, who during the first month was the Executive Committee's *porte-parole* [spokesman] at meetings of the Provisional Government and the Contact Commission, was regarded by him with hostility and contempt. Often after a meeting, or in *à parté* [asides] during it, Kerensky denounced Prince L'vov's

57. A reference to the "July offensive," which opened June 18 (O.S.) and was smashed in a massive German counterattack on July 6 (O.S.). The Russian General Staff promoted the offensive, hoping to instil some discipline in their restless troops, and Kerensky and the Petrograd Soviet leaders supported them. The offensive was a disaster not only because of German might but because of poor planning by the military command and the failure of the civilian leadership to question that planning. See Robert Feldman, "The Russian General Staff and the June 1917 Offensive," *Soviet Studies* 19 (April 1968) : 526–42; B. & K., 2 : 921–76.

excessive leniency in regard to Steklov. But Kerensky himself decidedly avoided polemics with Steklov, and he himself never once tried to defend the position of the Provisional Government. He always managed to maneuver so as to maintain his position as "the hostage of democracy"—a basically false position which often greatly embarrassed the Provisional Government.

My personal relations with Kerensky passed through several stages. He greatly mistrusted me in the very beginning when I accepted the post of Head of the Chancellery. It apparently seemed to him that I was strengthening the purely Kadet element within the Provisional Government, and he tried to prevent me from playing any political role. I was perfectly conscious that any attempt on my part to participate in the discussion of this or that question, even in the closed sessions of the Provisional Government, would have elicited a sharp protest from Kerensky—in the name of the Provisional Government's prerogatives—and thereby put me in an extremely awkward position. In point of fact, specifically thanks to Kerensky's presence, my role proved to be so incompatible to that which I had expected, that in the early days I questioned myself whether or not I should remain at my post. If I did not answer this question in the negative immediately, withholding my resignation when the first crisis occurred in the makeup of the Provisional Government, with Miliukov's (and Guchkov's) exit [58] and the entrance of Chernov, Tseretelli, Skobelev, and Peshekhonov,[59] I so acted in

58. Guchkov resigned May 1/14 and Miliukov May 3/16.

59. Viktor Mikhailovich Chernov [Iu. Gardenin] (1876–1952), founder, Peasants' Brotherhood, 1895; cofounder, Socialist Revolutionary party, 1902; a leading Socialist Revolutionary theoretician; minister of agriculture, May–September 1917; member, Executive Committee, Petrograd Soviet, 1917; member, Contact Commission, 1917; president, Constituent Assembly, January 1918; emigrated 1919. See his *The Great Russian Revolution* (New York, 1966), *Pered burei* (*Before the Storm*) (New York, 1953), and *Rozhdenie revoliutsionnoe rossii* (*The Birth of Revolutionary Russia*) (Paris, 1934).

Irakli Georgievich Tseretelli (1882–1959), Georgian; youthful Menshevik leader, Second State Duma; sentenced to ten years at hard labor in a police fabrication; released after February coup, 1917; member and dominant figure, Executive Committee of the Petrograd Soviet, 1917; minister of posts and telegraphs, May–August 1917; minister of the interior, July 23—August 7, 1917; prominent in Menshevik government of Free Georgia until it was overrun by the Bolsheviks; emigrated to the interest of a post that I wanted to leave well-organized and in good order. Subsequently, when Kerensky was quite sure that I held no personal designs, he changed his attitude. This was reflected, not only by offers made to me to occupy a ministerial post, but in the entire character of his personal attitude toward me. Finally, in the last phase, Kerensky tried, through me, to influence the Party of People's Freedom and to receive its support in the Council of the Russian Republic.[60] I will discuss this below.

After all that has been said, I will hardly be suspected of bias if I nevertheless am unable to join in that torrent of abuse and anathematization which now always accompanies any mention of the name Kerensky. I do not deny that he played a truly fateful role in the history of the Russian Revolution, but this occurred because an inept and unconscious mutinous elemental force (*stikhiia*) [61] by chance raised an insufficiently strong personality to a quite inappropriate height. The worst that can be said of Kerensky pertains to an appraisal of the qualities of his mind an character. One may repeat those words concerning him which he recently, with such amazing lack of moral feeling and elemental tact, used regarding Korni-

---

Paris and then to New York City, where he died. See his *Vospominaniia o fevral'skoi revoliutsii* (*Recollections of the February Revolution*), 2 vols. (Paris, 1963).

Aleksei Vasil'evich Peshekhonov (1867–1933), journalist; organizer and leader, Popular Socialist party; minister of food, July–August 1917; served under the Bolsheviks; banished in 1922; later worked for Soviet government abroad. See his "Pervyia nedeli (iz vospominanii o revoliutsii)" ["The First Weeks (Recollections of the Revolution)"], in *Na Chuzhoi Storone* (*On Foreign Shores*) (Berlin, 1932) 1 : 255–319.

60. The Council of the Russian Republic was first called the Democratic Council, but then was enlarged by the inclusion of delegates from bourgeois groups and was renamed the Provisional Council of the Russian Republic. Actually, this body not only represented parties but also social organizations and the army. It acted as a consultative body to the Provisional Government until such time as the Constituent Assembly met. The council convened on October 7. Trotsky withdrew the Bolshevik delegation at this first meeting. See B. & K., 3 : 1721–45.

61. The *stikhiia,* or elemental force (the crowd, "street people"), is discussed by Bertram Wolfe in Richard Pipes, ed., *Revolutionary Russia: A Symposium* (New York, 1969), pp. 163–75.

lov: [62] "in his own way" he loved the Fatherland. He did, in fact, burn with revolutionary pathos, and there were occasions when genuine feeling penetrated the actor's mask. We may recall his speech about ["the free Russian state is a state of"] rebellious slaves, his cry of despair when he realized the abyss into which Russia was drawn by unbridled demagogy. Of course, here one did not feel either genuine strength or a clear command of reason— there was a sincere although unfruitful impulse. Kerensky was a prisoner of his mediocre companions and of his own past. He was incapable by nature of acting directly and boldy, and despite his conceit and vanity, he did not have that calm and inexorable self-confidence which is characteristic of really strong men. There was decidely nothing "heroic" in the sense of Carlyle. The blackest stain on his short-lived career is the story of his relations with Kornilov, but I am not going to discuss that, since I know only what is generally well known.

It will be necessary to return to Kerensky more than once in the course of my story. For the present I will restrict myself to what I have written and will pass on to another man on whom all of Russia placed colossal expectations which he did not justify.

I knew Prince G. E. L'vov from the time of the First Duma. Although he was listed as a member of the Party of People's Freedom, I do not remember whether he undertook any active participation in party life and sessions of the factions or of the Central Committee. I do not think I am violating the truth if I state that he had the reputation of being a most upright and honest man who was, however, not distinguished by political strength. After the dissolution of the First Duma he also was in Vyborg, but he took

62. General Lavr Georgievich Kornilov (1870–1918), commander, Petrograd Military District, March–April 1917; commander-in-chief, Southwestern Front, July 1917; Supreme Commander, July–August 1917; arrested and imprisoned after the "Kornilov affair"; with General Alekseev organized the Volunteer Army, 1918; killed in battle. See Kerensky, *The Prelude to Bolshevism: The Kornilov Rebellion* (London, 1919); J. D. White, "The Kornilov Affair," *Soviet Studies* 20 (October 1968) : 187–205; Harvey Asher, "The Kornilov Affair: A Reinterpretation," *The Russian Review* 29 (July 1970) : 286–300.

no part in the conferences and did not sign the appeal. I remember that he stayed at the same hotel as D. D. Protopopov [63] and I, but he fell ill immediately on arrival, so that he did not leave his room until his departure from Vyborg. Protopopov attributed L'vov's illness to his agitated state. Like many of us, in his heart L'vov did not sympathize with the appeal, did not believe in it, and considered it a mistake; but he realized that he was powerless to impede it, having no other acceptable and striking plan of action. I remember his pale, distraught face and his limp figure. Eleven years passed before I met him again. Like everyone else, I considered him an excellent organizer and set great hopes on his enormous popularity with the zemstvos of Russia and the army. I have already mentioned the impression Prince L'vov made on me at our first meeting in the Tauride Palace on the day of the formation of the Provisional Government. I would say that this impression was prophetic. It is true that in the next few days Prince L'vov outwardly changed, was sparked by feverish energy, and, as it seemed to me, at least for the first time, had faith in the possibility of establishing order in Russia.

The task of the minister-president in the first Provisional Government was actually very difficult. It demanded great tact and the ability to subordinate, unite, and lead men. Above all, it required a strictly defined plan, systematically put into action. In the first days after the coup the authority of the Provisional Government and of L'vov himself stood very high. It was necessary to take advantage of this circumstance, first of all for the consolidation and reinforcement of power. It was necessary to understand that disruptive forces were in readiness to begin their destructive work, to take advantage of the colossal upheaval in the minds of the masses, which could not but accompany a political coup that developed and was completed in such a manner. It was necessary for him to know how to find energetic and authoritative collaborators and either give his entire attention to the Ministry of the Interior or, once it became impossible to combine efficiently his obligation as minister of the

63. D. D. Protopopov, Zemstvo liberal; Kadet deputy, First State Duma; member, Kadet Party Central Committee, 1917; Assistant to the Commissar on the Affairs of the Grand Duchy of Finland, 1917.

interior with his role of premier, to find a genuine substitute for the first post.

I have no wish to say anything slighting, let alone bad, about D. M. Shchepkin or Prince S. D. Urusov,[64] but I think that it is difficult to expect from them what Prince L'vov himself was unable to give. Shchepkin is a conscientious and industrious worker, an excellent fellow full of energy and *bonne volonté*. But he was not a commanding figure on the basis of experience, social standing, or his personality; he himself well realized this, and this awareness paralyzed him in all independent actions. Prince Urusov was apparently at a complete loss in his new surroundings, was badly oriented, and felt totally out of place. After all, his bureaucratic career was spent in conditions radically contrary to those in which he now found himself. He passed by like some pale ghost, inspired by the very best intentions but powerless to fulfill them. He would have been able to be an assistant or an executive, but it was impossible to expect from him determination, initiative, and creativity.

The fact that the Ministry of the Interior—in other words, the whole administration and police force—was left totally disorganized, contributed in very large measure to the general process of Russia's disintegration. Initially, there was a strange faith that everything would somehow take care of itself and would start working in a correct and organized way. Just as the revolution was idealized ("great," "bloodless"), so the population was idealized. It was naïvely thought, for example, that the huge capital, with its riffraff and vicious criminal elements always ready to make trouble, could exist without a police force, or with an outrageous and ridiculous improvised militia that was lavishly paid and in which were enlisted escaped professional thieves and convicts. The all-Russian campaign against the police and the gendarmerie quickly achieved a natural consequence. The apparatus, although rather feeble but still operative, was smashed to pieces. Large numbers of police and gendarmes swelled the ranks of the Bolsheviks. In Petersburg and Moscow anarchy gradually began to develop. Its growth immedi-

64. Assistant ministers of the interior, March–July 1917. Shchepkin was a Moscow liberal; Urusov, a conservative nationalist; both members, "Moscow" Center, 1918.

ately increased in an alarming manner after the Bolshevik coup.
But the coup itself was made possible and so easy to carry out only
because of the disappearance of the consciousness of an authority
that would be prepared decisively to maintain and preserve public
order.

It would, of course, be highly unjust to put all the responsibility
for what happened on Prince L'vov. But one must say, however
severe the verdict may sound: Prince L'vov not only did nothing,
but did not even attempt to do anything, to counteract the over-
shadowing decomposition. He sat in the driver's seat but made no
attempt to take up the reins. How many times I experienced agonizing sessions in which the Provisional Government's total impotence
emerged with a kind of inexorable clarity, with disharmony, inner
dissension, and the smouldering or obvious hostility of some individuals toward others. I do not recall a single occasion when the
minister-president used a tone of authority or spoke out decisively
and definitively. Prince L'vov was literally besieged from morning
till night. A spate of urgent telegrams incessantly flowed from all
parts of Russia, demanding instructions, clarifications for the immediate implementation of pressing measures. On all possible pre-
texts, serious and trivial, L'vov was consulted both as head of government and as minister of the interior; he was constantly
summoned to the telephone, and was visited at the ministry and at
the Mariinskii Palace.

I originally tried to set a time for my daily report and for receiving all necessary instructions, but very soon I became convinced
that these attempts were quite futile, and on the rare occasions
when my efforts were successful, they proved to be completely
useless. I never received a firm and definite decision from him; he
was usually inclined to agree with the decision that I proposed to
him. I would say that he was the very embodiment of passivity. I
do not know whether this was conscious policy or the result of his
awareness of his own powerlessness, but it sometimes seemed as
though L'vov had some mystical faith that everything would somehow work out by itself. At other moments it seemed to me that he
had a completely hopeless attitude toward events, that he was completely permeated by an awareness of the impossibility of influenc-

ing their course, that fatalism possessed him, and that he only continued for appearance's sake to play that role which, without any desire or aspiration on his part, had fallen to his lot.

Miliukov had played an active role in the selection of L'vov for the position of minister-president and in the removal of Rodzianko, and I subsequently heard from Pavel Nikolaevich that he had often asked himself the agonizing question whether it would not have been better to have left L'vov alone and appointed Rodzianko, a person in any case capable of acting decisively and boldly, who possessed his own opinion and knew how to rely on it.

Prince L'vov's attitude toward Kerensky produced a sad impression. It not infrequently aroused the indignation of my assistants in the chancellery, who saw it as an insufficient awareness of his dignity as head of the government. It often resembled timid favor-seeking. Of course, there were no personal motives here. Prince L'vov possessed absolutely none of these; ambition was alien to him, and he never clung to power. I think he was profoundly happy the day he was relieved of his burden. It is that much more surprising, then, that he did not know how to take advantage of the moral authority with which he came to power. It was not he who spoke with an air of authority in the Provisional Government, but Kerensky.

In following a natural sequence I now must speak about Guchkov, but this I find most difficult of all.

First of all, I had few opportunities to observe Guchkov as a member of the Provisional Government. He was absent for a considerable part of the time, occupied with trips to the front and Stavka; in mid-April he was ill. But the main thing was that while he occupied the post of war and navy minister he was almost impossible to observe. Now, looking back on the same period, I am inclined to think that from the very beginning Guchkov felt in his soul that the cause was lost and only stayed on *par acquit de conscience*.[65] In any case, the note of utter disappointment and skepticism never sounded so strongly in anyone as it did in him when-

65. "For conscience's sake."

ever the question of the army and the fleet arose. When he started to speak in his quiet, soft voice, gazing into the distance with his slightly squinting eyes, I was seized by a sense of total despair. Everything seemed doomed.

The first session wholly devoted to the question of the situation at the front must have been on 7 March, on the evening of the day when sessions of the Provisional Government were transferred to the Mariinskii Palace. I can recall this date because at that session it was resolved to draft an appeal to the army and population, which appeared on 10 March. It was entrusted to me, written by me on the next day, the 8th, discussed at the day session on the 9th, and was adopted almost without amendment. (For some reason it was not put in the published compilation of the state chancellery, and is preserved only in the *Vestnik Vremmenago Pravitel'stva* and in newspapers.) I recall that at this session two points of view were expressed about the significance for our military operations of the events which had taken place.

One view was that officially expressed in speeches and reports. According to this point of view, a causal relation was established between the tsarist government's poor conduct of the war and the revolution. The outburst of protest against the undistinguished, clumsy, and traitorous (Stürmer!) [66] conduct of this tsarist government was concentrated, as it were, in the revolution. The revolution was to change this and to establish a broader, more sincere, and therefore more fruitful bond between ourselves and the great European democracies, our allies. From this point of view the revolution could be considered a positive factor in the cause of the conduct of the war. It was assumed that the Command would be renovated, that talented and energetic generals would be found, and that discipline would be quickly restored. Sad to say, our party's policy constantly strove to maintain this official optimism. For some people, like A. I. Shingarev for example, the optimism survived until very late, until the autumn of 1917.

66. Boris Vladimirovich Stürmer (1848–1917), governor, Novgorod and Iaroslavl, 1894–1902; member, State Council, 1904; chairman, State Council, 1916; minister of the interior, March–July 1916; minister of foreign affairs, July–November 1916; imprisoned, March–September 1917.

I consider that the incorrect understanding of the significance that the war had as a factor in the revolution, and the reluctance to consider all the consequences the revolution must have had in relation to it, played a fateful role in the events of 1917. I remember how on one of my trips somewhere by automobile together with Miliukov (this was while he was still minister of foreign affairs), I expressed to him my conviction that one of the basic causes of the revolution was weariness of the war and reluctance to continue it. Miliukov decidedly disagreed. What he said essentially was: "Who knows? Perhaps it is due to the war that everything here is somehow still holding together, and without the war everything would soon collapse." Of course, the realization alone that the war was destroying Russia would not have made it easier. No sage, neither then nor later, could have found the means to end it without colossal damage—both moral and material—to Russia. But if it had been clearly realized in the first weeks that for Russia the war was hopelessly lost and that all attempts to continue it would lead nowhere, there would have been a different orientation to this basic question and—who knows?—catastrophe perhaps would have successfully been avoided.

I am not implying that the revolution alone destroyed the army, and less than anyone am I inclined to underestimate the disastrous importance of that criminal and traitorous propaganda which had begun from the first. Least of all am I inclined to justify the Provisional Government's placidness and indifference toward this propaganda. But I am still profoundly convinced that any kind of successful conducting of the war was incompatible with those problems which the revolution raised inside the country and with the conditions under which the problems had to be resolved. It seems to me that Guchkov also realized this. I remember that his speech at the session of 7 March, which was entirely devoted to the theme, "There is no question of getting fat, let us try and stay alive," was so pervaded with despair that, when he asked me at the end of the meeting, "What is your opinion concerning this question?" I replied that, in my opinion, if his assessment of the situation was correct, then there was no other conclusion than the necessity of a separate peace with Germany.

Guchkov, admittedly, did not agree with this, but he was unable to refute such an inference. On that same memorable evening, he suggested after the meeting that I accompany him to the war minister's apartment (which Guchkov had already occupied at that time) and be present during his direct conversation by wire with General Alekseev: "Let us see what he has to tell us." General Alekseev's information was extremely gloomy. In the enormous chaos that was created during the first days of the revolution he had soon detected elements of the future collapse and the enormous danger threatening the army. Guchkov repeated to him the content of the proposed appeal and asked whether he thought such an appeal would be useful. Alekseev answered affirmatively. Incidentally, I may note that, almost coincidentally with the appeal I composed, an analogous appeal written by the Ministry of War and also an order to the troops appeared. They all developed the same ideas, and all were completely fruitless.

Guchkov—and this is his characteristic—was the first member of the Provisional Government to become convinced that the task of the Provisional Government was hopeless and futile and that "it was necessary to resign." He spoke repeatedly on this theme in the second half of April. He constantly demanded that the Provisional Government surrender its authority, writing its own epitaph with a diagnosis of the situation and a prognosis for the future. The Provisional Government's well-known declaration of 23 April (about which I will subsequently speak) derives its origin from these conversations. "We must account for what we have done and explain why we can no longer work. We must produce a kind of political testament." The declaration of 23 April, however, turned out to have a different tone and different conclusions. I think this was the last drop that made the cup overflow and elicited Guchkov's resignation from the Provisional Government.

In the course of those two months in which Guchkov occupied the post of minister of war, his role in the Provisional Government remained undefined. As I have already said, he was rarely at its meetings. Even more rarely would he express an opinion. He would attempt to bring a conciliatory note into conflicts that arose, but in that memorable clash between Kerensky and Miliukov on the question of war aims and the goals of foreign policy, he somehow remained in the background and did not provide support for either side. Moreover, he apparently withdrew into the background intentionally. His resignation from the Provisional Government was unexpected. I recall Nekrasov saying that this resignation was a "stab in the back." But Guchkov himself decisively proved that Prince L'vov certainly should have expected the minister of war's resignation and that he, Guchkov, had emphatically warned him of it.

I. V. Godnev, the state controller, was an extremely typical figure in the Provisional Government. I did not know him at all, even on sight, until I met him at the sessions of the Provisional Government. From the constant reference to his name in Duma reports, in connection with various kinds of legal questions and with disputes about the interpretation of the law, I had formed an image of him as an expert on our law, who although perhaps without a formal legal education, had yet acquired the appropriate knowledge in practice and knew how to orient himself in juridical questions. Furthermore, I supposed Godnev to be one of the important political figures in the State Duma.

I well remember my first impression of Godnev. He himself, his manner, and of course his approach to political or legal questions, were all imbued with a very simple-minded philistinism, with the deepest provincialism; everything about him reflected extreme naïveté and narrow-mindedness. In his veneration of the principle of legality, there was something estimable and even touching, but because he was utterly incapable of understanding the continual conflicts of the new order with the unrescinded rules of the Fundamental Laws, he fell into an impasse at every step, experienced agonizing bewilderment, and was generally disturbed. As a political figure he remained completely passive, and moreover became upset in all cases when in the midst of the government some sharp clash or discord would take place. An absolutely honest man, full of the very best intentions and deserving sincere respect, he was utterly out of place as a member of the Provisional Government, and he apparently only stayed at his post out of sheer inertia and the lack of a more suitable candidate. As soon as Kokoshkin was nominated (in July), Godnev, who had sat meekly with Tseretelli and Skobelev, handed over his duties to Kokoshkin, just as meekly and probably with an unburdened heart.

The Ober-Procurator of the Holy Synod,[67] V. N. L'vov, was also, like Godnev, inspired by the very best intentions but also displayed naïveté, as well as an incredibly frivolous approach toward matters. This was not so much toward his own special affairs but the general problems that were daily placed before the Provisional Government. He always spoke with great fervor and animation and invariably evoked amusement, not only among the members of the government, but also in the ranks of the chancellery staff.

Speaking of V. N. L'vov I cannot but record here an episode which occurred much later but which is closely connected with L'vov's general characteristics.

It was Tuesday of the week of the twentieth of August 1917, at the end of which Kornilov moved on Petersburg. L'vov telephoned me in the morning and said he had important and urgent business he wanted to discuss with Miliukov as chairman of the Central Committee and Vinaver as deputy chairman, but he was not successful in reaching either of them (they were apparently away), and therefore he was asking me for an appointment. We arranged that he would come to my place at 6 P.M. I was somewhat late returning home, and when I arrived I found L'vov in my study. He had a very important and mysterious air. Without a word he handed me a small piece of paper on which was written approximately the following (I could not copy the text, but I remember it precisely): "The general who sat across the table from you requests you to warn the Kadet ministers to resign on a certain day of August" (the date given was the one on which Kornilov's advance took place, five days later, it seems, the 28th of August; for the moment I cannot recall it definitely, but this could easily be done from the newspapers) "with the object of creating new difficulties for the govern-

67. The Holy Synod was established by Peter the Great and was the highest administrative organ of the Russian Orthodox Church. The ober-procurator was a layman and the synod's superviser. For 1917, see B. & K., 2 : 803–11.

ment and in the interests of their own safety.'' These were a few lines in the middle of the page, without a signature. Understanding nothing, I asked L'vov what this enigma meant and what precisely was demanded of me.

''Just bring this to the attention of the Kadet ministers.''

''But,'' I said, ''such anonymous instructions of even the slightest importance would hardly convey a warning.''

''Don't question me, I do not have the right to add anything.''

''In that case, I repeat, I do not see what practical use I can make of your message.''

After a few mysterious phrases and innuendoes, L'vov finally revealed that he would speak openly but obtained from me my word that what was said would remain between ourselves, ''Otherwise they may even arrest me.'' I replied that I wished to reserve the right to share what I learned from him with Miliukov and Kokoshkin, and he at once agreed. Then he told me the following: ''When I leave you, I am going to see Kerensky, and I am taking him an ultimatum; a coup d'état is being planned, and a program for a new government with dictatorial powers has been established. It will be proposed that Kerensky accept this program. If he refuses, that will be the final rupture, and it will only remain for me, a person close to Kerensky and well-disposed toward him, to try to save his life.'' To my subsequent questions asking for more definite information on this matter L'vov maintained a consistent silence, revealing that he had already said too much as it was. As I remember, Kornilov's name was not mentioned, but it was undoubtedly said that the ultimatum originated from Stavka. With this the conversation ended and L'vov went to see Kerensky.

As far as I can judge from the information published later, L'vov in this first conversation with Kerensky certainly did not carry out the plan about which he told me. He did not present an ultimatum (this was done at the end of the week, after L'vov had gone to Moscow and returned again), and he merely discussed various positions and demands originating from certain public groups. That, at least, is how Kerensky reported the conversation, and L'vov did not deny it. Unfortunately, I had no further occasion to encounter L'vov, and to the present time the whole incident remains for me insufficiently clarified. I am certain of one thing. Either L'vov drastically changed his intentions on the way to the Winter Palace, or Kerensky had known for five days what was being planned. I personally am more inclined toward the latter assumption. Unfortunately, at the time I am writing these lines,* I am still not familiar with the book in which Kerensky sets forth the evidence on the Kornilov affair, which is embellished with various, very recent additional material. But if it is true that such an important mission was entrusted to such a person as V. N. L'vov, then this attests to the fact that the initiators of the coup were very bad judges of human character and acted exceedingly thoughtlessly. Miliukov subsequently expressed the supposition that L'vov "had badly blundered" in this entire incident. I repeat, for me it remained a mystery. It is necessary to add that I reported our conversation that same evening to Kokoshkin, as well as to our other ministers (Ol'denburg and Kartashev) [68] whom I met almost daily at A. G. Khrushchev's [69] apartment. I remember that I asked them to notice Kerensky's behavior at the evening session. Subsequently they informed me that Kerensky had behaved as usual.

To my characterization of V. N. L'vov I can add: when Miliukov in two meetings acquainted the Provisional Government with our "secret" treaties,[70] nothing could have been more genuine,

* The end of July 1918.

68. S. F. Ol'denburg (1863–?), philosopher, scientist; permanent secretary, Academy of Sciences; member, Kadet Party Central Committee, 1917; minister of education, July–August 1917.

Anton Vladimirovich Kartashev (1875–1960), onetime professor, St. Petersburg Theological Academy; Kadet; ober-procurator, Holy Synod, July–August 1917, then minister of confessions; emigrated to France.

69. Aleksandr Grigor'evich Khrushchev, landowner, banker; Zemstvo activist; Kadet deputy, First State Duma; member, Kadet Party Central Committee, 1917. See his *Andrei Ivanovich Shingarev ego zhizn' i deiatel'nost'* (*Andrei Ivanovich Shingarev, His Life and Work*) (Moscow, 1918).

70. "Secret" treaties refers to the agreements concluded in February 1917 between Imperial Russia and the other Allied governments of England, France, and Italy, by which Russia obtained approval for the annexation of the Bosphorus, the Sea of Marmora, and the Dardanelles, along with a sizable area of land on both the east and west coasts, including Constantinople, plus some islands necessary to the defense of this region. In return, Russia agreed to let the other Allied governments

more direct, more naïve, than L'vov's indignation. He characterized those treaties as brigandage and swindling, and it seems he
expressed the desire for an immediate repudiation of them. He was
particularly indignant about Italy and the "annexations" (it had not
yet become a popular expression) which she reserved for herself.
With the same directness, he spoke of the "idiots and scoundrels"
sitting in the synod. His reports were imbued with an almost comic
despair. Undoubtedly V. N. L'vov had one positive feature: he was
not a political plotter, and with his entire soul he devoted himself to
the goal of cleansing the highest administration of the Church. Unfortunately, this task was decidedly beyond him. Like Godnev,
when his position was needed for another, he surrendered it without
a murmur. In spite of all his activity in five months' tenure at the
post of ober-procurator, I do not know whether his activity left
even a slight trace in the "Department of the Orthodox Faith."

I have already indicated above my surprise at the appointment of
M. I. Tereshchenko to the post of minister of finance. At first I
could not believe that this could be that brilliant young man who a
few years before had appeared on the Petersburg horizon, penetrated theatrical circles, become well known as a passionate music-
lover and patron of the arts, and from the beginning of the war,
thanks to his colossal wealth and connections, became a prominent
figure in the Red Cross. Later, I knew he had become head of the
Kiev War Industries Committee,[71] and at a certain congress held in
Petersburg had made a speech which could be characterized as the
speech of a "repentant capitalist." This was his only public appearance of which I knew. I did not know that he was in apparently

carve out their own spheres of influence in the Ottoman Empire. France and Russia
agreed secretly to Russia's redrawing her western frontier in return for France doing
the same with her eastern border. The Declaration of London of August 23/Sep-
tember 5, 1914, in which the Allies agreed not to conclude a separate peace, was really not part of the "secret" treaties.

71. The War Industries Committees were created by leading industrialists of all
Russia in the summer of 1915. Its central committee was a liaison between industrialists and representatives of workers' groups. The government unwillingly accepted the aid of these committees, which did excellent work in promoting the war
effort.

close relations with Guchkov and Nekrasov and enjoyed the favor of Rodzianko. Up to this time I do not know exactly who brought up his candidacy. I heard that he had obstinately refused it.

At present he is remembered primarily as the minister of foreign affairs who occupied this post for six months, from the beginning of May until the end of October, when the Provisional Government was overthrown. As minister of finance, in his two months' tenure at that post, he does not seem to have left any noticeable trace. He was mainly occupied with the issuance of the famous Liberty Loan.[72] I remember that when he had to report to the Provisional Government, his reports were always very clear and not long-winded but, on the contrary, concise and excellently stated. In fact, I am not going to pass judgment on his qualities as minister of finance. He excellently grasped the external facets of things, knew how to orient himself and how to talk to people, saying just what his listener wanted to hear and conforming to the latter's views. In his activities as minister of foreign affairs, his goal was to follow Miliukov's policy, but in such a way as not to be hindered by the Soviet of Workers' Deputies. He wanted to dupe them all and for some time succeeded in doing so. In September 1917 the socialists became disappointed with him and expected nothing further from him, but Sukhanov-Gimmer [73] had much earlier begun a campaign against him in *Novaia Zhizn'*. During July and August he, together with Nekrasov and Kerensky, comprised a triumvirate which directed the whole policy of the Provisional Government, and in

72. The Liberty Loan was an attempt by the Provisional Government to eliminate the issuance of more paper money by floating a loan utilizing some 12 billion rubles of free funds in banking institutions. The Petrograd Soviet openly supported it on April 22 even though socialists considered it a tax on future generations. By July, only one-third of the available 12 billion rubles had been subscribed. See B. & K., 2 : 485–92.

73. Nikolai Nikolaevich Sukhanov [Gimmer] (1882–193?), journalist, economist; Social Democrat Internationalist; onetime Socialist Revolutionary; coeditor, *Novaia Zhizn'*, 1917; member, Executive Committee, Petrograd Soviet, 1917; sentenced to prison for ten years, 1931; vanished; authored extensive chronicle of 1917; *Zapiski o revoliutsii (Notes of the Revolution)*, 7 vols. (Berlin, 1922–23), abridged and issued as *The Russian Revolution 1917: An Eye-witness Account*, 2 vols. (New York, 1962).

this capacity he bears responsibility for the weakness, duplicity, unscrupulousness, and fruitlessness of that policy, which constantly maneuvered and searched for a compromise just when the only solution to this situation lay in a rejection of a compromise, in resoluteness and determination.

In October, mainly from the time of the formation of the "Council of the Russian Republic," Tereshchenko demonstrably broke with the socialists. I happened to witness the stormy scene with Kerensky in which Tereshchenko insisted that the Provisional Government release him from the Ministry of Foreign Affairs' portfolio, and at this time he designated me as his successor. But all this was too late. M. I. Tereshchenko met a sad fate. He wanted to win general sympathy and general approval. Nevertheless, he did not put down firm roots anywhere, neither in any social circle, nor in any political group, and no one valued him or had a high opinion of him. *Ce n'était pas un caractère.*[74] What is remarkable is that our allies' diplomatic representatives related to Tereshchenko better than to Miliukov. His *souplesse,* his good manners, the absence of firm convictions or well-thought-out plans, and his complete dilettantism in questions of foreign policy, made him, under the circumstances, a man estraordinarily easy to talk to—and during the whole existence of the Provisional Government our entire international policy was indeed nothing but talks.

Toward the end of the existence of the Provisional Government, after N. V. Nekrasov's resignation, Tereshchenko was inflamed with hatred for the socialists. This was a change of attitude. I have reason to believe that such a change of mood was influenced by the Kornilov affair. I do not know how Tereshchenko conducted himself at the time this affair was developing, but he was greatly shaken by the suicide of Krimov,[75] having been on friendly terms with him. The "socialist front's" badgering of Kornilov was for him most trying and unpleasant, and aroused his indignation; he told me so himself. I think on this basis a certain coolness developed between him and Kerensky. At the same time, he believed—

74. "He had no personality."

75. General A. M. Krimov (1871–1917), commander of the Third Cavalry Corps, committed suicide after being arrested for his part in the Kornilov affair.

or wanted to believe—right up to the very last, in the possibility of the rebirth of the army and the restoration of the front. I spoke with him regarding this in September or October 1917. He maintained categorically that Alekseev could prepare a new army by the spring of 1918. When the Provisional Government's last minister of war, General Verkhovskii [76] declared plainly in the Military Commission of the Council of the Republic that Russia could not fight any longer, Tereshchenko responded very sharply. His clash with Verkhovskii in the session of the commission was one of the most memorable episodes in the last days of the existence of the Provisional Government.

Alas, we must acknowledge that Verkhovskii was essentially correct.

Summarizing my opinion of Tereshchenko, I can say that, despite his outstanding ability and undoubted *bonne volonté,* he was not, and could not be, up to the political task that fell to him. His role was head and shoulders beyond him, as it was beyond the majority of the other ministers. He was as incapable as they of "saving Russia." And between March and October 1917 it was necessary to save Russia, in the literal sense of the word.

Finally, among the members of the Provisional Government whom I hardly knew was A. I. Konovalov, the minister of trade and industry. I first met him at the Tauride Palace in the first days of the revolution, and I observed him during the two months I occupied the post of Head of the Chancellery of the Provisional Government. After that I completely lost sight of him and did not meet him again until the last formation of the Provisional Government, in which he was deputy minister-president.

Here is a man about whom I could not say the least word of blame from my personal point of view. Both as minister of trade and later, when to his misfortune he considered it his patriotic duty to heed Kerensky's insistent request and again entered the Cabinet,

76. General Aleksandr Ivanovich Verkhovskii (1886–1941), commander, Moscow Military District, summer 1917; minister of war, September-October 1917; emigrated; joined Red Army, 1919; professor, Red Army Military Academy, 1927–41; author, *Rossiia na golgofe (Russia at Calvary)* (Petrograd, 1918).

accepting, moreover, the very responsible and burdensome role as Kerensky's deputy, he was a perpetual martyr, and he suffered deeply. I do not think he believed for one moment in the possibility of a favorable outcome from this situation. As minister of trade he could see clearly and at close hand our catastrophic path toward economic collapse. Later, as deputy president, he had to face all the negative aspects of Kerensky's character. At the same time, Konovalov was already perfectly well aware in October 1917 that for Russia the war was over. At this time (or earlier, in September but after the formation of the last Cabinet) a conference was held in Prince Grigorii Nikolaevich Trubetskoi's apartment (on the Sergievskaia, in Wiener's house, where my family and I had lived in the winter of 1906–07). Neratov, Baron Nol'de, Rodzianko, Savich, Maklakov, M. Stakhovich, Struve, Tret'iakov,[77] Konovalov, and I were present (I think I have named everyone; Miliukov was not there but in the Crimea, where he had gone after the Kornilov affair) for the discussion of the question of whether it was possible and right to orient subsequent Russian policy toward a general peace. Konovalov very decisively supported the view of Baron Nol'de who, in a detailed, profound, and shrewd report, proved the necessity for such an orientation. Unfortunately all this was already too late.

But all these recollections relate to Konovalov's second period of activity. I do not remember him playing a notable role in the first Provisional Government. He spent most of the time, it seems, complaining that the Provisional Government was not sufficiently concerned with the industrial deterioration which was growing, not daily but hourly, due to the excessive and increasing demands of

77. A. A. Neratov, highly respected assistant minister of foreign affairs under the tsar, in the Provisional Government and in Denikin's Special Council in the Civil War. Miliukov called him the walking encyclopedia of the Foreign Ministry.

Nikanor Vasil'evich Savich, Octobrist deputy, Third, Fourth State Dumas; chairman, Commission to Revise Naval Regulations, 1917. Miliukov called Savich the chief oracle of the Octobrists.

Sergei Nikolaevich Tret'iakov, industrialist; president, Moscow Stock Exchange; president, Economic Council, September–October 1917; minister of trade and industry, Kolchak government; member, Wrangel's financial council; emigrated after the Civil War.

the workers. He was never eloquent, and spoke very simply and sincerely—artlessly as it were—but I think that a note of panic could be heard in his addresses to the Provisional Government. In private conversations, too, he would often turn to these themes as though seeking approval and moral support. How Konovalov could have entered the Provisional Government a second time with Kerensky as president is, for me, an unsolved mystery. Apparently he thought it his patriotic duty not to refuse and thought that he would be successful in holding out until the Constitutent Assembly. At the time that mirage, the Constituent Assembly, excited in many minds quite incomprehensible hopes. But the importance of the idea of the Constituent Assembly to the Provisional Government I will discuss in a separate place.

I met A. I. Konovalov for the last time in tragic circumstances, on the day the Provisional Government was overthrown, October 26. I shall also have to talk about that day at the appropriate time.

Until now I have touched upon the character and role of those individuals in the Provisional Government who were not my party compatriots. Several of them I met for the first time in these circumstances. Now it remains for me to talk about the four Kadet ministers, Miliukov, Shingarev, Nekrasov, and Manuilov, whom I had known for a long time, although I was on close personal terms only with Miliukov.

Manuilov was the one I knew least of all. This is, of course, explained by the fact that Manuilov is a Moscovite and never took a particularly active part in the meetings of the Central Committee, and outside of those meetings I hardly ever encountered him. I must say that during the two months of my participation in the affairs of the Provisional Government Manuilov remained constantly in the background. Very rarely, if at all, did he take part in the heated political debates that went on in the closed sessions. I recall that in the main controversy of the first month, concerning the question of foreign policy in relation to war aims, Manuilov gave very feeble support to Miliukov; in fact, I would even say that he gave no support at all. On the other hand, a sense of the hopelessness of the Provisional Government's task somehow penetrated

Manuilov sooner than the others, and he spoke of the necessity of leaving the Provisional Government in view of the impossible working conditions that resulted from the control and constant obstruction by the Soviet of Workers' Deputies.

His special field of activity in the capacity of minister of education was not distinguished by the authority one would have expected from him. It is very possible that this may not have been his fault, that is, not the fault of his personal qualities. In other, more normal conditions, these qualities would have made him an exemplary minister of education, since there can be no doubt of his breadth of view, great knowledge, nor in general of his virtues as a politician and administrator. But essentially, his was not a combative nature, he was no fighter. Even earlier, his main method of struggle was to hand in his resignation. This may have been all right under Kasso,[78] but at this particular moment something else was needed. Manuilov might have been perfectly suited for the post of minister of agriculture, although I imagine that by temperament and mood he was actually not the man suited to this particular revolutionary moment. He did not impress anyone. Together with this, his balanced nature as a spiritual European was deeply irked by the atmosphere of unbridled, demagogic radicalism which lent itself to all sorts of manipulation by people like [V. I.] Charnolusskii. I remember Manuilov's despair at the time of the Teachers' Congress. It was namely in the sector of education that our Jacobin radicalism was manifest most boldly, and if eventually the educators received Mr. Lunacharskii [79] as their director, then we can properly say: *"Tu l'as voulu, Georges Dandin."*

Of all the ministers, Manuilov received an exclusively "bad press." Both the Right and the Left attacked him: the Right, for his inactivity and for apathy in the face of the growing revolutionary

78. Lev Aristidovich Kasso (1865–1914), minister of education, 1910–14; in 1911 purged Moscow University faculty of more than one hundred instructors and replaced them, in the words of Miliukov, with his own henchmen; sought to isolate the school from society.

79. Anatoli Vasil'evich Lunacharskii [Voinov] (1875–1933), dramatist; Bolshevik starting in 1903; commissar of education, 1917–29; ambassador to Spain, 1933. Charnolusskii chaired the Teachers Congress; see B. & K., 2 : 773–74.

wave, and for the Spelling Reform [80] (which, as we know, had nothing to do with him, the Academy of Sciences has that disgrace on its conscience); and the Left, for bureaucratism, for preserving red-tape, and for appointing officials of the old regime. Gerasimov's [81] appointment was a cause of particular irritation. Manuilov did not know how to defend himself against attack. He would give way to depression and despair. Essentially speaking, perhaps he was completely right in recognizing a hopeless situation. But even so he should have acted differently, more decisively—I would even say more demonstratively. Despite all his virtues, he remained a rather dim figure, and if all welcomed his appointment, his resignation and replacement by S. F. Ol'denburg not only caused no regret, but was positively rather than negatively received, even in circles sympathetic to him.

I find it most difficult to discuss Nekrasov. At the beginning of my notes I mentioned that, as a result of my prolonged absence from the Central Committee, I was very ill-informed about the personal interrelationships which had formed there (and in the State Duma). Only a considerably long time after I had become Head of the Chancellery of the Provisional Government did a talk with A. I. Shingarev open my eyes. He told me about the ''underground war'' that Nekrasov had long conducted against Miliukov. Only then did I understand the behavior of Nekrasov, whom, until then, I had through force of habit considered one of Miliukov's most devoted friends. But all the same it remained unclear to me what Nekrasov was striving for. However, each day provided clearer and clearer indications that he was gravitating toward the socialists, drawing closer to Kerensky, with whom he possessed greater and greater influence and with whom he was more and more in accord. Nevertheless, I do not know Nekrasov well enough to judge him with confidence; yet I fear that during his tenure in power he was guided

80. The Spelling Reform was a change in orthography and the dropping of four letters from the alphabet; it had been under discussion since 1905 and was only implemented in 1917. See B. & K., 1 : 482, 781–84.

81. Peter Vasil'evich Gerasimov, lawyer; Kadet deputy, Fourth State Duma; member, Kadet Party Central Committee, 1916–17.

first and foremost by motives of ambition. He sought to play the leading role—and he achieved his aim, but only to the extent that he inspired Kerensky's shameful behavior in the Kornilov affair, following which he withdrew from the scene with a damaged political reputation, abandoned by all his former friends (even such devoted and intimate friends as I. P. Demidov) [82] and nicknamed the "evil genius of the Russian Revolution."

Nevertheless, I am firmly convinced that Nekrasov is one of the few outstanding men to have emerged in the political arena in recent years. He has immense administrative capabilities, he knows how to orient himself, his outlook is broad, and he has a practical keenness. An intelligent, resourceful, eloquent man, he known how to appear sincere and open-hearted when necessary. But apparently his ethical attitude (I am, of course, speaking of his social and political, not personal, qualities) were not up to his intellectual qualities. I am quite prepared to believe that in the end he was striving essentially for the victory of those ideas which united him with his fellow party members. But for this he chose an extraordinary, tortuous path that finally ended in a cul-de-sac. I imagine that at this time (1918) he must be a most unhappy man and that his political career is finally over. He will never again inspire confidence in anyone, and confidence is, after all, an absolutely essential condition for a politician. Once duplicity appears it is never forgotten. Nekrasov left precisely an impression of duplicity, a mask concealing his true face. It was particularly perceptible because his apparent geniality was so disarming. A *faux bonhomme* as the French so accurately express it, is perhaps the most unpleasant type of human being in general, and of politician in particular.

Finally, if one considers that the Kadet element in the membership of the Provisional Government was personified above all in Miliukov, one must say that Shingarev alone, without a doubt, gave by support and assistance his entire soul to the party.

As I write these lines, more than six months have passed since Shingarev's tragic death—yet, even in these notes, it is somehow

82. I. P. Demidov (1873–?), Kadet deputy, Fourth State Duma; member, Kadet Party Central Committee; member, Paris Kadet Committee.

difficult to speak about the deceased with complete freedom. He paid far too high a price for the heroic feat of his life. Nevertheless, I will try, here also, to write the entire truth as I understand it. The truth here lies in the fact that throughout his life Shingarev remained essentially what he would have been in more normal conditions: a provincial Russian intellectual, a representative of the third estate, very capable, very industrious, warm-hearted, and high-minded, moved by crystal-pure motives, personally extraordinarily charming and likeable, but ultimately not meant for the national but for the provincial or district level. He became a financier purely by chance. Thanks to his talent and industriousness, he was so accustomed to this field that he could successfully make a speech at the tribune of the Duma from an opposing viewpoint and win a victory.

But he was quite unable to impress real experts, either theorists or practical men. His dilettantism, his poor training, and the limitations of his interests, were too obvious. Thanks to his personal qualities and his amazing attractiveness, he was one of the most popular and favored members of the Duma. The press made much of him. The government was very attentive to his views. Large masses of people, for one reason or another swarmed around him daily. His popularity within the party was enormous. If it fell short of Miliukov's, this was perhaps so only in the sense that Miliukov stood higher as an intellectual eminence, as spiritual leader and guide, and as a statesman; but Shingarev was better loved, particularly in the provinces, where his speeches, addresses, and lectures always enjoyed exclusive success.

The middle classes felt a greater spiritual affinity with Shingarev than with Miliukov. He was closer to them, more like one of them. As an orator Shingarev was certainly not comparable to Maklakov and Rodichev (when the latter was at his best). Strength could rarely be felt in him. One could not find imagery or brilliance in his speeches. He was quite unable to rivet attention, to stir emotions, to shock. Further, one did not sense in these speeches, which were always very verbose, that enormous reserve of ideas and knowledge that was so clearly felt when Miliukov spoke. He did not charm his listeners as Maklakov did, he did not move or petrify the nerves like Rodichev, but he spoke easily and freely, his train of thought was always very clear and accessible, in debate he was quite often resourceful and witty, and his voice and manner were very winning. If one could stop listening to him without any regrets, one was almost never made to feel that he had not been worth listening to. In *The Possessed,* Dostoevsky says that one cannot listen to one speaker for more than twenty minutes. This is absolutely not true of our provincial audiences. They love verbosity and accept their boredom as proof of the seriousness and importance of the speech or lecture; no wonder such dull mediocrities as Gredeskul' [83] have always enjoyed enormous success in the provinces.

By the end of the Fourth Duma, Shingarev's authority stood very high. To any objective observer it was obvious that his conceit and self-confidence had increased, particularly after members of the Duma made their trip abroad in the spring of 1916. One felt that Shingarev was feeling slightly dizzy from the height to which he, a humble country doctor, had been elevated, not by chance or by outside help but through his own efforts. Without the State Duma, Shingarev would have lived the honest and pure life of an intelligent local figure, a selfless toiler. The State Duma brought him to the forefront and prepared everyone to accept Shingarev as one of the most indisputable candidates for a ministerial portfolio as soon as the old bureaucracy fell.

He was at once submerged in a sea of excesses that was too much for the strength of any one man. There were few people whom he trusted or relied on. He wanted to do everything himself, and this was physically impossible. He probably worked fifteen to eighteen hours a day, soon tired himself out, and very quickly lost his vitality and cheerfulness. He often spoke at the Provisional Government's sessions, but it was precisely here that his powers proved inadequate. At these sessions, too, he felt himself to be on the rostrum in the State Duma, spoke at length and was terribly wordy, and fatigued himself and the others to the utmost. But the worst insult one could give him was to say? "Andrei Ivanych, can

83. Nikolai Andreevich Gredeskul' (1864–?), jurist, publicist; deputy chairman, First State Duma; member, Kadet Party Central Committee, 1906; resigned Kadets, 1916; editor, *Russkiia Vedomosti;* author, *Rossiia prezhde i teper'* (*Russia Then and Now*), (Moscow, 1926).

you not make it a bit shorter?'' In such instances he would reply: ''I can stop speaking completely,'' thereby compelling one to entreat him to go on.

His attitude to Kerensky and the whole socialist Swamp [84] was negative and hostile; yet not only could he not fight them energetically but, on the contrary, with such measures as the creation of the Land Committees [85] and the handing over to them of uncultivated estate lands, as well as later (while he was minister of finance), with the total unjustifiable and completely absurd raising of the income tax, he played into the hands of the socialists, making for himself many implacable enemies among landowners and the propertied classes in general. He personally had little faith in his own law introducing a grain monopoly. Incidentally, the prices fixed by the law were being changed incessantly right up to the last minute; in the long run, apparently, many of them had to be given up as lost. Concerning questions of general politics and foreign policy, Shingarev was constantly on Miliukov's side, but I cannot remember his making powerful or vivid speeches.

After his final resignation from the Provisional Government, Shingarev became extremely short-tempered and atrabilious—I am inclined to say embittered. It was difficult to argue with him in the Central Committee, where he interpreted as abusive any argument, as though it were directed against him personally. He sometimes spoke very sharply. Presumably, the personal misfortune he suffered during this period (the death of his wife) strongly shook his already strained nerves. He became difficult, and maintained his former manner and attitude toward only a few (of whom I was one). N. I. Lazarevskii told me it was very hard to work with Shingarev. He was, in Lazarevskii's words, unusually suspicious and mistrustful in relation to everyone around him, with the exception of a small circle of intimates of his personal choice. His de-

84. From the time of the French Revolution, politically unstable individuals of shifting views; a term used by the socialists themselves in 1917.

85. The Land Committees were to accumulate factual data and deal with specific, local land problems. The committees consisted of appointed and elected representatives, including local soviet delegates. The government, with the urging of the Petrograd Soviet, undertook to establish the committees as early as March 10/23. See B. & K, 2 : 528–32, 618–21.

mise in January 1918 is one of the most tragic, and at the same time most senseless, episodes in the bloody history of bolshevism.

It seems to me I have already stated that Miliukov was without doubt the most important figure, intellectually and politically, in the first Provisional Government. I consider him in general one of the most remarkable of Russians, and I would like to attempt to give a more detailed characterization of him.

I have often had occasion to listen to Miliukov: in the Central Committee, at party congresses and gatherings, at meetings and public lectures, in state institutions. His qualities as an orator are closely related to the basic features of his intellectual personality. He is most adroit whenever he has to make a polemical analysis of various tactics. He is a master of irony and sarcasm. His splendid exposés, with their captivating logic and clarity, can crush an opponent. At political meetings no orator from opposing parties has ever been successful in confusing or side-tracking him. He worries little about the outward form of his speech. In it there is no imagery, no rhythmical beauty. But it also never has what the French call *du remplissage* [padding]. If he is usually wordy in his speeches and writings, it is only because he needs copious detail to express his thought. Here, too, his complete disregard of extenuating circumstances, together with his unusual tirelessness, expresses itself. When his turn comes, late at night after a full day of heated debate, he begins his speech slowly and methodically, and immediately for him all attendant considerations vanish: his listeners' fatigue has no meaning for him; he gives no consideration to the fact that perhaps they are simply in no condition to follow the trend of his thoughts. Likewise, in his newspaper articles he does not care about purely journalistic considerations. If he needs two hundred lines, he writes two hundred lines; but if his ideas and his argument will not fit into them, he is totally unconcerned should his editorial spread over three newspaper columns.

Like many others, Miliukov, too, is living and has lived at a historical moment highly unpropitious for his personal talents. According to the will of fate, it transpired that Miliukov was in power at a time when what was needed above all was a strong authority that would not hesitate when faced with the most decisive actions—when the highest degree of unity and solidarity among the members of the government, and their complete trust, were required of one another. He found himself at the head of the department that implements foreign policy just when a deepseated disagreement about the prerequisites of this policy existed between himself and those who followed Kerensky's line. In my presence Kerensky aligned himself, if not directly with the Zimmerwaldians, in any case with elements spiritually very close to Zimmerwaldism. Both in the press and on the rostrum of the State Duma, Miliukov carried on a stubborn struggle with Zimmerwaldism from the beginning. He was absolutely alien and hostile to the idea of peace without annexations and indemnities. He considered that it would be absurd and simply criminal of us to renounce the "greatest prize of the war" (as Grey [86] called Constantinople and the Straits) in the name of the humanitarian and cosmopolitan ideas of international socialism. But most importantly, he believed that this prize had not really slipped from our grasp. This belief turned up in relation to his general views on the revolution's significance for the war. Here is the very key to the Russian tragedy one has experienced.

It is well known how Miliukov regarded the threat of impending war in June and July 1914. He wrote that it was an awesome danger fraught with enormous disasters. Of course, neither he nor any other politician realized or could realize how the war would transform Europe and what it would do to Russia. Above all, no man on earth would have believed, if he had been told in 1914, that boys then thirteen years old would be participating in the war, or that four years later the war would be raging at its height and that, even then, there would be little hope of its quick termination. Nevertheless, Miliukov well realized, first, the terrible risk for Russia entailed in the declaration of a European war, and second, the fallacy of expecting that the "historical power," whose rule in Russia had proved so hopelessly and immeasurably inept during peacetime, would be equal to the task that would fall to it. He

---

86. Sir Edward Grey (1862–1933), British foreign secretary, 1905–16.

therefore, in a series of articles in *Rech'*, appealed with all the force of his conviction, for composure, self-control, and moderation.

It is also well known how maliciously he was attacked by our militant, nationalist press, headed by *Novoe Vremia*.[87] The question was "intervention for Serbia," and since Miliukov was considered a "Bulgarophile," and consequently a "Serbophobe," hostility to "little Serbia" and indifference to Russia's international prestige were read into his speeches or attributed to him. A furious campaign was raised which resulted in the closing of *Rech'* (admittedly, only for a short time) on the day of the declaration of war. War began, and at once Miliukov took a perfectly defined posture toward it. In the State Duma, in the party, and on the pages of *Rech'*, he led an energetic campaign oriented toward stirring up enthusiasm for the war. The slogan War to a Victorious Conclusion relates to a later time, but its roots derive from the very first days of the war.

When it became clear that England was joining France and Russia, there was a widespread conviction that the war would end quickly with the defeat of Germany. I vividly remember, in August or September, meeting Count P. N. Ignat'ev [88] for dinner in a restaurant (he was an old friend to whom I was close in my student days) and his telling me that Rennenkampf [89] was marching straight on Berlin, circumventing strongholds and leaving behind covering detachments, and that he swore he would be in Berlin within two months; the count was quite serious, and apparently faithfully believed in the fulfillment of this plan. I also remember

87. *Novoe Vremia* (*New Times*), conservative St. Petersburg daily established in 1865; in 1917, edited and published by A. S. Suvorin.

88. Count Pavel Nikolaevich Ignat'ev (1870–1926), landowner; official, Department of Agriculture from 1909; minister of education, 1915–16, resigning over the government's rejection of his plan of reform for the gymnasiums; emigrated after the Bolshevik coup.

89. General Pavel Karlovich Rennenkampf (1854–1918), General Staff, 1882; distinguished in Russo-Japanese War, 1904–05; prominent in putting down uprisings, 1905–07; commander, First Army, 1914; suspected of treachery for his inaction at Tannenberg; recalled and dismissed, 1915; killed by the Bolsheviks.

writing to A. I. Kaminka [90] for the first time from Staria Russa, where my detachment was forming, saying that I was more convinced each day of the enormity of the undertaking and of the impossibility of its being quickly implemented. But our first successes in East Prussia and then in Galicia considerably strengthened our hopes, and only the terrible surprises during the second half of the winter of 1914–15 showed how rash such hopes had been.

At the same time, the State Duma's tactics toward the government abruptly changed. The *mot d'ordre* [watchword] in the autumn of 1914 was support for the Cabinet, something of the nature of the French *Union Sacré*.[91] But by the spring of 1915 it was clear that to support Sukhomlinov, Maklakov, and Shcheglovitov meant to lead Russia knowingly to defeat and catastrophe.[92] So the struggle began. The course and peripeteia of this struggle are well known. The role played by Miliukov is also well known; and so, at the very beginning, the tragic misunderstanding which influenced the entire course of the Russian Revolution and led to the ruin of Russia. In the name of what was the struggle carried on? Obviously, first and foremost and *ex professo,* so to speak, in the name of establishing in Russia a government capable of correcting the blunders and errors which had already been made, and of successfully organizing supplies and reinforcements for the army. In other words, the purpose of the struggle was to form the kind of authority that could conduct a better and more efficient war. Meanwhile, all the governmental changes took on more and more the character of a kind of mad ministerial leapfrog. Decent and effective persons like

90. Avgust Isaakovich Kaminka (1877–?), Kadet leader and coeditor with Nabokov and Gessen of *Rul'*, Berlin; head, Russian Academic Group, an adjunct of the University of Berlin, 1920.

91. A war fought in the defense of the fatherland which binds the nation together. See Paul Miliukov's chapter, "The 'Sacred Union,' " in *Political Memoirs, 1905–1917* (Ann Arbor, Mich., 1967).

92. Vladimir Aleksandrovich Sukhomlinov (1848–1926), minister of war, 1909–15; charged with treasonable conduct of the war; under house arrest, 1915; later sentenced by the Provisional Government; released by the Bolsheviks; emigrated to Germany; authored notorious memoirs, *Erinnerungen* (Berlin, 1924).

Ivan Grigor'evich Shcheglovitov (1861–1918), notorious anti-Semite; minister of justice, 1906–15; chairman, State Council, 1916–March 1917; imprisoned by the Provisional Government; shot by the Bolsheviks.

Prince Shcherbatov or Polivanov [93] did not remain long at their posts. Their places were taken either by seedy mediocrities like General Shuvaev or by sinister figures like Aleksei Khvostov [94] and, later, Stürmer. One sensed insanity and death in the air. Behind the scenes Rasputin, Prince Andronnikov, [95] and other rogues were handling everything. The tsar, from the outbreak of war until the catastrophe which befell him in the early days of March 1917, was absolutely unaware of the fatal significance of the events that were unfolding.

Those who experienced the winters of 1915–16 and 1916–17 in Petersburg well remember how a sense of some inevitable catastrophe grew daily. I was informed as early as 1914, immediately after the beginning of war (I was then already in Staraia Russa), that Rodichev, at a session of the Central Committee of the Kadet Party, had exclaimed: "Do you really think we can win with these fools?" It gradually became clear that the folly of our domestic policy, the shadowy spirit of irresponsible adventurism and total contempt for the Fatherland's interests by those who darkened a throne that was completely estranged from the entire country and was occupied by an insignificant, hypocritical weakling, must all end inevitably either in a separate peace or a coup d'état. Progressive Russian public opinion, which had long ago lost faith in Nicholas II, gradually realized that, as Kokoshkin eloquently expressed it in his speech on the republic and monarchy, it was impossible to be at one and the same time for the tsar and for Russia, that to be for the tsar meant to be against Russia.

93. Prince N. B. Shcherbatov (1868–?), minister of the interior, June–September 1915; died in emigration.

Aleksei A. Polivanov (1855–1920), deputy minister of war, 1906–12; minister of war, June 1915–March 1916; removed for being too cooperative with the Duma; Soviet government military expert.

94. General D. S. Shuvaev (1854–?), minister of war, March 17, 1916–January 3, 1917.

Aleksei N. Khvostov (1872–1918), minister of the interior, 1915–16 (replaced by his uncle, A. A. Khvostov, July–September 1916); member, State Duma Party of the Right; arrested by the Provisional Government, 1917; executed.

95. Prince M. M. Andronnikov (1875–1919), journalist; onetime accomplice of Rasputin, or as the prince described himself, "Aide-de-Camp of Our Lord Above."

On 1 November 1916 Miliukov made his famous speech, "Stupidity or Treason?".[96] Though directed against Stürmer, this speech was actually aimed much higher. The name of Empress Aleksandra Feodorovna was directly mentioned in it. Everyone remembers the tremendous impression it made, but probably not everyone realized its future consequences. Only much later, after the coup, was it commonly stated, particularly by Miliukov's friends, that the beginning of the Russian Revolution dated from the speech of 1 November. Miliukov himself, I believe, looked at the matter differently. He was fighting for a Cabinet with public trust, to isolate and render the tsar powerless (once it became clear that the tsar could not be, by any means and under any circumstances, a positive factor in the direction of the country and the conduct of the war), to make it possible for creative forces to engage in active and responsible participation in government work. I think it was in the course of the winter of 1916–17 that he thought a decisive overthrow necessary, particularly with reference to Nicholas II. But I suppose that he imagined it, as many others did, rather like an eighteenth-century palace coup d'état, and did not comprehend the profundity of the forthcoming shocks.

On the other hand, Miliukov's attitude toward the war became more and more definite, more closely tied to the position of our allies, England in particular, and more implacable toward Germany. I well remember the influence he had on me and a few close friends who had met for dinner at I. V. Gessen's house on the day a telegram brought news of Germany's first peace proposals. For us this was news of tremendous significance, chiefly because it was the first ray, even though weak and very distant, but anyway a ray of hope for the possibility of peace. It was from this point of view that we appraised the news in the first place. Miliukov immediately and resolutely doused us with ice water. Calmly and cheerfully, he declared that the German proposals were important only insofar as they testified to Germany's grave situation, that they should be understood and welcomed only in this sense, but that the only feasible

96. The speech is given in Frank A. Golder, ed., *Documents of Russian History* (New York, 1927), pp. 154–66.

response was a categorical rejection of them in the sharpest terms possible.

Apparently, Miliukov's attitude was dictated solely by a very profound belief in a "victorious conclusion" and in the possibility of Russia bringing the war to such an end so as to enjoy its fruits. In a recent letter, Miliukov himself has referred to the mood that prevailed in the ruling circles of Europe as "war fever." I think that this fever was the undercurrent of all international policy from the beginning of the war. Italy's entry into it, then Rumania's, and last of all America's were not dictated by any correct understanding of their legitimate national interests, and even less were they provided with any considerations or motives of political ethics; it was simply a fever of the sort which develops in the soul of one who is present at a huge game with colossal stakes and who knows that it is incumbent upon him to participate in this game and secure for himself a future share of the spoils.

The well-known treaties with Italy and Rumania have no more significance than a division of the spoils. Of course, such spoils were sought not for personal gain but in the name of national interests. Certainly Miliukov, too, grasping hold of and clinging to the very end to the promise of Constantinople and the Straits, was thinking only of Russia's good. But ultimately all aggressive aspirations can always be justified by a concern for a country's good. Miliukov's real attitude toward the war was always much closer to Romain Rolland's than to Barrès's and *"L'Action Française."* [97] That set of ideas and moods which possessed Miliukov from 1914 to 1917 was only a superficial froth; Miliukov even felt they were alien to himself, and his escape from this net of ideas and moods must have seemed to him to be a "spiritual" liberation. As I see it, this liberation consisted of a return to objective criteria which corre-

97. Romain Rolland (1866–1944), French Nobel Prize author; pacifist, World War I; later, a mouthpiece for Fascist and Nazi opposition.

Maurice Barrès (1862–1923), French novelist; archpatriot; sought the promotion of French national unity in terms of "traditional development" with decentralization and harmonizing of the forces of nationalism and socialism, an ideology in some respects foreshadowing national socialism. *L'Action Française* was a French paramilitary group.

sponded with certain fundamental concepts of justice and humanity and with the rejection of bloodshed and violence, rather than with an immediate, practical political aim.

Anyhow, it is clear from what I have said that any future conflicts that ensued within the Provisional Government, and between it and the elements around it most deeply involved in the revolutionary movement, were, in the truest sense of the words, utterly inevitable. The most influential figure in the Provisional Government proved to be "the hostage of democracy," Kerensky. If on the day the Provisional Government was formed it had occurred to anyone to nominate Kerensky as minister of war, I think even Kerensky, in spite of his boundless aplomb, would have been embarrassed. Everyone else would have taken such a nomination as a mockery, a stupid joke. Nevertheless, within two months Kerensky emerged as the "providential" minister of war.

One must say this to an even greater degree regarding the post of Supreme Commander. I remember a prolonged session in the Mariinskii Palace devoted to the discussion and solution of the question of who was to be appointed to this position, Alekseev (the former chief of staff of the Supreme Commander at the time) or Brusilov.[98] Rodzianko especially stood for the latter. I can imagine what an effect would have been produced under these conditions if the candidacy of Kerensky had been proposed. It also would have been simply taken as a joke in bad taste. Yet this too came to pass several months later. I think there are no better criteria of the speed with which the Zimmerwaldist ideal triumphed in this matter, and brought about the destruction of our army, than these two appointments. But, essentially speaking, the source of future decay was already inherent in the fact that, when the Provisional Government was formed the fundamental question concerning the war was circumvented; otherwise how was it possible to include in the same government both Miliukov and Kerensky, since the latter's views were sufficiently well known from his speeches in the State Duma?

It should be pointed out that during the first days and even weeks

98. General Aleksei Alekseevich Brusilov (1853–1926), commander-in-chief, Southwest Front, March 1916–May 1917; Supreme Commander, May–July 1917; commanded the Bolsheviks' 1920 Polish campaign; Soviet government inspector of cavalry, 1924; author, *A Soldier's Notebook, 1914–1918* (London, 1930).

of the Provisional Government's existence, foreign policy in relation to the war was not raised. The grave inner contradiction of the
coup d'état remained unrevealed. Actually, it came as a result of a
military mutiny and essentially had to lead to a breakdown of discipline and disintegration, first in the Petersburg garrison; and then,
as this garrison became a hotbed of bolshevism and a breeding
ground of infection, the disintegration necessarily spread further.
But according to the official ideology, the revolution was supposed
to increase our military strength, since our troops henceforth would
be fighting not for a hated autocratic regime but for a liberated Russia. It is known that at first many naïve people thought (and even
wrote in the newspapers) that Germany seemed to be embarrassed
by the burst of patriotism of the Russian Revolution. Germany, it
was said, had at first placed great hopes on the revolution, but now
she would have to be convinced that a politically "conscious" Russian army, which had won its freedom, would be much more of a
threat, etc. I do not know whether anyone really believed such
twaddle, but I repeat, it was not only developed in the pages of
newspapers but also repeatedly and persistently formally declared
(for example, at embassy receptions and at receptions for the numerous military deputations that began to arrive at the end of
March).

Meanwhile, imperceptibly and little by little, the slogan War to a
Victorious Conclusion was undermined in the name of another,
Peace without Annexations or Indemnities. Gradually, within the
Provisional Government, complaints arose that Miliukov was conducting a quite independent international policy of his own. An internal split began to emerge, but at first rather vaguely and timidly.
If I am not mistaken, the issue initially was pointedly raised after
an interview with Miliukov on the question of war aims appeared in
the press about a week later (in the 23 March issue of *Rech'*), following the publication of the notorious appeal of the Soviet of
Workers' and Soldiers' Deputies to the peoples of the whole world
(on March 14), an appeal in which the leaders of the Executive
Committee showed their true face for the first time.[99]

It is impossible to imagine anything more contradictory than

99. For the Soviet's declaration, see B. & K., 2 : 1077–78.

these two documents. I do not know whether it was under the influence of his own friends or whether it was spontaneous, but Kerensky was in a state of extreme agitation because of the publication of the Miliukov interview. I believe he had just returned from Moscow. I vividly remember that he brought the issue of *Rech'* with him to the meeting, and before Miliukov's arrival, in his own peculiar manner, he burst into unnatural laughter, tapped his fingers on the newspaper, and repeated, "No, no, this trick will not work." When the question was raised, Miliukov revealed that his interview had appeared to counterbalance an interview with Kerensky which had been printed, if I am not mistaken, in the Moscow newspapers.

I do not remember whether it was at this or a subsequent meeting that Kerensky proved in a very harsh manner to Miliukov that if under "tsarism" (one of those infamous expressions of revolutionary jargon alien to the spirit of the Russian language) the foreign minister could not and should not have any policy but the policy of the emperor, so now the foreign minister could not have his own policy but only that of the Provisional Government. "We are for you, Sovereign Emperor." Miliukov, outwardly calm but inwardly violently agitated, answered approximately this way: "I have considered and still consider that the policy which I am following is the policy of the Provisional Government. If I am wrong, then let me be told so straightaway. I demand a definite answer, and what I shall do in the future will be dependent on this answer." Here was a direct and decisive challenge, and this time Kerensky retreated. Prince L'vov, speaking for the Provisional Government, attested that Miliukov was following, not his own independent policy, but that which corresponded to the views and plans of the Provisional Government. A way out of this awkward situation was found by adopting the guideline that in the future no private political interviews should be given. At the same time, the wish was expressed that Miliukov as soon as possible make a detailed report for the purpose of fully acquainting the Provisional Government with all aspects of the international situation, and in particular with all the famous "secret treaties." This was done as early as the first half of April, but even before that, at the end of March, the Provisional Government's declaration on the aims of the war was published.[100]

The initiative for this declaration came from Tseretelli. About the middle of March he returned from exile, and on the 20th he appeared in the Contact Commission, having replaced Steklov. From the very start, probably even at the first session he took part in, he advocated with particular insistence that no time should be wasted in making a solemn declaration to the army and the people—that it should contain, first, a definite break with imperialist ambitions, and second, an assurance that steps for concluding a general peace would be taken without delay. He argued that, if the Provisional Government would make such a declaration, the army's morale would rise to an unprecedented degree, and he and his confederates would then proceed with complete faith, and doubtless success, to rally the army around the Provisional Government, which would thereby gain enormous moral strength. "Say it," he said, "and everyone will back you to a man." I remember that at the time his tone and manner were truly persuasive. In them one felt a fervent and genuine conviction. In his objections Miliukov touched mainly on the second point and argued that in the present circumstances it was absolutely intolerable and, at best, fruitless, to propose any sort of peace negotiations to the Allies. Tseretelli persisted, and his assurances that, if only the basic sense of the directive were acknowledged Miliukov would be able to find some subtle diplomatic ways by which the directive could be implemented, made a somewhat comic impression. But Miliukov would not make any concessions on this second point. He also stood firm on the issue of annexations and indemnities.

I ask myself now whether it would not have been better for Miliukov actually to have handed Kerensky an ultimatum then, not solely because of those ill-fated words, but also because of the very meaning these words encompassed, the meaning which was, in the end, included in the declaration, although admittedly in somewhat milder and intentionally ambiguous expressions. In retrospect, this question has personal significance for me. As in the very begin-

100. For the Provisional Government's declaration, see B. & K., 2 : 1045–46.

ning, when Miliukov threatened to resign over the question of [Grand Duke] Mikhail, so now, too, it seemed to me that his resignation would have fateful consequences from the point of view of the international situation and of our allies' attitude toward us. I believed that, if need be, we should make even the greatest concessions simply to keep Miliukov in the government. Here I thought a little Machiavellianism might be justified.

I recall that Miliukov and I were discussing and correcting the text of the declaration during lunch at the European Hotel, having come directly from the Congress of the Party of the People's Freedom, which had opened on 25 March in the auditorium of the Mikhailovskii Theater. I was trying to persuade him to agree to include such expressions in the declaration (an explanation of what Russia did not want from the war) so that "annexations and indemnities" would only figure allegorically. I said that these words allowed a very broad and subjective interpretation, that, as far as they included a rejection of aggressive policy, they corresponded to our views too, but that they had no meaning at all that could bind one in the future at a peace conference should the war end to our advantage. I remember that we changed the text several times before we finally found expressions which proved acceptable to Miliukov. There was still a certain *reservatio mentalis* in his acceptance.

But, to take another example, compare Wilson's successive declarations—the one, for example, which maintained that the present war must end without any victors—with those which dramatized and accompanied America's declaration of war; do they not contain obvious contradictions? It is beyond reason to believe that a simple governmental declaration which has no contractual nature is binding on all subsequent governments. But even the government that has issued a declaration is bound by it only insofar as it contains in it certain immutable principles of government policy. It was proven long ago that the "principle" of "without annexations or indemnities" could not be accepted, that this precept is ambiguous and in practice gives no solution to a series of questions. It is not in vain that subsequent terminology invented the expression, "deannexation."

It would naturally be difficult to reconcile the transformation of the Dardanelles and the Bosphorus into a Russian channel with a strict interpretation of the words of a declaration. But if the circumstances ever made such a transformation possible, who would remember the words of this declaration and would decide to use it as an argument against Russia? It would be another matter if the Russian government, *expressis verbis,* rejected possible gains that were secured by international treaties and were to reveal this renunciation to the other contracting parties. But this was not, and indeed could not be, done by Miliukov. He himself, at a party congress after his resignation, quite sincerely and very convincingly maintained and proved that he had not conceded anything concrete and had not damaged Russia's interests in any way. But on the other hand, it is difficult to deny that this entire position was somewhat artificial. This artificiality, though, was not to be found in this or that interpretation of the individual expressions of the declaration, but in the fact that, essentially, an abyss existed between Miliukov's attitude toward the war and its goals, and those of the socialist group that influenced Kerensky.

I recall an occasion when this artificiality was somehow particularly accentuated and painfully felt. It happened a few days after the reception by the Provisional Government of a delegation of French and English socialists.[101] Miliukov made a speech that was wholly consistent and characteristic in tone, and that essentially conformed to Russia's traditional foreign policy in wartime. Kerensky spoke after Miliukov. He spoke Russian, which Miliukov translated into English (and one of the Frenchmen translated from English into French). This is where a striking contradiction was really felt, a contradiction in spirit, in the basic outlook itself. Now it became clear that within the Provisional Government there were two fundamental tendencies that were hostile to each other. There was no doubt that sooner or later—rather sooner than later—the ar-

101. The British and French socialists who came to bolster the Russian war effort included Marcel Cachin, Ernest Lafont, Marius Moutet, and later, Albert Thomas of France; Emile Vandervelde and Henri DeMan of Belgium; Will Thorne, James O'Grady, William S. Sanders, and later, Arthur Henderson of England. See B. & K., 2 : 1050–52, 1115–18.

tificial combination of Kerensky and Miliukov would have to collapse.

It is here that I find an answer to the question I raised above, whether it would not have been better if Miliukov had given an ultimatum before the 28 March declaration and resigned from the Provisional Government without waiting for the revolutionary action of the troops of 20–23 April, which was provoked by the foreign minister's note of 18 April. I think that Miliukov entered the Provisional Government for the right reasons, and for those same reasons he should have remained in it, fighting to the end in the interests of the cause he was serving. From the very beginning the revolution created compromises, artificial combinations. Just as compromising as the Provisional Government's relationship with the Soviet of Workers' and Soldiers' Deputies was the coexistence in the Cabinet of two men who were radically incapable of walking hand in hand, Kerensky and Miliukov. These compromises turned out to be foul and did not halt the catastrophic course of the Russian Revolution. But under the prevailing conditions they were inevitable, and for us Kadets to have renounced them would have meant taking the view "the worse, the better," or at the least washing our hands of everything. We then would have even more bitterly realized our responsibility for subsequent events.

In what I have said up to now about Miliukov's role in the Provisional Government, I was concerned only with his role in international politics. In my memory, at least, this remains the most brilliant aspect [of his career]. I do not recollect that Miliukov ever raised questions point-blank about domestic policy or insisted on any particular decisive measures. Apparently he believed, more than he should have, both in the political instinct of the Russian people and in their healthy understanding of their own interests. He could not and would not understand, and would not be reconciled to, the fact that the three-year war remained alien to the Russian people, that they continued it unwillingly, from under the lash, not understanding its meaning or aims, that they were exhausted by it, and that the revolution was received with ecstatic sympathy because they hoped that it would lead to a swift end to the war. He did not know that the poisonous seeds which irresponsible agitators had started to sow in the army from the very first days would fall on such propitious soil.

For that reason he did not take a decisive, unyielding stand against allowing the passengers of the famous sealed railway car [102] inside the borders of Russia. One must say that in relation to these passengers the Provisional Government had profound illusions. It was even thought that the fact of the "importation" of Lenin and Co. [103] by Germany would absolutely discredit them in the eyes of public opinion and somehow prevent their propagandizing from having any success. Indeed, at various meetings this theme of "the sealed car" always had great success. But that did not hinder the development of the most rabid and destructive propaganda in *Pravda, Okopnaia Pravda,* [104] and a number of other anarchical papers.

Now, of course, the Bolsheviks are showing us how a brazen power can, without any quibbling, suppress a press hostile to it. The Provisional Government was bound by its own declarations about the freedom of speech, by its whole ideology. This passivity also in part revealed the Provisional Government's awareness of its own impotence, which prevented it from taking decisive measures against such phenomenal and frankly criminal actions as the seizure of Kshesinskaia's residence and its conversion into a citadel and public rostrum of unbridled bolshevism. Now, of course, it is easy to reproach the Provisional Government for this passivity. But if one thinks back to that period and again recalls the prevailing mood, then it is clear that the government could not have acted differently without the risk of placing itself in complete isolation. Who would have supported it? The Petersburg garrison was not in its hands. The "bourgeois" classes, unorganized and nonmilitant,

102. This was a sealed car in that it had diplomatic immunity.

103. The "importation" of Lenin and his associates through Germany into Russia by way of Sweden and Finland is the subject of W. Halweg's thorough study, *Lenins Rückkehr nach Russland 1917* (Leiden, 1957).

104. *Pravda (Truth)* and *Okopnaia Pravda (Trench Truth).* The former was the news organ of the Central Committee of the Bolshevik party in Petrograd; the latter, the news organ of the Bolshevik Military Organization for the Northern Front in Riga.

would have eventually been on its side, but it would have been nothing more than platonic sympathy. But between them such sympathy was insufficient, although it came from a great many groups of the population.

I had occasion not long ago to talk over these matters with Miliukov. We concentrated on the question of whether there would have been a chance of preventing the catastrophe if at the very beginning the Provisional Government had raised outright the question of authority, relying on the State Duma, and if it had not allowed the Soviet and Executive Committee any political role, and in case of resistance had arrested the ringleaders. I considered, and still consider, this possibility as purely theoretical. But Miliukov maintained that in the first days of the overthrow the garrison was in the hands of the State Duma and, if this opportunity had not been missed at that instant, the situation could have been saved. Obviously, connected with this is the question of Mikhail. If the dynasty had retained the throne, its authority and prestige would have been preserved. But I do not see how the Provisional Government could have been successful without a monarch. What forces would have preserved its prestige and authority? Or, more importantly, how would it have coped with the war problem, that touchstone of the whole revolution?

I well remember that Miliukov repeatedly raised the question of the need for a more determined and decisive struggle against the growing anarchy. Others did so too. But I do not remember any definite practical measures ever being proposed or discussed by the Provisional Government. It was paralyzed by the absence of both a well-organized police force and a military that was unquestionably loyal to the government. Here, too, were the seeds of ruin, and its growth could not be hindered by all the Provisional Government's enormous energy manifested in the matter of basic legislation. Besides, every one of the ministers was so hard pressed by his own department that none of them had time to give any practical thought to the concerns of other departments and to suggest any concrete measures. In private discussions only general political questions were discussed. Of course, Miliukov repeatedly turned his attention, for example, to the necessity of terminating the disgraceful scandal that continued unhindered both outside and inside Kshe-sinskaia's house. But how was this to be done? To this question we had no answer.

The story of Miliukov's resignation, most likely, has been very fully stated in the already completed first volume of his history of the Russian Revolution.[105] His resignation was in fact, of course, the work of the socialists, aided on this occasion by Albert Thomas, who had arrived in Petersburg on 9 April. I do not remember whether it was before Thomas's arrival or already on 10 April that Miliukov told me during one of my morning visits that he was really considering whether it would not be better for him to hand over the Foreign Ministry portfolio to Tereshchenko ("At least he is not completely illiterate in these questions and will be able at any rate to talk to the ambassadors"), so that Manuilov could take over Finances (or perhaps Shingarev, Finances, and Manuilov, Agriculture) and hand the portfolio of the minister of education over to him, Miliukov. But I did not support this idea and Miliukov himself soon thereafter gave it up.

It was just at this time that Chernov returned to Russia and the campaign against Miliukov began full scale. At the Provisional Government's joint session with the Committee of the State Duma and the Executive Committee of the Soviet deputies, at which matters of foreign policy were discussed, Chernov declared that it was time for Russia to stop talking to Europe like "a poor relative." He said directly, with his typically vulgar grimaces, sugary smile, and affectations, that he and his friends infinitely respected P. N. Miliukov and considered his participation in the Provisional Government a necessity, but in their opinion he could better deploy his talents in some other post, even if only as minister of education.

At the same time a sharp incident involving Kerensky occurred, in connection with a semiofficial communiqué which he passed to the Press Bureau, announcing that a government statement on the subject of foreign policy was about to be published. That this communiqué had come from Kerensky I learned from L. L'vov (who played the leading role in the bureau). I knew perfectly well that

105. *Istoriia vtoroi russkoi revoliutsii,* 1 vol. in 3 parts (Sofia, 1921–23).

the Provisional Government had not even mentioned anything of the sort, and I saw Kerensky's action as an intolerable stunt, if not a provocation. I immediately reported this to Miliukov at the Provisional Government's session that was taking place at the time. At the termination of the session Miliukov asked who had given the press such a deliberately inconsistent communiqué. Kerensky appeared somewhat embarrassed and tried to hedge the issue by saying that he was not responsible for the way the press reported his words, but in the end he declared that under the present circumstances he considered a statement essential. Then Miliukov told Prince L'vov that, if Kerensky did not disavow the report, he, Miliukov, would hand in his resignation at once.

As it was already late and everyone was tired, it was decided to thrash out the question in the evening. A very stormy session took place, at which Kerensky felt himself quite alone, since even his staunchest supporters found the device he had used completely improper and impossible. He had to yield, and telephoned (from my office) the demanded denial. At the same time, however, the question was raised that the declaration of war aims had not been officially communicated to our allies and would therefore seem to be a document only for internal consumption—which would, of course, subvert its meaning. Accordingly, it was requested that diplomatic representatives be officially informed of the view of the Provisional Government concerning this question. It was difficult to dispute this, and Miliukov had to agree; at the same time it was decided to discuss the foreign minister's note with the full membership of the Provisional Government, which was done. At the time, A. I. Guchkov was down with a weak heart, and so the session occurred at his place.

I remember very clearly that the first reading of Miliukov's draft impressed everyone, even Kerensky, as unquestionably acceptable; and moreover, Miliukov in this manifested maximum compliancy and a willingness to meet his opponents halfway. That is why there was scarcely any debate at first to get tied up in; but when Kerensky began to carp at individual expressions, and offered most unsatisfactory variants, the mood began to deteriorate, and the usual personal antagonism made itself felt by a heightened tone and sharp outbursts. All the same, they finally were successful in circumventing differences and agreed on a text, the one that was published. At the end of the session, I remember, Miliukov emphasized that the government was, therefore, totally united on the document and was accepting responsibility for its contents. Kerensky did not object. Evidently, on this occasion his common sense and a judicious handling of the matter proved stronger than blind party loyalty. On the other hand, he apparently did not consider it opportune to consult his friends, being honestly convinced that for them, too, the note would be quite acceptable. It was published on 20 April. Then notable events occurred which were reported in detail in the newspapers of that time. Since the demonstrations were directed against Miliukov, the Provisional Government was forced to announce officially that the note had been approved without objection on anyone's part.

As a matter of fact, all of these demonstrations were only a perpetrated bluff and elicited imposing counterdemonstrations. But they created a strained and tense atmosphere. Probably, the fact that in this matter of the note Kerensky had been forced to unite at least nominally with Miliukov, aggravated his personal antagonism. The socialists persistently continued their work; Thomas played an ambiguous role and spoke slightingly and with hostility about Miliukov.* But since by that time Miliukov had decided not to yield, it was clear that a crisis had to come, this time on the initiative of the Provisional Government. And it occurred. What part the other Kadet ministers played in it I am not now ready to say. Miliukov was offered the portfolio of the minister of education; he categorically refused it, and he left the session no longer a minister. The next morning Vinaver and I went to his place on behalf of the [Kadet] Central Committee and for a long time insistently pressured him to remain and accept the portfolio of the minister of education.

We felt that Miliukov's resignation coming at the same time as the introduction of the socialists into the makeup of the government

---

* At this same time the Provisional Government came to the decision that it was necessary to reinforce its membership with socialists (see the declaration of 23 April). Miliukov was against this in principle, and very reluctantly agreed to the text of this declaration. I am going to discuss this again by itself.

would be the beginning of disintegration. Of course, we also thought that Miliukov, if he stayed in the government even as minister of education, would have the opportunity to influence foreign policy and at all times follow its course. This was feasible in connection with a project which arose at that time, to form a special commission consisting of some members of the Provisional Government and to empower them to attend to questions of national defense, as well as to general questions of foreign policy. This commission had been conceived as anti-Miliukov. We proposed to him that, in the changed conditions, he utilize it in the interests of his cause and remain in the government with the condition that he be one of the members of the commission. Miliukov did not agree. He argued at first; but then, when all arguments had been exhausted, he said the following, verbatim: "It may be that all your arguments are correct, but I have an inner voice which tells me that I must not follow them. Whenever I have this kind of clear and definite awareness, even though motiveless, that a given line of conduct is necessary, I follow it. I cannot act otherwise." We understood that the question was exhausted and gave up. From that moment began the fundamental break between Miliukov and the Provisional Government.

I have already referred to the declaration and appeal of 23 April, in which it was vowed that the socialists would be invited to participate in the government. This appeal was a development of the notion (almost from the very outset pressed by Guchkov, and later by Manuilov) that the Provisional Government should resign after telling the country what it had done and why it considered any further efforts fruitless, in the genre of an epitaph or political testament. But actually the appeal did not announce the government's resignation. It exposed, as a matter of fact, a complete picture of what was happening in the country and drew the conclusion: either the ruin and downfall of the "conquests of the revolution," or support for authority by the people who were asked to submit willingly to it. The composition of this document was entrusted to Kokoshkin.

Miliukov later on maintained that, thanks to Kerensky, Kokoshkin's text was transformed into an abstract sociological discourse devoid of any practical force. This is an exaggeration. Kerensky—

and not even he himself but the editorship of *Delo Naroda* [106]—introduced into the appeal only a few lines which actually rather vaguely and abstractly stated the reasons for the disorder that was occurring and saw its roots in the fact that the old social and political ties had broken down before new bonds had time to form and strengthen. Of course, this was "sociology," but it was completely harmless, and it did not impart the underlying tone to the appeal. If it was a weak document (and I consider it one of the weakest), it was not Kerensky's fault—and even less, of course, Kokoshkin's. It was weak in its underlying tone, and it cannot be stated that its ideology—which placed above all else the voluntary submission of the citizenry to their chosen authority—was much akin to the ideology of anarchism.

In any case, the heart of the matter did not lie in these admonitions but in the appeal to the socialists. Apparently, the Provisional Government itself did not believe they would respond. But the socialists realized that another rejection could be used as a powerful weapon against them and would put them in a position of "irresponsible critics" and "watchdogs," a trying quandary. They became ministers. In fact, from that moment one could say that the days of the Provisional Government, which had been established by the "victorious revolution," were numbered; that we had entered a period of all sorts of ministerial crises, each of which weakened authority; and that it was not possible to call a halt on the path which led to the triumph of Bolshevik aspirations. Even if Miliukov had not resigned in the first days of May, he still could not have gone along the same path with Tseretelli and Skobelev.

The "Contact Commission," of which I have already spoken several times, was formed by the Soviet of Workers' and Soldiers' Deputies on 10 March, and its first members were Chkheidze, Skobelev, Steklov-Nakhamkes, Flippovskii, and Sukhanov.[107] At

106. *Delo Naroda* (*The People's Cause*), Petrograd (March 1917–18) was a daily news organ of the Socialist Revolutionary Party Central Committee and its Petrograd Committee. Appeared after the Bolshevik coup as *Delo Narodnoe, Delo Narodov, Dela Narodnye, Delo,* and was finally suppressed in March 1919.

107. Nikolai Semenovich Chkheidze (1864–1926), Georgian Social Democrat; later, Menshevik deputy, Third, Fourth State Dumas; chairman, Social Democratic

the end of March, Tseretelli replaced Steklov. However, if my memory does not fail me, they initially served together. Chernov appeared considerably later. In the course of the first weeks of the existence of the Provisional Government, sessions of the Contact Commission occurred frequently, about three times a week and sometimes more, always in the evening and rather late, after the Provisional Government sessions, which in these instances were always abbreviated. The principal character at these sessions was Steklov. I first met him then, and I did not suspect that he was a Jew or that his euphonious pseudonym hid his far from euphonious real name. Even less, of course, was the story known—it was later uncovered by L. L'vov—that Nakhamkes had resorted to the most indignant and servile petitions to "legalize" his pseudonym and officially substitute it for his real surname. Somehow or other, from our very first encounter he produced in me a loathsome impression of his manner, thereby perfectly suiting his surname, which somehow inherently combined the words "impudent" (*nakhal*) and "boor" (*kham*).

His tone was that of a man who believed that the Provisional Government existed only by his kindness and only as long as it was convenient to him. He behaved like a tutor observing how the pupil entrusted to him conducted himself, [making sure he] did not play pranks, carried out his assignments, and always remembered what he was permitted and what he was forbidden to do; with this went an awareness of his own might, which constantly surfaced and accentuated his magnanimity. How many times had I to listen to phrases which directly or indirectly meant: "You (that is, the Provisional Government) know perfectly well, after all, that if we desired it, we could take power into our hands without hindrance, and under us it would be the strongest and most authoritative power. If we have not done this and for the moment do not do so, it

---

Duma group; member, Provisional Committee of the State Duma, 1917; chairman, Petrograd Soviet, March–September 1917; chairman, Georgian Constituent Assembly, 1918; emigrated 1921; eventually committed suicide.

Lieutenant Vasilii Nikolaevich Filippovskii, Socialist Revolutionary; member, Executive Committee, Petrograd Soviet, 1917; member, Committee for the Salvation of the Fatherland and the Revolution, 1917.

is merely because we consider that, for the time being, you better satisfy the historical moment. We have agreed to accord you power, but for that very reason you must remember your place with respect to us and must never forget yourselves or undertake any important and crucial steps without consulting us and receiving our approval. You must remember that we only have to wish it, and at once you will no longer exist, since you have no independent importance and authority.''

He never let slip an opportunity to develop these thoughts. I remember that on one occasion Prince L'vov mentioned the torrent of greetings and good wishes arriving daily in hundreds of telegrams from all corners of Russia, promising the Provisional Government help and support. ''We,'' objected Steklov instantly, ''could show you right now far more, ten times as many, telegrams endorsed by hundreds and thousands of organized citizens, which demand that we take power into our own hands.'' Another facet of this same position went: ''We''—that is, to say the Executive Committee—''are shielding you with our bodies from hostile blows; we are instilling in the masses, submissive to us, a trust in you.''

This position was particularly disagreeable to Kerensky, who from the very beginning had aspired to show, or wanted others to think, that he, ''the hostage of democracy,'' who still formally carried the title of deputy chairman of the Executive Committee, was winning the hearts of the ''broad masses'' for the Provisional Government. For that reason he could brook Nakhamkes less than anyone, and he reacted to his tone with great irritation. He also thought that his position in the Provisional Government did not give him the opportunity to be polemical with Steklov and ''dress him down.'' He would, therefore, often refrain from participation in sessions with the Contact Commission, and whenever he did participate, it was only to be ''present,'' sitting as distant as possible, maintaining a tenacious silence, and glancing only angrily and contemptuously with his ever-narrowed, short-sighted eyes at the speaker and others. But when the session was over and he was alone with his ministerial colleagues, he would often with great passion attack Prince L'vov, accusing him of being too mild and tactful and expressing astonishment that L'vov had allowed some statement or other of Nakhamkes to pass without answering him as he deserved.

It must be said that on occasion Steklov whet the temper of even his own "friends"—or rather, of the other members of the Contact Commission, since he evidently had few friends. Sometimes Chkheidze or Skobelev would interrupt one or another of his declarations, or immediately afterwards would note that Steklov was speaking only for himself on the given question, or that he was expressing his private opinion and that "this had not been decided by us." This, however, did not embarrass Steklov in the least. Occasionally he would even try to engage in polemics with his colleagues then and there. In point of fact, I do not know if any of them was actually capable of opposing Steklov's unlimited aplomb and his brazen talent for identifying his own voice with that of the "toiling masses."

Later, when the story of his most servile application ("self-prostration") became known, it was freely used against him, and he was forced to retire into the background for a time, even for a long time. But in the first weeks he actually played some kind of a role. At the First Conference of delegates of the Soviets of Workers' and Soldiers' Deputies on 29 March, he recounted the history of the relationship between the Provisional Government and the Executive Committee, and he formulated a draft resolution for introducing Soviet commissars into all departments "for the vigilant surveillance of all activities of the Provisional Government." This concept of commissars created one of the most excruciating points of conflict. It was only abandoned when the entry of the socialists into the Provisional Government made the latter appear more "trustworthy" to the Soviet of Workers' and Soldiers' Deputies.

Of the other members of the Contact Commission, two, Filippovskii and Sukhanov, hardly spoke at all, at least not during the time that I participated in the affairs of the Provisional Government. After Steklov, the most frequent speaker was Skobelev. I had not known him before at all. He was one of the most insignificant of men, sparingly endowed and highly limited, who accidently became famous throughout Russia as a *porte-voix* [spokesman] of the "working masses," thanks to the fact that the State Duma had created an all-Russian platform for their political speeches, which were inspired and at times directly dictated from behind the scenes. He endeavored, and endeavored conscientiously, to be a *porte-voix*. Yet it would appear that he did not have the least gift with words. I am unaware, perhaps, that he may have made an impression as an orator at rallies among those sympathetic to him, but here, where there could be no clichés and one had to succeed by the substance of his speech, he invariably appeared singularly deficient, feeble, boring—and timid. All the same, one cannot deny that he was more attractive than his associates. He seemed straightforward, more sincere, more honest than they. Very likely, he was under the influence of the atmosphere of the State Duma and was more fully aware of the enormity of the difficulties that had arisen.

Recently, in Kiev, I had occasion to hear from Shul'gin that even in the first days, if not hours, of the revolution, Chkheidze gave way to utter despair, grasped his head, and declared that all was lost. Chkheidze is a much more colorful figure than Skobelev. There was always, in my opinion, something tragicomical about him, even in his overall appearance, the expressions of his face, his manner of speaking, his Caucasian accent. Of course, the real tragedy was that a man like Chkheidze should become the ''leader of democracy'' for all of Russia, the chairman of the Soviet Workers' Deputies, an influential figure, and, at least at that time, a future candidate for the chairmanship of the Constituent Assembly and perhaps for the presidency of the Russian Republic. At sessions with the Contact Commission he spoke whenever a statement of an enquiry needed additional emphasis. It seems that he, too, regarded Steklov with disapproval.

Sessions with the Contact Commission occurred neither daily nor on set days. The initiative for a meeting issued most often from the commission itself: the message (Chkheidze usually did this) would state that the commission would like to have a conference with the Provisional Government to discuss several questions. However, in the majority of instances the government was not notified beforehand what questions would be raised, thereby sometimes leading to some quite amusing surprises, revealing the full extent to which views on the relative importance of some fact or measure ranged.

I remember that one of the questions which at first attracted the most attention was the funeral for the victims of the revolution. The Soviet of Workers' Deputies, with considerable insolence, wanted to monopolize this ceremony. Without informing the Provisional Government, the Executive Committee set the date, published the ceremony of the funeral, and chose the site for the fraternal graves—Palace Square, where, as is known, they even proceeded to dig the graves. After long, tedious, and absurd arguing, this question was finally settled; the government came to an agreement with the Executive Committee, and there followed one of those grandiose demonstrations, the success of which depended partly on the propensity of the masses of idle people prepared to become spectators of the solemn procession, and partly on an attitude which thirsted for satisfaction through some sort of demonstration.

As I have already said, at the end of March Tseretelli appeared at the sessions of the Contact Commission. To me he was a completely unknown figure. At the time of the Second Duma I had often heard him speak from the rostrum, but I had not had occasion to meet him. One's first impression undoubtedly won favor for him. His name was enveloped by an aura of the most genuine and tragic of political martyrdoms. His brief career in the Second Duma,[108] which attracted everyone's sympathy, ended with a ten-year term of exile which was spent, at least in the beginning, in very distressing conditions. His outward appearance somehow corresponded to that image created by his moral character. His oriental face is handsome and refined, and his big dark eyes now blaze, now grow dim in melancholy reverie. He is a very outstanding orator. His accent is less marked, less coarse than Chkheidze's, and at times it imparts an especially expressive force to what he is saying. He can achieve great strength, especially in a sympathetic atmosphere and when he speaks on favorite Social Democratic themes. But at the same time he can be, and not infrequently is, intolerably garrulous, insipid, and false.

In this regard I am especially reminded of two of his speeches,

108. The Second Duma lasted from March to June 3, 1907 (O.S.).

one, delivered at the solemn session of all four Dumas [109] on 27 April, the other, at the Moscow State Conference. It was particularly distressing to listen to the latter, so obvious was it that Tseretelli himself absolutely did not believe what he was saying. However, his speeches usually conveyed a sense of great conviction and sincerity, and this is one of the reasons for his success. Of course, if one expects from his speeches profundity of content, a wealth of ideas, and diversified learning, then one will be badly disappointed. The scope of Tseretelli's dominant ideas is limited and is essentially made up of ordinary Marxist platitudes heartily assimilated in student days. Everything beyond these platitudes, anything that requires deep insight, individuality, or independent thought, leaves Tseretelli absolutely helpless.

I had occasion to meet him more intimately in mid-September 1917, at the conference with representatives of the political parties that Kerensky organized, as a result of which the organization of the last Cabinet (with Kishkin, Konovalov, Tret'iakov, Smirnov, Maliantovich, and Maslov) [110] was formed with the Council of the Russian Republic established. The most characteristic feature of his frame of mind at that time was fear of the growing power of bolshevism. I remember how in a tête-à-tête conversation between us

109. "All four Dumas" refers to the meeting of the available members from the First, Second, Third, and Fourth State Dumas to commemorate the occasion and the work of the Dumas and to discuss national issues. See B. & K., 3 : 1258–67.

110. Nikolai Mikhailovich Kishkin (1864–1930), physician; member, Kadet Party Central Committee, 1907–21; commissar of Moscow, March–August 1917; minister of welfare, Sept. 25–Oct. 25, 1917; in charge of Petrograd defense, Oct. 25, 1917; an anti-Bolshevik movement; later served under the Bolsheviks, People's Commissariat for Health.

Sergei A. Smirnov, Kadet; editor, *Utro Rossii* (*The Dawn of Russia*); chairman, Moscow War Industries Committee, 1915–17; state controller, Sept. 25–Oct. 25, 1917; imprisoned by the Bolsheviks; emigrated after the Bolshevik coup.

Pavel Nikolaevich Maliantovich, Menshevik; minister of justice, Sept. 25–Oct. 25, 1917; emigrated after the Bolshevik coup. See his "In the Winter Palace on October 25–26, 1917," in *Petrograd, October 1917: Reminiscences* (Moscow, 1957), and his *Revoliutsiia i pravosudie* (*Revolution and Justice*), (Moscow, 1918).

Semon Leontevich Maslov, Right Socialist Revolutionary; minister of agriculture, Oct. 3–25, 1917.

he spoke about the possibility of the Bolsheviks seizing power. "Of course," he said, "they will not last more than two or three weeks, but just think what destruction there will be! We must avoid this at all cost."

There was a note of genuine panic in his voice. At the time he believed in the redeeming influence of the Council of the Russian Republic. He (or his confederates) had thought up this title. He proposed it to me on the evening I arrived, as arranged, at Skobelev's apartment to discuss the draft of the ministerial declaration which Tseretelli had drawn up. That evening I had a very pressing personal appointment elsewhere, and I wanted to be free as early as possible. I confess that, owing to the force of the circumstances, I probably did not pay sufficient attention to the text of the declaration and the suggestion to name the newly established body the "Council of the Russian Republic." I must add, however, for my own justification, that previous experience had made me skeptical toward declarations of any sort. I gradually arrived at the conviction that this eternal bargaining over separate words and expressions, this sectarian stubbornness in defending some and disputing others—all was pitiful and fruitless Byzantinism, of importance and interest only to party circles, various central committees, and so on, but utterly without affect on and alien to daily life. The entire contents of the declaration had been revealed beforehand at a conference in the Winter Palace, where the ministry's program had been drawn up. The editing of this program had seemed to me of secondary importance. Because of this, the original draft, which Tseretelli authored and I accepted, contained two or three unfortunate passages which were corrected or removed by A. Ia. Gal'pern, who was then Head of the Chancellery of the Provisional Government (I cannot now remember the content of these *lapsus*). Tseretelli protested by telephone but in the end yielded.

As to the name "Council of the Russian Republic," I, as a Kadet, of course, had to make a resolute objection, since we considered it absolutely improper to affix a formal qualification to a provisional regime that had been established in the days of the coup d'état and was to last only until the Constituent Assembly. I remember Tseretelli declared to me with a certain enthusiasm: "We have come up with the title 'Council of the Russian Republic.' Truthfully, don't you agree with it? What do you think, Vladimir Dmitrievich? Right away I think It will make a great impression and create empathy.'' I replied that a more fitting title would have been ''Council of the Russian State'' or ''Council Attached to the Provisional Government,'' * even though the first title too closely approximated that of the former State Council and the latter brought it to the level, as it were, of a common government consultative board. In any event, I did not oppose Tseretelli's proposal.

I shall have to return to the entire matter of the ''Council of the Russian Republic,'' which I have touched upon here only in connection with Tseretelli's characteristics. As is known, he left for the Caucasus at the same time,[111] the end of September, and returned to Petersburg only at the beginning of November, after the Bolshevik takeover. Then, when he met me in the Municipal Duma, he said: ''Yes, of course, all we were doing then was a futile attempt to hold back a destructive, elemental force (*stikhiia*) with paltry chips of wood.''

Here I wish to include just one more episode that has nothing to do with Tseretelli. But it easily has an essential place in the story of the creation of the Council of the Republic.[112] When the text of the ''statute'' establishing this body had been settled, we arranged with P. N. Maliantovich, the newly appointed minister of justice, that I would communicate to him the final edited text. He suggested to me a very late hour, 12 o'clock, and I agreed. I found him in the study which I remembered so well from my childhood recollections of the apartments of the procurator-general. He was very worried. He disclosed to me the cause of his anxiety. It concerned the notorious N. D. Sokolov, who two or three months previously had been appointed a senator of the First Department by Kerensky.

* It is noteworthy that this latter title was later staunchly defended by A. A. Dem'ianov at the session of the Prov. Gov't. at which the draft was heard and ratified. [Dem'ianov was assistant minister of justice in 1917.]

111. Tseretelli was suffering from tuberculosis and had to go to a warmer climate to recuperate.

112. For a discussion of the establishment of the Council of the Russian Republic, along with relevant documents, see B. & K., 3 : 1687–91.

Sokolov had had a knockdown drag-out with those present on the question of formal attire. He refused to submit to the decision adopted by the senators, to continue to wear formal dress at open sessions and general meetings. He had appeared at one session in a frock coat, and apparently had a violent wrangle with Vraskii (I was not at this meeting), as the result of which he was compelled to leave. Then he had sent a written statement to the minister of justice, pointing out that the Senate had raised absolutely illegal and arbitrary demands by insisting that senators put on "the emblems of slavery" (these are the words he used to designate the buttons on the formal attire, which depicted a double-headed eagle above that of the law). He even demanded, in turn, that the question be resolved by means of legislation in a democratic spirit. Maliantovich was terribly perplexed. "What do you think should be done?" he asked me. I answered ironically that I had not sufficiently thought over this grave and complicated question, and I added that, if I were in his place, I would throw N. D. Sokolov's statement into the wastepaper basket under the table. "Impossible! After all, you know Nikolai Dmitrievich. He will never leave it at that. I am thinking of organizing some sort of commission to decide this matter. The main problem is that at present it is very difficult to introduce new buttons. Where would you get them? And they would be a big, new expense for the senators." As I did not answer, he concluded with a sigh, "Perhaps later on you will think of something regarding this question——."

It was with such paltry, pathetic nonsense that a member of the Provisional Government was concerned a month before the coup d'état. The issue of the buttons apparently remained undecided to the very end.

Now, after the passage of more than a year, when I wish to recollect the first two months of the Provisional Government's existence, a rather chaotic picture arises in my mind. I recall separate episodes, stormy clashes that sometimes arose quite unexpectedly, endless debates which at times caused a session to drag on until late at night. I remember the feverish daily activity, beginning in the mornings and interrupted only by lunch and dinner. I was living at my home on the Morskaia, five minutes' walk from the Mariinskii Palace, and this was very convenient. I remember incessant telephone calls and daily visitors, which made concentration almost completely impossible. I primarily remember an atmosphere in which everything that was experienced seemed unreal. It was impossible to believe that we could successfully realize our two main tasks: to pursue the continuation of the war and to lead the country safely to the Constituent Assembly.

The Provisional Government's resolution to summon a special conference to draw up the laws concerning the elections to the Constituent Assembly was adopted only at the end of March. This institution was to be constituted in such a way (the members designated by groups and parties) as to ensure full confidence in it. But unfortunately its staffing dragged on a very long time. The Executive Committee of the Soviet of Workers' Deputies, which was terribly late in nominating its candidates, was, in fact, mostly at fault. It must, however, be said that the whole manner in which the question of the Constituent Assembly elections was handled was inherently defective, and this was innately felt even from the first days. Later I often had occasion to hear the following remarks: the Provisional Government, in the very first days, should have immediately named a small commission of the ablest and authoritative jurists, charged them with drafting in two weeks' time the election laws, and scheduled elections as soon as possible—in May, for example. I remember that, among others, L. M. Bramson [113] (somewhat surprisingly), expressed this thought. Since my very first days as Head of the Chancellery, I personally had repeatedly and persistently discussed with Prince L'vov the necessity of establishing a commission as soon as possible, so as to settle the question. But there were always other more urgent matters to cope with that brooked no delay. When at last this special conference was formed and the work of drafting the law began, the entire apparatus proved to be so complicated and clumsy that it became impossible to count

113. Lev Moissevich Bramson (1869–?), lawyer and journalist; Popular Socialist; member, First State Duma; member, Executive Committee, Petrograd Soviet, 1917; emigrated after the Bolshevik coup.

on finishing the work quickly and scheduling an election in the near future.

Does it therefore follow that the other plan—the formation of a small commission, a quick drafting of the laws, and scheduling of elections as soon as possible—was both feasible and advisable? I do not think so. First of all, I have no doubt that a campaign would have immediately commenced against the government, accusing it of intending to formulate the laws by academic and bureaucratic means. Every defect in the law would have been reckoned at the expense of the government. The authority of the framers and, of course, the plan they implemented would have been undermined. I think that even the framers themselves would have run into difficulties on certain basic decisions of principle, such as, for example, the matter of whether the electoral system should be by majority or proportional; or whether active army and navy personnel should take part in the elections; or, finally, of how elections in outlying districts should be organized.

Assume that all these difficulties could have been surmounted. How was it possible to organize elections in a Russia shaken from top to bottom by a revolution, in a Russia which still had neither democratic self-government nor a correctly functioning local administrative apparatus? And what about elections in the army? But, of course, the greatest risk would have been the actual convocation of the Constituent Assembly. Naïve people could theoretically imagine this assembly and its role in the following form: It would convene, establish the Fundamental Laws, settle the question of the form of government, appoint the government and invest it with plenary powers to end the war, and then would dissolve. It is possible to imagine this, but who believes that it could actually have happened like that? If any authority had somehow survived until the Constituent Assembly, its convocation would undoubtedly have been the beginning of anarchy.

Now the Constituent Assembly experiment has been carried out. Probably the Bolsheviks themselves did not think in October that this assembly would be abolished so easily and as early as the beginning of January, two months after the coup d'état. As is known, one of the charges the Bolsheviks raised against the Provisional Government was that it had put off the elections . . . but when the Constituent Assembly no longer suited them, they dispersed it without hesitation. If the Provisional Government had felt it had genuine strength, it would have promptly announced that the Constituent Assembly would be convened at the war's end; and, of course, this would in fact have been the only right way of deciding the question once Mikhail Aleksandrovich's repudiation of the throne made it necessary to raise the question of the form of government. But the Provisional Government had no sense of real power. From the first days of its existence that struggle began in which those public elements that were sensible and moderate but—alas—timid, unorganized, accustomed only to obeying and incapable of commanding, stood on one side; and, on the other, was organized rascality with its narrow-minded, fanatical, and frequently dishonest ringleaders.

The center of gravity of the entire situation at once became the problem of the army.

About three weeks after the coup, beginning with 20 March, deputations from the front began to arrive in Petersburg. The purpose of their coming was, on the one hand, to declare to the Provisional Government their readiness to support the new regime and to defend freedom, and on the other, to ascertain for themselves the true relationship between the Provisional Government and the Soviet of Workers' Deputies. Deputations arrived daily, from various fronts and various units, more or less numerous in composition and headed by commanders and officers with red badges and red banners. The Provisional Government nearly always received them in the rotunda of the Mariinskii Palace. I remember how surprised I was in the beginning by the scene of the interior of this palace, and how difficult it was to reconcile it with old memories of the epoch of the pre-reform council and my service in the State Chancellery.

Then, the Mariinskii Palace had been the sanctuary of the higher bureaucracy. It housed the State Council with the State Chancellery, the Council of Ministers and its secretariat, as well as the Office of Petitions addressed to His Imperial Majesty. In the splendid halls of the palace, with their velvet carpets, gilded furniture, and heavy draperies, singularly stately footmen moved silently about in embroidered liveries and white hose, serving tea and coffee. On Mondays, the day of the plenary sessions, a sort of agitated solemnity reigned. There were the imposing figures of generally very aged dignitaries decorated with ribbons and orders, there were military and court uniforms, subdued conversations, and all this created an atmosphere of inaccessibility, somehow, a separation from vulgar, everyday life. In those days a man in a jacket would have appeared as an indecent and wild anomaly if he had suddenly found himself among those well-groomed, elegantly dressed, and stately personages.

Now all that had disappeared without a trace. The Mariinskii Palace had undergone a transformation to radical "plain living." Its splendid halls were invaded by crowds of disheveled and carelessly dressed people in jackets and blouses of the most proletarian kind. The splendid footmen exchanged their liveries for grey, double-breasted jackets, and lost all their dignity. The grand and solemn ceremonial of days passed was replaced by a vociferous bustle. All this may have happened gradually, but it seemed only a short period of time. In the first weeks only the Provisional Government and the Juridical Conference met in the Mariinskii Palace. The "revolutionary" mayor of those days, Iu. N. Glebov, [114] persistently asked for the great hall of the State Duma with its antechamber to be put at the disposal of the Municipal Duma for its sessions. I equally and persistently opposed this attempt, which finally fell through. But nevertheless, the Mariinskii Palace very quickly became the center of all sorts of commissions, and when the conference began its work on drafting the electoral law for the Constituent Assembly, there were days when every hall, including the rotunda, was occupied by a commission. During March this had still not occurred and the rotunda was nearly always free and was used for the arrival of military deputations.

How painful, how distressing, it now is to recall those deputations! How often we listened to declarations of readiness to support with all their strength the "People's Provisional Government," to

114. Iu. N. Glebov, mayor of Moscow; chief, Republican-Democrats (formerly Octobrists), 1917.

join together to defend the freedom and inviolability of the home-land, to ignore seditionists, and not fall prey to schemes of the enemy! What fiery and often exalted speeches! True, the soldiers' faces at best expressed a kind of obtuse perplexity; true, one did not feel in the officers' words any sense of self-confidence or authority, and their revolutionary phrases often grated—all ruinous to their spirit. True, this sudden revolutionary awareness seemed in-comprehensible and improbable, and the question stirred in one's soul: is this not simply the voice of mutiny, is that not an elemental protest expressed against any sort of discipline, any subordination? The main theme of the speeches was almost invariably the rela-tionship between the Provisional Government and the Soviet of Workers' Deputies. It was often said that the army was disturbed and puzzled by the impression of what appeared to be some kind of dual power,[115] that it needed a unitary power. In reply, government representatives made rather unctuous statements to the effect that there was no dual power and that there was complete unity, mutual trust, and the best of relations between the Provisional Government and the Soviet of Workers' Deputies. The war was also mentioned, but here confidence could be felt least of all.

The first deputations made a strong impression on both the Provi-sional Government and the delegates themselves. It seemed that somehow a spiritual link with the army was being established and that it would be possible to retain, or even to re-create, a strong and stable military force. But it only seemed so. The deputations arriv-ing from the front came into contact not only with the government but also with the Soviet deputies. The government confined itself to receiving them in the halls of the Mariinskii Palace, listening to them and responding; the deputations shouted ''hurray!'' and then they went off to the Tauride Palace, where first of all a belief in the greatness and omnipotence of the Soviet of Workers' Deputies and its Executive Committee was instilled in them, and all sorts of irre-sponsible people engaged in demagogic and anarchical propaganda. They met with this same propaganda everywhere, at street rallies

115. ''Dual power'' (*dvoevlastie*) refers to the division of authority between the Provisional Government and the Petrograd Soviet. Miliukov, Lenin, and others gave currency to the term. See B. & K., 3 : 1210–35.

and in the barracks; they came into contact with the licentious and profligate elements of the Petersburg garrison, who prided themselves on the fact that "we made the revolution"; and they were themselves corrupted. As a result, the pilgrimage of army deputations to Petersburg brought about the poisoning and demoralization of the troops, and not their stabilization.

When in mid-April General Alekseev arrived in Petersburg at sessions of the Provisional Government (which took place in the apartment of A. I. Guchkov, who was ill) and described the mood of the army, I well remember the feelings of horror and despair that gripped me. The conclusion was quite obvious. Despite all reservations, it was clear even then that the revolution had struck our military strength a most terrible blow, that demoralization was proceeding at a colossal pace, and that the commanders were powerless. Two tendencies, two types of men, appeared among the complement of commanders. Some realized very soon that they could maintain themselves at their post only by indulging the revolutionized soldiers and currying their favor, by exaggerating the new "comradely" relationships, or, plainly speaking, by demeaning themselves before the soldiers. These men, of course, only facilitated the collapse of discipline and the loss of a sense of military duty, to the general demise of the army. Others did not want to become reconciled to the new order and the new spirit and tried to oppose it and display authority, and either became involved in tragic incidents or proved an inconvenience to the higher command and were relieved of their duties. In this way the best, strongest, and most conscientious elements gradually disappeared, and only pathetic dregs or particularly adroit persons who knew how to balance between the two extremes remained.

Among my papers are still a few letters I received at the time, or later, from Count N. N. Ignat'ev, a man who had dedicated his whole life to military service and had commanded the Preobrazhenskii Regiment in wartime, a genuine officer who was also a highly sensible, thoughtful, and serious man. If I am not mistaken, the revolution broke out while he was either chief of staff of the Guards Corps or commander of the Guards Infantry Division. These letters of his made an immense impression on me. They confirmed my worst suspicions. I do not have them at hand presently and so cannot verify the dates, but I remember that very soon the following theme appeared in those letters: We have to understand clearly that the war is finished, that we cannot and must not go on fighting because the army overwhelmingly does not want to fight. Intelligent people must find a painless way to end the war, otherwise a catastrophe will occur. I showed one of the letters to Guchkov. He read it and handed it back to me, saying that he was receiving mounds of such letters. "What do you think about it, then?" I asked. He only shrugged his shoulders and said something to the effect that we must hope for a miracle. But the miracle did not happen, the process continued on its natural and necessary course and toward its natural and necessary end.

2

The Bolshevik Coup D'Etat

During a break in one of the March sessions of the Provisional Government, amidst continuous conversations about the steady spread of Bolshevik propaganda, Kerensky declared, between his usual little bursts of hysterical laughter: "Just wait, Lenin himself is coming . . . that's when things will really begin!" This led to a brief exchange of opinions among the ministers. It was already known that Lenin and his friends were intending to avail themselves of the Germans' services in order to get from Switzerland to Russia. It was also known that Germany, shrewdly appraising the results, was apparently willing to accommodate them. If I am not mistaken, Miliukov (yes indeed, he!) asked: "Gentlemen, are we really going to allow them in under such conditions?" But he got a fairly unanimous reply to the effect that there were no formal grounds for refusing Lenin entry; on the contrary, Lenin had a right to return, inasmuch as he had been granted amnesty, and inasmuch as the means to which he was resorting in order to make the journey were not formally criminal. It was added that, from the point of view of political expediency, Lenin's use of Germany's services would so destroy his authority that there was no need to fear him. On the whole, they all took a fairly casual view of the dangers that might arise from the return of the Bolshevik leader. This set the general tone. Bound by its own proclamations about freedom and preoccupied with its own constant meetings, the Provisional Gov-

ernment did not consider it possible to counteract even the most extreme and destructive propaganda that was beginning to spread orally and in the press.

Lenin's arrival and his speech made a strange and unexpected impression, which found expression in the newspapers at the time. Even Steklov-Nakhamkes thought it necessary to say that Lenin had evidently lost contact with Russian reality. *Pravda* did not immediately dare to rise to the level of its ideological leader.[1] The Executive Committee's initial perplexity quickly changed to defiant hostility. But Lenin's colossal perseverance and self-confidence could not, of course, be overcome so easily. Everything that followed showed how lucidly the plan had been elaborated even in its detail. It was implemented immediately, step by step; its principle levers were the exhaustion of the army by the war and the decomposition of the army that had begun rapidly and, one might say, catastrophically, at the front as a result of the direct influence of the Petersburg coup.

From my recollections I must say that the Provisional Government was surprisingly passive in the face of this destructive activity. Lenin was hardly ever mentioned. I recall Kerensky saying as early as April, some time after Lenin's arrival, that he wanted to visit and talk with him, and in answer to puzzled questions he explained: "After all, he is living in a completely isolated atmosphere, he knows nothing, he sees everything through his own imagination; he has no one nearby to give him the slightest help in understanding what is happening." As far as I know, the visit did not take place. I do not know whether Lenin turned it down or whether Kerensky himself gave up his idea. Then, as I think I have already noted, the Provisional Government repeatedly discussed the disgraceful business of Kshesinskaia's villa, a private property bla-

1. *Pravda* responded to Lenin's April 8 statements: "Comrade Lenin's scheme is unacceptable to us, since it is based on recognizing the bourgeois-democratic revolution as finished, and calls for an immediate transformation of this revolution into a socialist one." Only the first of Lenin's "Letters from Afar," his view of the revolution as seen from Switzerland, appeared in *Pravda*. J. V. Stalin edited the Bolshevik organ at the time, and though he did not support Lenin at first, he soon came to do so.

tantly seized by force and daily subjected to damage and destruction. But the matter never got beyond talk. When Kshesinskaia's lawyer brought suit before the justice of the peace in order to have the organization which had arbitrarily taken possession of the building ejected, Kerensky pointed out with pleasure that at last the right way had been found. But when he was asked how the justice of the peace's verdict could be executed, he replied that that was not his business but the business of the administration, the executive authority of the minister of the interior—that department being at the time nonexistent. As is known, the Bolsheviks eventually were successfully evicted; but the damage was done; they had made full and thorough use of their public rostrum.

The Bolsheviks' role is still unclear concerning the initial and partly organized demonstration against the Provisional Government from 19 to 21 April, when troops arrived at the Mariinskii Palace with placards demanding Miliukov's resignation. This demonstration was quelled without any trouble, as is known. An enormous number of the Petersburg population came out most definitely on the side of the Provisional Government. In those days Guchkov was ill and sessions took place at his apartment. I remember that stormy day which began with the appearance of troops on the Mariinskii Palace Square and ended without a pause in enthusiastic ovations for Miliukov and Guchkov at a protracted meeting outside the Ministry of War. On that day the great moral strength of the Provisional Government could still be felt but remained—alas!—utterly neglected. Petersburg sensed then, as though for the first time, the possibility of further shocks and responded en masse that it did not want them.

The history of the July days—when troops came out a second time and bore the character of what appeared to be a genuine attempt at rebellion—will be researched in all its details and its whole secret development clarified.[2] I only wish to recall my own personal experiences and impressions. I had long ago ceased to be Head of the Chancellery of the Provisional Government. My of-

2. For a thorough, scholarly treatment of the July days and the Bolsheviks, see Alexander Rabinowitch, *Prelude to Revolution* (Bloomington, Ind., 1968). See also B. & K., 3 : 1335–82.

ficial activities were, however, fairly varied, since I was working in the Juridical Conference and on the commissions and plenum of the conference to draw up the electoral laws for the Constituent Assembly. In addition, I was a member of a commission to review and implement the Criminal Code. How painful it is, incidentally, to recall now that strenuous work that absorbed so much labor, energy, and time—labor which was often of the very highest excellence (I mean, of course, the work of the collective whole, not my own participation), and which has remained absolutely fruitless and half-forgotten!

For some time there had been rumors that the Bolsheviks were preparing an armed action. Kerensky was at the front. Propaganda in the streets, at public meetings, and in the newspapers daily grew more and more unrestrained. After the first news of success during the first days of the advance on the front (18 June), alarming rumors began to spread. An atmosphere of anxiety and depression developed.

We had set a meeting for 2 July at the quarters of the [Kadet] Central Committee, at 8:30 P.M. as usual. On my way there after dinner I noticed considerable animation as I approached the quay. Along the Millionnaia were many soldiers, and some units were standing on the Field of Mars, near the beginning of that street. Loud conversations could be heard, with talk of demonstrations coming from the other bank of the Neva. Suvorov Square was blocked by people. Already as I passed the British Embassy, I saw a great throng carrying banners and placards coming across the Troitskii Bridge from the Petersburg side. I walked on. On the French Quay I was overtaken by a car with armed soldiers inside and lying on the front fenders with rifles aimed forward. They had the same dull, vacant, brutal faces that we all remembered from the February days. An armored car hurtled past in the same direction. When I got to the quarters of the Central Committee I met a woman clerk in the secretariat and learned from her that the meeting was not there but in the Furshtadtskaia. At the corner of the Shpalernaia and Liteinaia it was difficult to advance. There stood a solid mass of people, ugly shouting was heard, and an armed throng of workers was moving from the Liteinaia, then turning left along the

Shpalernaia toward the Tauride Palace and the Smol'nyi. On their placards were Bolshevik inscriptions: Down with the Capitalist Ministers, All Power to the Soviets, and others. Their faces were grim and angry.

I went along the Liteinaia to the Furshtadtskaia, but when I arrived at the residence to which I had been directed, I concluded that I had evidently been given the wrong address. I had to return to the French Quay, clear up the misunderstanding, and then return again to the Furshtadtskaia once I received the right address. The meeting was in an apartment in a big house with two main entrances. There I found a rather large number of the Central Committee members. Miliukov was presiding. The draft of an address to the population was being discussed. The exchange of opinion was somewhat lackadaisical—people continually milling around in the next room, the phone ringing, private discussions taking place.

We had already been there for more than an hour when a message was brought in stating that an armored car had pulled up to the building and that the exit onto the street was occupied by soldiers. This news gave rise to a lively discussion as to whether Miliukov and Shingarev * ought not to be hidden somewhere, somehow; perhaps taken out the back way or to another apartment. But they both said they would remain if their stay did not trouble the owners of the apartment. The meeting continued and discussion ended without further incident. It seems that Miliukov and Shingarev spent the night in the apartment. It turned out that the armored car had left and the street exit was clear.

It was near midnight, sultry and dusty. I was faced with a long return trek. I decided to go along the Liteinaia and the Panteleimonovskaia, past the Summer Gardens and the Field of Mars to the Moika, and across Palace Square straight to St. Isaac's. In spite of the late hour, the Liteinaia was quite as lively as in daytime. Every now and then clusters formed, soldiers walked about with rifles, [and] sailors—cars were honking. It became quieter and more deserted near the Fields of Mars. I went my way without any kind of

* Shingarev had just resigned from the membership of the Provisional Government together with Manuilov.

incident and, arriving (by Admiralty Prospekt) at Voznesenskii Prospekt, I turned left. A small group of worried guests was standing outside the Hotel "England," among them my cousin Katia D. [Catherine Danzas], who told me that troops were on the Morskaia, along the square (Mariinskaia), and in the streets, and it was unlikely I would be allowed through. However, I made my way past Miatlev's house and the Germany Embassy to the Morskaia and went through without hindrance. The troops were deployed in two long ranks and were occupying the Morskaia about as far as the Italian Embassy.

Evidently these were troops called out by the government to guard the Mariinskii Palace.

I have a hazy recollection of the course of events of the next few days. The appearance of the city changed quickly. Automobiles of private citizens vanished, armored cars and vehicles darted through the streets, packed with armed workers and soldiers. Every now and then shooting would break out from various places, and the crackle of shots would start up from various directions. The multitude of people overflowing the pavements of the Nevskii Prospekt would suddenly dash to one side and flee in a headlong rush, nearly knocking down those they met. Every now and then large detachments would appear, marching off somewhere and carrying red banners and placards of the type already noted. The days were lovely and hot, the sun was shining—a kind of striking contrast between life and nature and the alarming, uneasy effect of all that was happening.

The Mariinskii Palace was deserted, hardly anyone appeared at the sessions of the commission. I walked along the streets, visited the editorial offices of *Rech'*, and tried to orient myself to what was happening. Prince L'vov and some of the ministers were at District Headquarters (in Palace Square). It was said that an unsuccessful attempt to arrest the Provisional Government had been made on the first day [of the July uprising]. Everyone was tensely waiting for something. The whole episode came to an end, as we know, with the arrival from the front of loyal government troops (a cavalry division), the rebels were cut off and subsequently disarmed, a complete victory for the government, and momentarily—alas!—

bolshevism was liquidated. This was the moment which the Provisional Government could have finally utilized to eliminate Lenin and Co. But it did not venture to do so. The new government declaration contained only new concessions to socialism and Zimmerwaldism. Then Prince L'vov left his post, and the government was turned over to Kerensky.

After the July crisis, the formation of the new ministry and the convocation of the Moscow State Conference, the Kornilov affair, and the temporary functioning of the so-called Directory [3]—the founding of the "Council of the Russian Republic" and the urging of representatives of trade and industry (Tret'iakov, Smirnov, Konovalov) and also of prominent Kadets (Kishkin) to enter the government—were last attempts to check the ever-growing wave of bolshevism. I was taking an active part in this final phase of the Provisional Government's existence. Miliukov and Vinaver being absent at that time, I actually stood at the head of the [Kadet] Central Committee. I have already described some episodes relating to that period. When it became known that Tseretelli, who had played the most prominent role (among the socialists) in the negotiations, was going off to the Caucasus and would not participate in the meetings of the Soviet, I asked him with whom we should deal in party negotiations and agreements. He specified F. Dan (Gurvich).

As is known in the establishment of the Council of the Republic the coalition parties (mainly the socialists and the Kadets) pursued a definite aim: to reinforce the Provisional Government in its struggle with bolshevism. It was necessary to clear the atmosphere, to give the government a platform from which it could speak officially and openly before the whole country, and to give it real support in the person of the parties that had entered into the coalition and were represented in the government itself. This demanded above all, of course, a firm and clear decision of all the parties on two counts: the struggle with bolshevism and the support of authority. When

3. The Directory consisted of four socialists and one nonparty affiliate appointed by Minister-President A. F. Kerensky on September 1, following the mass resignations from the Cabinet in the midst of the Kornilov affair. Kerensky also declared Russia a republic on that same date. The Directory lasted until September 25, when it was replaced by the Third Coalition. See B. & K., 3 : 1659–61.

the work of designating the future members of the Council of the Republic was concluded, Adzhemov and I came to an arrangement with Gots, Dan, and Skobelev and agreed to meet (in Adzhemov's apartment) in order to clarify a subsequent plan of action and to establish a tactical plan.

If I am not mistaken, we met twice at Adzhemov's place, and I vividly remember the despair and irritation that gradually took possession of me during those discussions. I scarcely knew Dan, whom I had met in 1906 and had not seen since. His attitude toward the developing state of affairs bore little resemblance to Tseretelli's. In answer to Adzhemov's and my definitive statement that we considered that the newly constituted council's chief task was to create an atmosphere of public confidence around the Provisional Government and to support it in its fight with the Bolsheviks, Dan replied that he and his friends were not inclined to promise their confidence and support in advance, that everything would depend on the government's mode of action, and that in particular, they could not see the possibility of taking the position that bolshevism must be fought above all else regardless of the outcome. "But this is the very crux of our agreement," we objected, "and your present attitude is once again the old ambiguous, uncertain, 'insofar as' kind of confidence which is no help whatever to the government and does not facilitate its task." Dan equivocated, he mumbled and countered with pedantic arguments. . . . We parted with heavy feelings, knowing that the old precrastination had begun again, that our "leftist friends" were incorrigible, and that all our efforts to reach an agreement and support for authority in its fight with anarchy and rebellion had almost gone to waste.

In the end, as is well known, that is how it turned out. The Provisional Government did not have the support of a definite and reliable majority in the Council of the Republic. The demonstrative withdrawal of the Bolsheviks was, it seems to me, of decisive importance, because after that the Internationalists,[4] who were fairly

4. The Internationalists were a group of Russian socialists headed by the Mensheviks Martov and Dan and the Socialist Revolutionary Chernov, who blamed the First World War on the "international bourgeoisie" and demanded a "general democratic peace without victors and vanquished" (which was the program of the Zimmerwald majority).

closely connected with the rest of the socialist Swamp,[5] became the far Left. The council proved to be a very cumbersome machine, and much time was spent organizing it and making it operative. The Council of Elders [6] could frankly have been called the Sanhedrin.[7] The predominant portion of its membership were Jews. The only Russians were Avksent'ev, myself, Peshekhonov, and Chaikovskii.[8] I remember that my attention was drawn to this circumstance by Mark Vishniak [9] who, in the capacity of secretary, was sitting beside me (I was deputy chairman).

In the preliminary negotiations it was decided that Avksent'ev would be appointed chairman, Peshekhonov, Krokhmal',[10] and myself deputy chairman, and Vishniak, secretary. I had not known Avksent'ev before, but his confused and meaningless speech at the Moscow State Conference (which he made in his capacity as minister of the interior), had made a very unfavorable impression on me. Closer acquaintance during the course of October and November changed this impression. Personally, Avksent'ev is very attractive, undoubtedly sincere, and quite without conceit, and he well rea-

5. The Swamp was largely composed of political newcomers in the Soldiers' Section of the Soviet and shifted to the far Left only after the Workers' Section had done so.

6. The Council of Elders was the steering committee of the State Duma and later of the Provisional Council of the Russian Republic; it was composed of the leaders of each of the Duma factions. (Nabokov sometimes used the term *Sen'oren konvent* for Council of Elders).

7. The highest court and council of the ancient Hebrew nation.

8. Nikolai Vasil'evich Chaikovskii (1850–1926), Popular Socialist leader; member, Union of Regeneration; head, Northern Russian government at Archangel, 1918; emigrated.

9. Mark Veniaminovich Vishniak (b. 1883), journalist; Socialist Revolutionary; secretary, Constituent Assembly, January 1918; emigrated in 1918 to Paris, then in 1940 to the United States; author, *Dan' proshlomu* (*Tribute to the Past*) (New York, 1954), *Dva puti (fevral' i oktiabr')* (*Two Paths: February and October*) (Paris, 1931).

10. Nikolai Dmitrievich Avksent'ev (1878–1943), Right Socialist Revolutionary; imprisoned and exiled, 1906–17; minister of the interior, chairman, Democratic Conference; president, Council of the Russian Republic; member, Union of Regeneration; president, Ufa Directorate; emigrated.

Viktor Nikolaevich Krokhmal' [Fomin] (1873–1930), lawyer; Menshevik; member, Menshevik Central Committee, 1903–07, 1917; arrested several times after October 25; harbored by Dzerzhinskii until the latter's death.

lized that Russia was on the brink of an abyss. As chairman of the council he behaved unimpeachably and was both polite and pleasant in his personal relations. For all that, however, he was the very last whom one would call an outstanding and strong personality, capable of winning the respect of others and persuading them to follow him. As chairman he showed complete objectivity and impartiality, but of course it was difficult for him in one month, even less, to achieve authority.

One of our party's practical aims in the council was to secure the removal of General Verkhovskii from the post of war minister. He revealed himself from the very beginning as utterly bankrupt, and acted like some kind of enigmatic personality, a sort of psychopath undeserving of any trust. At the conference Adzhemov spoke out first, sharply and vehemently, against Verkhovskii, then K. N. Sokolov spoke (using material supplied to him by Adzhemov). Some time later—it must have been the 10th of October—as I departed one morning from Avksent'ev's office, where meetings of the Presidium took place, to the council conference hall, I found Shingarev, Miliukov, and Adzhemov conferring with one another. They told me that a messenger from General Verkhovskii had come to the Mariinskii Palace to inform them that he would like to discuss serious questions with the leaders of the Kadet party and asking, in case of their agreement, to indicate any neutral place where they could meet. We suggested to Verkovskii that he should come to the Mariinskii Palace, but he telephoned to say that he would prefer somewhere less conspicuous. The option then came to my apartment on the Morskaia. The time was set for 2 P.M. It seems to me that, apart from the persons from the Kadet party named above, F. F. Kokoshkin also participated.

Verkhovskii arrived precisely at the designated hour, accompanied by his adjutant. We arranged ourselves in a circle in my study. Verkhovskii began at once in medias res, declaring that he would like to know the opinion of the leaders of the Kadet party, on the basis of the facts, as to whether immediate measures, including pressuring our allies, should be taken concerning peace negotiations. Then he began to give us the motives for his proposal and elicited a picture, with which in part we were familiar, of the complete disintegration of the army, the desperate situation with regard to procurement of provisions and supplies in general, the loss of horses, and the complete ruin of the means of communications. His conclusion was as follows: "In such conditions we cannot go on fighting, and any attempts to continue the war can only speed up the disaster."

My position was psychologically a very difficult one. No less than a month before I had participated in a private conference convoked by Prince Grigorii Nikolaevich Trubetskoi to discuss this same question. Tereshchenko and Neratov were at the meeting, and of those who had been invited I remember Rodzianko, Konovalov, Tret'iakov (the latter two were now ministers), Savich (a member of the State Duma), Mikhail Aleksandr Stakhovich, Maklakov, P. B. Struve, Baron B. E. Nol'de; that seems to be all. Miliukov was absent because he was not in Petersburg at the time. The question, essentially, was whether such an orientation was required by our military situation.

For quite a long time before this conference I had repeatedly and with ever-growing anxiety given this question considerable thought. Once, quite by chance, I had occasion to discuss the subject with Tereshchenko in the Winter Palace and to tell him my fears. As a matter of fact, essentially he shared them, but he still maintained that, according to General Alekseev, it was possible to normalize and reorganize the army and prepare for the spring campaign, and that for the time being it was necessary and possible to hold the front. I must admit that his considerations far from persuaded me. When later, chiefly at the initiative of Baron Nol'de and Adzhemov, the question was raised in our Central Committee (this must have been the 20th of September and also in Miliukov's absence), Baron Nol'de made a comprehensive report, the essence of which was: the longer the war continued, the greater and more irretrievable our losses would be; our army was ever faster falling prey to bolshevism; from the pattern of events it could already be foreseen that the war would end in a draw, without a decisive victory on either side; and we must make every effort to persuade our allies to open peace negotiations since a separate peace was naturally out of the question.

The overwhelming majority of the Central Committee reacted negatively to the report and the train of thought developed in it. As far as I can remember, it was defended only by A. A. Dobrovol'skii (firmly and resolutely) and by myself. No resolutions were passed, and it was decided to await Miliukov's return and then raise anew the entire question of the war and international policy. Such a discussion, incidentally, never took place. Miliukov did not return until 10 October (after our Moscow Congress), and within two weeks the Bolshevik coup took place.

At the conference at Trubetskoi's, Baron Nol'de repeated his argument more or less to the letter. This time also his reasoning was not accorded much sympathy. M. V. Rodzianko objected very sharply, as did Savich and others. The substance of the objections consisted partly in a denial of the fact of the total and irrevocable disintegration of our army, and partly in showing that we had no reason at all to expect our allies to be in the least favorably inclined toward any kind of peace negotiations that we could suggest. I now supported Nol'de. A. I. Konovalov, with tremendous zeal and candor, also subscribed to Nol'de's conclusions. I recall his words concerning the fact that the government which would succeed in giving Russia peace would achieve enormous popularity and become extraordinarily strong.

I had to leave before the meeting ended, and I did not hear Struve's and Maklakov's speeches, but as I was told later, only the latter partly supported Nol'de. It was decided to assemble periodically for an exchange of views, but there was no second meeting.

It stands to reason that my position was different at the discussion with Verkhovskii from what it had been in the Central Committee and in the conference at Trubetskoi's. He addressed us as the leaders of the Kadets. Miliukov and Shingarev were, of course, the most authoritative among us. They at once attacked Verkhovskii. I had to remain silent—all the more so because the baselessness and inconclusiveness of Verkovskii's argument was so obvious that no systematic and successful endeavor could be expected from him on this most complex and delicate question. Once again his whole personality produced an unmistakably negative impression. It was to be feared that, if he was left on his own initiative, he could lead us into a hopeless dead end. Besides that, his recent political past was so questionable that one could not disregard the possibility that he might simply play into the hands of the Bolsheviks.

The discussion ended with Verkhovskii asking: "So I cannot count on your support in this direction?" On receiving a negative answer, he rose and took his leave, but on the next day, at the evening session of a commission of the Council of the Republic (the Military Affairs Commission), he repeated his entire argument with additional viewpoints, along with the same conclusions. A clash then occurred with Tereshchenko, who put a question to him at once (a question to which he could not help answering in the affirmative): "Would he, Verkhovskii, confirm that all he had said had been stated by him for the first time at this meeting of the Commission, and that there had been no exchange of opinions concerning this question in the government?" Verkhovskii replied that, indeed, he had not made this report to the Provisional Government beforehand. This made a quite scandalous impression. Verkhovskii was sent on leave with the understanding that he would not return. A few days later, the Bolshevik coup took place.

In those October days the Kadet ministers (Kishkin, Kartashev, Konovalov, and Tret'iakov, who joined them), together with the members delegated to these conferences by the Central Committee, Miliukov, Shingarev, Vinaver, Adzhemov, and myself, met daily at 6 o'clock. These meetings were held at No. 19 Admiralty Quay, a house very well known to me, in the former apartment of my father-in-law, which was then occupied by A. G. Khrushchev (it belonged to the director of the Bank of the Nobility). The aim of these meetings was, first, that the ministers be in constant contact with the Central Committee, and second, to provide them with regular and accurate information about everything that was happening in the government.

At these meetings of ours Konovalov always looked extremely depressed and seemed to have lost all hope. "Ah! my dear Vladimir Dmitrievich, it is bad, very bad!" I well remember these phrases of his inasmuch as he repeatedly said them to me (he showed me more than the usual trust and kindness). It was Kerensky in particular who depressed him. By this time he had finally become disillusioned with Kerensky and had lost all confidence in him. What chiefly created his despair was Kerensky's indecisiveness, the absolute impossibility of taking him at his word, his susceptibility to all sorts of influences and pressures from the outside, sometimes even the most casual. "It quite often happens like this, almost every day," he would say. "You arrange everything, you insist on some measure or other, you reach agreement at last. 'So this is how it will be, Aleksandr Fedorovich, it is now firm, the decision is final, there will be no change?' You receive a categoric assurance. You leave his office, and within a few hours you hear that a completely different decision has already been implemented, or at best, that an urgent measure which had to be adopted at once, precisely today, is again being put off because new doubts have arisen or old ones which you thought had been eliminated have been resurrected. And so it is day after day. There is really no end to it."

He and all of us were particularly anxious about the possibility of martial law in Petersburg and the role to be played by Colonel Polkovnikov,[11] whom he did not trust in the least. In these days Kerensky was apparently going through a period of low spirits. It was quite impossible to make him adopt any energetic measures, time was passing, and the Bolsheviks were exerting themselves to the limit, with less and less constraint. The situation became more awesome every day. Rumors, which disturbed and alarmed everyone, were spreading in the city about a Bolshevik uprising within the next few days. During those days the—sheerly academic—order for Lenin's arrest was issued.

On the eve of the Bolshevik uprising, Kerensky, as is well known, appeared in the Council of the Republic, reported the uncovering of the plot, and asked for support and plenary powers. By accident I was not in the Mariinskii Palace at the time. I returned a little later and came upon a scene of total confusion. The usual agonizing process was taking place—which under these conditions was particularly shocking for its insignificance and irrelevancy: the

11. Colonel Georgii Petrovich Polkovnikov, commander, Petrograd Military District, October 1917.

search for such a compromise as might be agreeable to some kind of majority. In the end the Kadets did not propose their own formula, having decided to associate themselves with the Popular Socialists and the Cooperativists,[12] but the latter were by no means voting as a unit and, as a result, after validating the vote by means of a division, no majority was constituted.

At the most decisive moment the Council of the Republic had proved lacking. It had not given the government moral support but, on the contrary, had assaulted and battered its morale by revealing the government's isolation. I will not venture to say that a different vote would have staved off the course of events for any length of time or would have hindered the Bolsheviks, but the results of this sad and shameful day could have done nothing but raise the latter's spirits, give them hope, and add to their determination. On the other hand, this day exposed with unusual violence the negative features of our ''revolutionary democracy''—its shortsighted obtuseness, the fanaticism of its words and formulas, and its lack of any flair for governing. No reasonable, strong, genuine government with such elements could have worked. We dispersed, extremely depressed.

The next day, about 10 A.M., while I was still in my bath, a maid-servant knocked and told me that two officers wished to see me. I asked her to show them into the study and joined them there after a few minutes. These officers (one, as far as I remember, a staff captain; the other, a lieutenant) were unknown to me. They appeared extremely uneasy. The senior of the two stated his name and position and said: ''You are probably already aware of the

12. The Popular Socialists (*Narodnyi sotsialist*) were a group of moderate socialists led by Chaikovskii, Mel'gunov, Miakotin, and Peshekhonov, who advocated the democratization of Russia's political structure and the ''nationalization'' of the land, to be allocated only to those who tilled it.

''Cooperativists'' refers to those who established credit, consumer, and agricultural cooperatives after the 1861 emancipation of the serfs. Only with the turn of the century, however, did cooperatives really develop. In 1901, only 837 credit cooperatives existed: 600 consumer cooperatives, and 237 agricultural cooperatives. By 1915 these numbered, respectively, 14,000, 11,000, and 5,000. See B. & K., 2 : 611–14, for their activity in 1917.

course of events and know that the uprising has started; post, telegraph, and telephone services, the arsenal, and railway stations
have been seized. All the main centers are in the hands of the
Bolsheviks. The troops are going over to their side, and there is no
resistance. The Provisional Government is played out. Our task is
to rescue Kerensky and drive him by automobile as soon as possible to meet those troops which have remained loyal to the Provisional Government and which are moving on Luga. All our motor
cars have been seized or are out of service. We have come to ask
you whether you can provide two limousines or indicate to us
where we can turn. Now every minute is precious."

I was so taken aback that for a minute I thought it might be a
pretense to obtain a car and steal it. I inquired of the whereabouts
of Kerensky. The officer told me that he was in Polkovnikov's office at District Headquarters. I asked two or three more questions,
and then I had to explain to the officers that I had only one old,
low-powered, battered Benz landaulet for driving around town,
which was absolutely not appropriate for the object they intended;
and I found it difficult to suggest any other automobile, since, after
all the requisitioning, both before and after the coup, none of my
acquaintances had such automobiles. Thus I could not be of service. The officers left at once, saying that they were setting off to
look in other places. Having shown them out, I warned my wife of
the events that were taking place and soon afterward left the house
and went to the Mariinskii Palace, where the Presidium of
the Council of the Republic convened every morning about 11
o'clock.

There were already quite a few people there. An attitude of confusion, anxiety, and helplessness prevailed. The S[ocialist] R[evo-
lutionary] faction was absent altogether, and only a few Social
Democrats were present.[13] Avksent'ev did not know what to do.

13. The Socialist Revolutionary party was formed by the unification of a number
of populist groups in the 1890s. The Terroristic Organization of the party assassinated a number of tsarist officials, 1901–05. The first congress of the Socialist Revolutionary party occurred in late December 1905 and adopted a program of a federa-
tive state and democratic republic based on general franchise, along with the
"socialization of the land" controlled and owned by "democratically organized

There were too few members to open the meeting, but mainly, all of his own faction were absent. After a rather long wait, the members of the council who were present began to show signs of impatience and demanded either that the meeting be opened, or that it be declared that it should not take place. Then Avksent'ev called the *Sen'oren konvent* together to decide what to do. At this moment the council's sergeant-at-arms reported that Kerensky had just driven across the square in the direction of Voznesenskii Prospekt in an open (*sic!*) touring car with two adjutants, followed by a second, closed automobile. Where the other members of the Provisional Government were and what they were doing, no one knew.

The *Sen'oren konvent* convened. A very short time after the session opened, E. D. Kuskova [14] (who was not part of the membership of the *Sen'oren konvent*) asked permission to come in and reported that a detachment of troops with an officer at their head had arrived, that all the exits to the square were blocked, and that the officer wished to see the chairman. The reply was that the chairman was occupied, that a session of the Council of Elders was in progress, and that, when it was finished, it would be possible to confer with the chairman. Some time later, E. D. Kuskova came again with the message that the commander of the detachment advised all those at the meeting and all members of the council to

communities on the basis of the equalization of holdings.'' The party had several wings. As the party of toilers, it had the largest following of any Russian party. See Oliver H. Radkey, *The Agrarian Foes of Bolshevism* (New York, 1958).

The Russian Social Democratic Workers' party was formally created in 1898, through the Marxist Liberation of Labor, its predecessor, originated in 1883. Orthodox Marxism triumphed over the ''Economists'' only to split into Bolsheviks (Majority-ites) and Mensheviks (Minority-ites) in 1903. The Menshevik F. I. Dan found the major difference between these two groups to lie in the paradox that faced Russian Marxists, of socialism vs. democracy: the Bolsheviks increasingly stressed the former to the detriment of the latter; the Mensheviks, the opposite.

14. Ekaterina Dmitrievna Kuskova (1869–1958), onetime Marxist journalist; author, ''Credo'' of the ''Economists'' that Social Democrats should work for the betterment of workers and not exclusively for the overthrow of the autocracy; cofounder, Union of Liberation (1902–03); leading spokeswoman, left-wing Kadets; editor, *Vlast' Naroda* (*The People's Power*), 1917; arrested and exiled for aiding the starving in the 1921 famine, 1922; emigrated to Prague and then to Geneva.

leave the Mariinskii Palace at once, otherwise decisive measures, not excluding the use of firearms, would be taken.

A stupefying impression was created. Apparently no one was tempted by the prospect of laying down his life for the glory of the Council of the Russian Republic, and there was no motive to recall celebrated historical precedents, since the Council of the Republic was a purely incidental ad hoc institution in no way approximating the concept of a popular representative body. There was absolutely no ideological basis for defending it in any way. It was very clearly felt that the position of the council was closely tied to the situation of the Provisional Government. In answer to the ultimatum, a banal resolution was quickly drafted about coercion used against the council and stating that it would reconvene at the first opportunity. Apparently, someone suggested gathering all the members of the council still present in the general assembly hall, but this motion was not adopted because the number of members was quickly dwindling, and no enthusiastic demonstration was to be expected. When we went into the antechamber that directly adjoined the general assembly hall, the staircase and first waiting room upstairs were occupied by armed soldiers and sailors. They stood in two ranks on both sides of the stairs. They had the usual senseless, vacant, and malevolent faces. I do not think any one of them could have explained to you the reason why he was there, who had sent him, and who we were. I walked with Miliukov, as I wanted to make sure he left the palace unhindered. In the great entry hall downstairs was a large congregation of soldiers and sailors, standing in ranks as far as the door. The outside entry was occupied and a naval officer was letting people out. Everyone going out was showing his identity card. Thinking that this was for purposes of detection and under specific orders, I felt quite sure that Miliukov and I would be arrested. We were walking toward the door in single file. I was in front of him. Just as I was about to pass through the doorway, there was some hitch on the porch, and movement stopped. Two or three agonizing minutes passed. As at all such moments I have experienced in my life, I felt only a great nervous strain, nothing more. They let us out. I thought that the officer hesitated when he glanced at Miliukov's card, but in any case it all took only a second, and we both found ourselves out in the square. I invited him to my place for lunch, but he told me he preferred to go home; we shook hands and parted. We did not meet again until 1918, on 10/23 June, in Kiev, after a nightmare of seven and a half months.

Returning home, I stayed there for a time, and at about 3 o'clock went to visit some friends who lived on the Fontanka, not far from the corner of Voznesenskii Prospket. At about 4 o'clock I telephoned my home to inquire whether there was any news or not. My wife told me that a messenger (a journalist) had just come from A. I. Konovalov with a pressing invitation for me to come to the Winter Palace, where members of the Council of the Republic and representatives of public organizations were assembling. A session of the Provisional Government would apparently take place there in normal conditions, under the protection of a military force. I was surprised at this unexpected request but, understandably, I immediately decided to follow it up. I took a tram on the Pod'iacheskaia, went as far as Konnogvardeiskii Boulevard, changed trams, and proceeded to Palace Square.

The square proved to be cordoned off. Thin ranks of soldiers stood along the lane, parallel to the Aleksandrovskii Gardens, around the square, and along the grated fence which encircled the palace gardens. Many people crowded the pavements. It was difficult to understand what was happening and what purpose the troops could have. Observing my custom of refraining from making any inquiries on such occasions, I produced my pass to the Winter Palace (I had made use of the pass when I attended the last meetings of the Provisional Government), showed it without a word to the first soldier I came upon, and he let me through without a protest. I passed without hindrance through the gate and entered the palace by the usual way, through the Saltykovskii entrance, went up the stairs, and into the Malachite Hall.

There I found the following scene: all the ministers were present in the hall except N. M. Kishkin (who was at the time in the District Headquarters building in the Palace Square, "organizing" defenses, with, as we know, extremely pitiful results). Konovalov looked extremely agitated. The ministers were in small groups, some pacing up and down along the hall, others standing by the windows. S. N. Tret'iakov sat beside me on a divan and indignantly stated that Kerensky had deserted and betrayed them and that the situation was hopeless. Others were saying (I remember Tereshchenko in a very tense and excited state) that they had only "to hold out" for forty-eight hours and loyal government troops moving on Petersburg would arrive. My arrival was very welcome.

It turned out that Konovalov had sent messengers in all directions to summon "vital forces" who would be prepared to rally round the government and support it. A few of the messengers had been detained by the Bolsheviks, but others had reached their destinations and passed on the invitation. However, no one had responded except me. It goes without saying that my presence proved to be utterly useless. I could not help in any way, and when it became clear that the Provisional Government had no intention of undertaking anything and was preoccupied with a passive, wait-and-see attitude, I decided to leave, at the very moment (soon after 7 o'clock) that Konovalov was informed that dinner was served. In the corridor I encountered some journalists with L. M. Kliachko-L'vov at the head. They told me they intended to stick with the Provisional Government to the end. In reality they did not stay very long after me and had difficulty leaving the palace, yet I walked out quite freely and went home. About fifteen or twenty minutes after my departure, all exits and gates were blocked by the Bolsheviks, and they did not let anyone else out. So it happened that sheer luck alone kept me from "sharing the fate" of the Provisional Government and enduring all the subsequent ordeals which ended in the Peter and Paul Fortress.

I passed the evening of that stormy day, I remember, at home. The next day at about 2 o'clock I went to the Municipal Duma. Our Central Committee had met in the morning at Countess S. V. Panina's house, and it continued to meet daily during the next ten or fifteen days, either at Panina's or V. A. Stepanov's—once at Kutler's, the day when the Junkers [military cadets] tried to seize

the telephone exchange.[15] The Municipal Duma met every afternoon, and in the evenings, the newly formed post-coup d'état
"Committee for the Salvation of the Fatherland and the Revolution," which met in conference in the School of Jurisprudence,
thereby availing itself of the premises of the Peasants' Union.[16]

In those days the Municipal Duma resembled a huge, disturbed
anthill. All the halls, rooms, lobbies, and staircases were teeming
with people. Whom did one not come to meet there! But alas, it
was only in these very first days that one was able to indulge in the
illusion that the Municipal Duma, together with the Committee for
Salvation, might become an organized center of strong opposition
to the Bolsheviks. It very soon became clear that they had no actual
organized force behind the orders they issued. Among my most
grievous memories is the visit Avksent'ev and I and, as I recall,
Shreider (the mayor) and Isaev (the chairman of the Municipal
Duma) paid to the British ambassador, Buchanan.[17] This was done
on the day after the coup. The aim of the visit was to "calm" the
ambassador and assure him that the success of the Bolshevik upris-

15. Countess Sof'ia Vladimirovna Panina, step-daughter of Petrunkevich; member, Kadet Party Central Committee; assistant minister of public education and of
welfare, 1917; founder and director, People's House; prominent social worker; her
public trial and imprisonment demeaned the Bolsheviks; emigrated.

Vasilii Aleksandrovich Stepanov, Kadet deputy, Fourth State Duma; member,
Kadet Party Central Committee, 1917; acting minister of trade and industry, May–
July 1917; controller, General Denikin's Special Council; died on way to Paris,
1920.

Nikolai Nikolaevich Kutler (1859–1924), minister of agriculture under Witte;
Kadet deputy, Second, Third, Fourth State Dumas; member, Kadet Central Committee, 1907–16; arrested by the Bolsheviks; remained in Soviet Union.

16. The Peasants' Union was founded in Moscow at its first congress in 1905. In
1917 an All-Russian Peasants' Union was formed, competing with the Peasants' soviets. The union saw the soviets as temporary (until the Constituent Assembly) but
the union as the permanent political organization of the village. The union congress
in Moscow in July 1917 was a deflated affair that led to a struggle in the villages between the union and the soviets.

17. Grigorii Il'ich Schreider, Socialist Revolutionary; mayor of Petrograd, 1917;
expelled by the Whites, 1918.

Sir George Buchanan (1854–1924), British ambassador to Russia, 1917; doyen of
ambassadors in Petrograd; author, *My Mission to Russia,* 2 vols. (London, 1923).

ing was purely illusory and paltry, that Kerensky was bringing an entire army corps to rescue Petersburg and the Provisional Government. Lord knows to what degree we ourselves believed these soothing statements. Buchanan, whom I had met before my trip to England in January 1916, in the same study where he now received us, was upset and depressed. The conversation flagged, particularly because Avksent'ev had difficulty expressing himself in French. On mention of the anticipated army corps, the ambassador became somewhat animated, but on the whole this useless visit left me with a nasty impression. I recalled the alluring speeches at the Provisional Government's reception for ambassadors in the Mariinskii Palace, speeches ringing with confidence in the strength of the government and the greatness of the revolution, and I unwillingly contrasted that moment, which was not long ago, with the disgraceful experiences of the Bolshevik *coup de main*. As is well known, the next few days revealed the absolute vanity of placing hope in a military force, and ended with the complete rout of Krasnov's Cossacks and with Kerensky's flight.[18]

The sessions of the Municipal Duma were nothing but sheer hysteria. The fundamental tone was set by the mayor, G. I. Shreider, in many ways a respectable person but one apparently devoid of inhibitions. The absurd "All-Russian Council of the Land"[*zemskii sobor*] which he convened as if it were in execution of a Municipal Duma resolution (in fact, discussion was a muddle, only something in the way of a behest was adopted), turned out to be a complete failure; nothing else could have been expected under the circumstances. The Bolsheviks probably treated this attempt to "organize public opinion" with great irony and proceeded to deal with their own more realistic affairs.

18. Piotr Nikolaevich Krasnov (1869–1947), tsarist general, writer; Don Cossack Ataman, 1918–19; emigrated; fought with Germans in World War II; repatriated by the Allies; executed by the Soviets.

Under orders from Kerensky, Krasnov moved a force of 500–700 Cossacks toward Petrograd. After technically routing 30,000 Bolshevik sailors and soldiers at Pulkovo near Petrograd, Krasnov negotiated for Kerensky's surrender. Kerensky was spirited away to the countryside and remained in hiding until he could secretly reappear in Petrograd. He left the country in June 1918 by means of the forged papers of a Serbian captain.

As for the daily sessions of the Duma, they bore the character of one continuous rally. There was no agenda, no order of procedure. It was all carried on in the form of pressing, urgent, extraordinary declarations. More often than not, the mayor himself made them. Immediately afterward a stormy debate would begin. The mass of Bolsheviks stopped coming to sessions after the coup, but they left representatives of their faction: the city councillor, [Petr Alekseevich] Kobozev (a most repulsive individual), and someone else. These gentlemen at first added to their abuse, then they sat silent for the most part, and after a time they too stopped attending the sessions. Poor A. I. Shingarev played first fiddle in our faction. He spoke time and again with great ardor, invariably calling the Bolsheviks traitors and murderers. Alas, we had no way of knowing that these speeches were his swan song. A little later Vinaver arrived from Moscow (where he had been when the coup took place). But I do not remember that he made any striking speeches at this time.

The Kadet faction in the Municipal Duma delegated Countess S. V. Panina, Prince V. A. Obolenskii,[19] and myself to form part of the Committee for the Salvation of the Fatherland and the Revolution. We attended these meetings very regularly, especially in the first days when it still seemed that some effective force might unite around the committee and set something going. But our personal position on the committee was a rather peculiar one. Its membership was, *ex professo,* "democratic" in that special sense of the word which excludes all nonsocialist elements from the concept of democracy. Not one of us, therefore, were members of the committee's bureau. Yet all more or less real committee work was done in the bureau. From it came the organization of the military action (by the Junkers) which had such a tragic finale. The committee itself was preoccupied with resolutions, and they usually argued about every phrase, every single word, as though the salvation of the "Fatherland and the Revolution" depended on such phrases and

19. Prince Vladimir Andreevich Obolenskii, liberal activist; member, Union of Liberation; Kadet deputy, First State Duma; member, Kadet Party Central Committee, 1917; member, Petrograd Municipal Duma, 1917; emigrated.

words. The number attending kept dwindling, the pointlessness and fruitlessness of the sessions became more and more striking.

Thus passed the days immediately following the coup. In the morning, there were meetings of the Central Committee, conversations, so-called briefings, at which at least half of the information consisted of unconfirmed rumors and fantastic stories; then there would be long, wearisome, and utterly fruitless debates ending with the approval of the draft of an appeal or with a totally unnecessary resolution. Those fifteen or twenty people who assembled felt all too keenly and indubitably their complete impotence, their isolation, the absence of any organization on which they could rely. Such was the feeling in both the Municipal Duma and the Committee for Salvation.

In the first days it seemed as though the possibility of an electoral campaign of any sort for the Constituent Assembly had to be considered unfavorably. I recall that I expressed myself in this sense concerning the election in the Central Committee and the All-Russian Electoral Commission. The latter decided to cease its work temporarily and in fact did not meet for (approximately) two weeks. Everyone expected the Bolsheviks to start a campaign against the Constituent Assembly. They proved to be more cunning. As is well known, in their first manifesto they accused the Provisional Government of delaying the convocation of the Constituent Assembly, and during the course of the first month after the coup they made a great spectacle of their aspiration to convene it. Only when they began to feel their own strength, or better yet, when they were convinced of their protagonist's impotence, did they open their campaign, at first cautiously, then coarsely and flagrantly.

They did not hinder the electoral campaign in Petersburg during the course of November. The first meeting organized by our party was set, if I am not mistaken, for Sunday, 5 November. A. I. Shingarev was supposed to speak. We expected Bolshevik demonstrations, obstruction, and so on. Nothing of the kind happened. As is usually the case, the meeting attracted an audience exclusively of Kadets or Kadet sympathizers; likewise, it was held in the Tenishev School in the Liteiny district, that Kadet citadel, and it was marked, as was reported later, by great enthusiasm. After that there was a whole series of meetings in Petersburg and its environs. I spoke in the Tenishev School, in the hall of the Kalashnikov Exchange, in a gymnasium on the Kazanskaia, in Luga, and in Peterhof.[20] I also spoke by special invitation in the hall of the General Staff (for its officials) and at the "Salamander" Society (for the employees). Possibly there were other speeches that I cannot now recall. The representatives of the other (socialist) parties hardly spoke at these meetings, while the Bolsheviks were completely absent. The mood of the audience was, on the whole, alarmed and despondent.

At one of the first sessions of the Committee for the Salvation of the Fatherland and the Revolution, Countess S. V. Panina told me that my collaboration was desired at a session of deputy ministers of the Provisional Government to be held at A. A. Dem'ianov's apartment on the Basseinaia. If I am not mistaken, I went to only one session (the first), and I recall it with the greatest disgust. It was a gathering of people utterly confounded. Apart from the deputy ministers, three socialist ministers who had been released by the Bolsheviks from the Peter and Paul Fortress during the first days also participated. When they (Nikitin, Maliantovich, and Gvozdev)[21] came into the room, Dem'ianov endeavored to "welcome them with applause," but no one supported him.

More tactful people understood that there was nothing to applaud. The release of the socialist ministers occurred under circumstances that were by no means a credit to them. One would have thought that when it was announced they were free to go but the other "bourgeois" ministers were remaining in the fortress, a simple sense of the solidarity of colleagues would have motivated them to protest categorically against such discrimination (an absurdity

20. The gymnasium is roughly the European equivalent of the American high school and junior college.

21. Aleksei Maksimovich Nikitin, Menshevik; minister of post and telegraph, July 24–Oct. 25, 1917.

Kuzma Antonovich Gvozdev (1883–?), Menshevik; chairman, Labor Group, Central War Industries committees; member, Executive Committee, Petrograd Soviet, 1917; minister of labor, Sept. 25–Oct. 25; served Soviets.

emphasized by the fact that the head of the Provisional Government, you see, was a socialist), and besides, that they would have protested, not in words and written statements alone, but practically and actively, by refusing the freedom offered them under these conditions. It would have been another matter had they been turned out of the fortress by force; naturally, one cannot do anything about force. But to leave as they did was ethically intolerable, and I can well understand how, when Konovalov was told how they had left, he was extremely depressed. As if to complete the picture, one of the ministers (I think, Gvozdev) found it fitting and necessary to ask for a meeting with M. I. Tereshchenko, in order to "consult" with him and inquire how he and the other ministers remaining in the fortress felt about the release of the socialists! What could poor Tereshchenko say to that? Naturally, he said that they should take advantage of the Bolsheviks' courtesy, but he was not quite able to hide his feelings entirely and was apparently quite despondent, too, as whomever it was who went to see him reported.

Needless to say, there was no lack of plausible excuses to explain the conduct of the socialist ministers. They were said to have walked out in order to "carry on the struggle," in order to preserve the appearance of the "apparatus of power," and, first and foremost, in order to try to secure the release of the remaining members of the Provisional Government. In reality, it immediately became clear that they were powerless in all these intentions. A. M. Nikitin, apparently the most sensitive of them, was obviously pained by the situation. At the session I attended, he very excitedly interrupted Gvozdev, insisting that Gvozdev depart with him for Smol'nyi and demand categorically, "stopping at nothing," the release of the imprisoned ministers and, in the event of a refusal, insist that those who had been released be recommitted! However, Gvozdev showed not the slightest desire to follow this summons, and the others who were there—chiefly Dem'ianov—tried to show Nikitin that his plan was fanciful and impracticable, that their task was to "preserve" the fragments of the Provisional Government. In the end Nikitin gave up his plan.

The Nikitin episode is the clearest of my recollections of the entire meeting. It was all highly confused, and in the capacity of chairman, Dem'ianov did not know how to present questions or keep a debate to the point. There was the usual verbosity, the endless speeches to which no one listened. The general mood was disgusting, and some, especially Gvozdev, seemed to be in sheer panic. I think only one first-rate, concrete measure for struggle was discussed, a strike of functionaries; and it must be said that this strike and the heroically insane action of the Junkers were the only real manifestations of resistance to the Bolsheviks.

After that, I did not participate in these meetings any more, inasmuch as my official position in the Provisional Government certainly did not authorize me to be present, and my personal attitude toward them was negative.

In connection with the launched electoral campaign, the All-Russian Electoral Commission decided, about three weeks after the coup, to join the Chancellery for a plenary session in the Mariinskii Palace, from which the Bolshevik guard both inside and out had been removed, in order to discuss whether or not it should resume its work. Apart from the political uncertainties, this also raised serious juridical doubts. It was clearly foreseen that, in the conditions under which the electoral campaign was to be run and the elections held, many of the requirements in the electoral law (concerning postponements, the composition of commissions, and so on) could not be observed. In all such cases, previously, before the coup, the All-Russian Commission had made appropriate representations to the Provisional Government, with a draft resolution allowing (in a lawful manner) deviation from the general requirement of the law in this or that instance. The Bolshevik coup removed the possibility of such a course because the Provisional Government had actually been overthrown and the All-Russian Commission could not recognize the Soviet authority which had been formed.

Therefore, in all instances, for example, where it proved impossible in practice to observe the time limits laid down by law, or to form an electoral commission with the membership required by law, we were confronted with a hopeless situation. In relation to its own position, the All-Russian Commission could work only in conjunction with a government. In accordance with these considerations, immediately after the coup we decided to halt the work of the commission, after we had taken measures to ensure the preservation of its correspondence and documents. It should not be forgotten that at that time everyone, including ourselves, did not believe for a minute that the Bolshevik regime would last; everyone anticipated its quick liquidation. Independent of these considerations, the general confusion and chaos which followed the coup interrupted the activities of all electoral institutions and—temporarily, at least—brought to a halt the activities of the All-Russian Commission that was directly concerned with them.

However, days passed, and the situation began to change, in that the All-Russian Commission's inactivity could easily have been interpreted as a malicious intent to impede the elections, or "sabotage" them. Telegrams were coming from the provinces with enquiries about what was to be done, whether the elections would be held, what directives as to elections were to serve as a guide to local institutions. On the other hand, the Bolshevik "government," which had impudently accused the Provisional Government of intending to "drag out" the elections, was itself supposedly preparing to promote the convocation of the Constituent Assembly at the appointed time, that is, 28 November. All these circumstances forced the commission to reconsider the question of its subsequent activity. With that end in view it was decided to hold a meeting.

When I arrived at the Mariinskii Palace on the prescribed day, I found some very embarrassed chancellery officials. It transpired that N. N. Avinov, the chairman of the commission, had departed urgently and unexpectedly for Moscow, and the duties of chairman had been passed on to me. The first thing I had to do in the capacity of chairman was to talk with representatives who had arrived on the instructions of the Soviet of People's Commissars: their head of secretariat, Bonch-Bruevich,[22] and some soldier. According to the

22. The Soviet of People's Commissars was established on October 26, 1917 (O.S.) by the Second Congress of Soviets, and was chaired by Lenin until his death in 1924; the executive branch of the Soviet government.

Vladimir Dmitrievich Bonch-Bruevich (1873–1955), member, "Emancipation of Labor" group; later, Social Democrat, then Bolshevik; instrumental in founding *Izvestiia* of the Petrograd Soviet, 1917; director, Museum of History of Religion and Atheism; personal friend of Lenin; author, *Na boevykh postakh fevral'skoi i oktiabr'skoi revoliutsii* (*At the Fighting Posts of the February and October Revolutions*) (Moscow, 1930).

chancellery officials, these two persons having arrived at the palace, inquired of the quarters of the All-Russian Commission and, once they were given directions, proceeded to the chancellery and demanded that they be shown the clerical work and be informed about the commission's activities in general. They had been told that the deputy chairman, who had taken the place of the absent chairman, was due to arrive soon, and they were requested to wait and talk with me.

I knew Bonch-Bruevich slightly from a meeting in Kiev in the autumn of 1913 concerning the Beilis case.[23] At that time he was most deferential. If I am not mistaken, I dined with him at S. V. Glinka's. As we spoke then only of the Beilis case, I could not form any further impression of Bonch-Bruevich himself. As I found out later, he had fallen into the position of head of the secretariat of the Soviet of Commissars through the influence of Steklov-Nakhamkes, being a creature of Steklov's. Bramson told me he had a very poor reputation and was considered to be a dishonest fellow. He played a role in the rise of the newspaper *Novaia Zhizn'* that was decidedly sordid, according to A. I. Konovalov. Here in the Mariinskii Palace he greeted me like an old friend, was ostentatiously polite, and declared that the Soviet of People's Commissars was keenly interested in the question of the Constituent Assembly elections and would like a clarification of the role of the All-Russian Commission. I invited him and his companion, the soldier, into the hall that was used as a tea room (adjoining the antechamber). L. M. Bramson (the second deputy chairman) came along, and we began to deliberate.

I explained to Bonch-Bruevich the All-Russian Commission's point-of-view, which was based on the nonrecognition of the newly arisen authority of "*Sovnarkom*"* Bonch-Bruevich tried to convince me that the basis of Bolshevik authority was just as lawful, if not more so, than the Provisional Government's, but I declined to discuss the matter any further. I added that a meeting of the commission was at hand just now, at which the question of its continued activity would be discussed again. "May I hope that you

---

* This vile term was not then in use. I call it "vile" by an association of ideas. [*Sovnarkom* (*Sovet narodnikh komissarov*) or Council of People's Commissars.]

23. See Introduction, p. 4.

will inform me of the result of the discussion?'' I replied that officially, the commission would almost certainly not have any dealings whatsoever with the Soviet commission, but that I was ready to tell him, Bonch-Bruevich, privately what decision was made, always provided that the commission had no objection to it. He was entirely satisfied with this.

The soldier who was with him took hardly any part in the conversation and only once joined in to declare ''in the name of the front'' that the elections were being awaited with great impatience and that everything must be done to bring them about. I indicated in reply that it was the Bolshevik coup on the eve of the elections and a month before the Constituent Assembly that had dealt the elections an enormous blow and had raised doubts as to the possibility of their implementation. With this the conversation ended and our two visitors left.

I opened the session of the commission, and after a brief debate we took the decision to resume the business of the commission, to ignore the Bolshevik government completely, and, in case questions arose requiring a legal solution, to leave it to the local bodies to circumvent the difficulties—however, by no means sanctioning any deviation from the law. It was assumed that the Constituent Assembly, in certifying its members, would consider the desperate situation that had arisen and recognize as immaterial any deviations (mainly concerning dates and the membership of commissions) that local organizations had allowed. The next morning I rang up Bonch-Bruevich and gave him the following information: ''First of all, I am charged to inform you that the All-Russian Commission has resolved to ignore completely the Soviet of People's Commissars, not to acknowledge its legal authority, and not to enter into any relations whatsoever with it. This ends the strictly official part of our conversation. Privately, and in accordance with the promise I made you, I can inform you that the commission resolved to resume its business and at once undertook to do so.'' Bonch-Bruevich thanked me effusively.

Here I must note that the Bolshevik government apparently did not have the slightest notion of the membership of the commission or its function, and evidently it assumed that the commission would actually conduct the elections and perhaps influence their course and outcome. However that may be, in the course of the next two or three weeks the commission was able to work without interference. We met daily in the Mariinskii Palace, and I repeatedly had to preside because of N. N. Avinov's frequent trips to Moscow. We had lively dealings with local organs; piles of telegrams arrived daily which proved the enormous difficulties being encountered in the provinces. For the most part, these telegrams asked the All-Russian Commission for permission to allow changes or deviations of one kind or another from the requirements of the electoral law, and the commission, being powerless to fulfill these requests, was compelled to leave them unanswered. At the same time, however, there were a great many cases in which we had to interpret the law and give all sorts of instructions. Naturally, out of the telegrams received, a general picture of the elections, although incomplete and fragmentary, subsequently took shape. After Bonch-Bruevich's visit, the Bolshevik authorities totally lost interest in the commission's activity.

About 20 November it was decided to transfer the clerical work and the sessions of the commission to the Tauride Palace. This was carried out during my absence. I left for Moscow on 19 November and returned toward the evening of Wednesday the 22nd. Upon returning, I learned that a session was set for the morning of the 23rd in the Tauride Palace. On the very day of my departure, an hour after I had left for the station, a search was made of my home, the details of which are unknown to me to this day. On the 23rd, about two hours after the commission had set about its work, the commandant of the Tauride Palace, a Bolshevik ensign whose name I have forgotten, appeared and in the name of the Soviet of People's Commissars ordered the commission to disband. N. N. Avinov was presiding, and his reply, on behalf of the whole commission, was a categorical refusal. The officer left, went to Smol'nyi for instructions, and came back with a document signed by Lenin and containing an order—very ridiculously edited—to arrest the ''Kadet'' Electoral Commission and send them to Smol'nyi.

Our detention at Smol'nyi lasted five days. We spent all five days in a narrow, cramped little room, which we had to reach by a short flight of stairs leading from a lower corridor. There were from twelve to fifteen of us, I do not remember exactly. About four or five persons went off to spend the night in another cell. ''Among those present'' I remember Avinov, Bramson, Baron Nol'de, Vishniak, Gronskii, two members of the State Duma (one an Octobrist, the other a Peaceful Reconstructionist—Progressivist—but I have quite forgotten their names), the editor of the commission's proceedings, Dobranitskii, three soldiers, representatives of the front, and V. M. Gessen,[24] who was not arrested along with us but appeared voluntarily, placed himself under arrest, and remained twenty-four hours (I believe) with us and had to be sent away almost by force the next day.*

The first day we were not very well off. In the room were wooden benches, chairs, two scanty beds on which our two eldest fellow companions, the members of the State Duma, slept, and nothing more. I slept on a narrow wooden bench, Vishniak on a table. We were not given linen or mattresses. On the first day, too, food or even tea was out of the question, and if Baron Nol'de's wife had not brought some provisions (she was the first to find out what had happened and succeeded in gathering a few things), we

---

* Dobranitskii and the other members of the Commission of the Front had not been arrested and were there at their own insistence. Attempts were also made to remove them, and they used military stratagems (including disguise) in order to return to our group.

24. Pavel Pavlovich Gronskii, law professor, St. Petersburg University; Kadet deputy, Fourth State Duma; member, Kadet Party Central Committee, 1917; commissar for press affairs, Provisional Government, 1917; deputy chairman, Internal Affairs Administration, Denikin's Special Council; emigrated; author, *La Chute de la Monarchie en Russie* (Paris, 1923).

The Octobrist party was founded in November 1905 as the ''Union of October 17'' and was based on fulfilling the promises made in the Imperial Manifesto of that date. It favored a constitutional monarchy, with a Duma having full legislative rights and ministers responsible to the throne, not the Duma. Gentry and bureaucrats made up most of its membership.

The Progressive bloc was formed in August 1915 by Kadets, Octobrists, and Progressive Nationalists plus three other groups, to force the government to conduct a more responsible war effort.

V. M. Gessen (1868–?), Kadet; assistant professor, Petrograd University; deputy, Second State Duma.

would have gone hungry. The second day everything was put right and we began to have our dinner in the common dining-room, families brought abundant provisions, camp-beds and linen appeared, two or three more mattresses were brought in, and we spent the remaining days quite gaily and animatedly. Our only worry was the complete uncertainty of our fate and the awesome prospect of departing to Kresty.[25] We were interrogated on the very first evening; the interrogation was conducted by a certain Krasikov,[26] a lawyer of the lowest type, and invariably included the question, to which we invariably answered in the negative: "Do you recognize the authority of the Soviet of People's Commissars?" At the end of the interrogation I categorically raised a question, What is the reason for our arrest? I received the answer, "Non-recognition of the authority of the People's Commissars."

At about 3 o'clock on Monday, 27 November, on the eve of the opening of the Constituent Assembly, a disheveled sailor, a member of the Commission of Inquiry, came to our room and, "in the name of the People's Authorities," told us that we were free. I cannot say that this news made me particularly happy. We were fully aware that our arrest and release were only mere chance among impending elemental calamities, that, though free today, we might be imprisoned again tomorrow, perhaps in much worse conditions. Before parting we had tea and a little something to eat for the last time, and were going to draw up a statement setting forth the procedure of our interrogation and release, but then decided to postpone it to another day and to meet on Tuesday morning in the Tauride Palace, gathering beforehand in L. M. Bramson's apartment.

However, certain circumstances prevented me from arriving at Bramson's on time, and when I did get to the apartment my col-

25. *Kresty* (The Crosses) was the common name for a prison used largely for political prisoners, which was built in 1893 on the American model and whose main cell-blocks formed a cross.

26. Petr Anan'evich Krasikov [Pavlovich] (1870–1939), Old Bolshevik; member, Central Executive Committee, Petrograd Soviet, 1917; chairman, committee of Inquiry in the Struggle with Counterrevolution, 1918; procurator, Supreme Court of the USSR, 1924–33.

leagues had already left for the Tauride Palace. I hastened after them. The nearer I got, the thicker were the crowds of people. I wanted to enter the palace from the Tavricheskaia side, but soldiers standing at the entrance would not let me pass. Upon my statement that I was a member of the All-Russian Electoral Commission and was going to a meeting of the commission, they said to me, "Ask the commandant."

"Where is the commandant?"

"At the other entrance, on the Shpalernaia."

I started toward the Shpalernaia, but it was utterly impossible to pass. The thick crowd became a wall around the grated fence, a clamor could be heard, and there was a fierce crush. I went back to the Tavricheskaia and pushed my way to another entrance, where there was a more hesitant soldier; and because I, on the other hand, showed great resolve, I got through.

As soon as I entered the palace, I learned of the arrest that morning, about two hours earlier, in Countess Panina's house, of the countess herself, Shingarev, Kokoshkin, and Prince Pavel Dmitrievich Dolgorukov.[27] The commission was already in session. It appeared that the commandant had already come and demanded that it disband, and armed soldiers had been brought into the room. The commission, however, refused to disperse and continued to sit in the presence of the soldiers. Some time later, G. I. Shreider and two or three other members of the Constituent Assembly joined us, having found out that the commission was being obstructed. They sent for the commandant, entered into a violent discussion with him, and demanded the withdrawal of the soldiers. The commandant referred to the orders he had received from Uritskii[28] (the commissar of the Tauride Palace) and went for further instructions from him.

27. Major-General Prince Pavel Dmitrievich Dolgorukov (1866–1927), prominent Zemstvo leader; Kadet deputy, Second State Duma; first chairman, Kadet Party Central Committee; emigrated 1920; returned 1927; shot by Soviet secret police; author, *Velikaia razrukha* (*The Great Devastation*) (Madrid, 1964).

28. Moisei Solomonovich Uritskii (1873–1918), revolutionary, 1890s; arrested and exiled to Siberia, 1897–1902; chairman, Krasnoiarsk Soviet, 1905; Interdistrictite and associate of Trotsky, 1905–17; Bolshevik from July 1917; member, Military Revolutionary Committee, 1917; head, Petrograd Cheka, 1918; assassinated by Socialist Revolutionary L. Kanegiser, Aug. 18, 1918.

After a while Uritskii arrived. I recall right now his impudent Jewish face and the repulsive figure of that seedy individual with a hat on his head. He also ordered us to disperse and threatened the use of arms. By this time Shreider and the other members of the Constituent Assembly had left and gone to the meeting. We demanded that Uritskii remove his hat, which he hastened to do. Further talk got nowhere. Uritskii left, and we continued the session, expecting that at any minute we would be ejected by force. This, however, did not happen. We finished our business after dealing with all the topics, and at about 2 o'clock we adjourned, agreeing to gather again at Bramson's house the next day and to act according to circumstances.

The next day I left the house about 10 o'clock, never dreaming that I would not cross its threshold again in 1917, nor probably in 1918.

On the way to Bramson's I read a decree outlawing the Kadet party and ordering the arrest of its leaders. When I got to Bramson's, I was received with lively greetings. They all thought I had been arrested.

The same day, under the influence of the counsel of close friends, I decided to leave for the Crimea, where my family had been located since mid-November, availing themselves of the hospitality of Countess S. V. Panina. By incredible luck I was with difficulty able to obtain at the ticket-office a first-class sleeper to Simferopol'. Without returning home, issuing all necessary orders by telephone, and taking only the most necessary items, I left that evening. I reached Gaspre safely on Sunday, 3 December. There I spent all winter, spring, and part of the summer, experiencing both the Bolshevik capture of the Crimea and then the German invasion. On 7 June I left for Kiev, intending to make my way to Petersburg. But I was not successful in doing so, and I returned to Gaspre on 22 July after putting in five and a half rather agaonizing weeks in Kiev. I am ending this section of my notes on September 25/8 October, just after receiving news of immensely important events in Germany and Bulgaria.[29]

29. The important events were the abdication of Tsar Ferdinand of Bulgaria on October 4 (N.S.), and the resignation of Count Georg von Hertling as chancellor of Germany and the appointment of the liberal Prince Max of Baden, October 4 (N.S.).

Index

Abdication. *See* Mikhail, Aleksandrovich, Grand Duke; Nicholas II
Academy of Sciences, 100
Action Française, L', 111 and *n*97
Adzhemov, Moisei Sergeevich, 25–26 and *n*25, 150, 152, 153, 155
Agapov, General, 46, 47
Aleksandr Feodorovna, Empress, 70 and *n*49, 110
Alekseev, Mikhail Vasil'evich, General, 26 and *n*26, 70, 81*n*62, 88, 112, 140, 153
Alexander I, 22*n*21
Alexander II, 2
Alexander III, 2
All-Russian Council of the Land, 164
All-Russian Electoral Commission. *See* Constituent Assembly
All-Russian Peasants' Union, 163*n*16
America, 111, 116
Andronnikov, M. M., Prince, 109 and *n*95
Anglo-Soviet Trade Agreement (*1921*), 7
April crisis. *See* Provisional Government
Archives of the Russian Revolution, viii, 18
Army: Nabokov's service in, 5, 15, 37–38, 60; Petersburg garrison, 15, 113, 119, 120, 140; in October crisis, 30, 158–65 passim, 176; General Staff, 37, 40, 42, 70*n*46, 78*n*57; Cossacks, 39, 164 and *n*18; Preobrazhenskii Regiment, 40 and *n*12, 47, 140; in February crisis, 40–41, 43, 146; in July war offensive, 78 and *n*57; Volunteer, 81*n*62; deputations from, 137, 140; disintegration of, 144, 153; in April crisis, 145; in July crisis, 145–49 passim; Junkers, 162–63, 165, 169
Arzub'ev. *See* Guber, P.
Aver'ianov, General, 45 and *n*21
Avinov, N. N., 170, 173, 174
Avksent'ev, Nikolai Dmitrievich, 26*n*28, 151–52 and *n*10, 159, 163–64

Barrès, Maurice, 111 and *n*97
Beilis case, 4–5, 9, 171
Beloborodov, A. G., 71*
Belosel'skii, S. K., Prince General, 44
Berlin: Kadet politics in, 6–8, 22*n*22
Black Hundred, 65 and *n*38
Blok, Alexander, 31 and *n*34
Bobrikov, N. I., 67
Bolsheviks: in Crimea, 6; and Constituent Assembly issue, 18*n*13, 136–37, 166–77; headquarters of, 30*n*33; first uprising, 35; move into power, 64, 84, 119, 143–77; murder royal family, 70*n*49; and Kerensky, 78, 143–45, 156; in Free Georgia, 79*n*59; growth of, 83; news organs of, 119*n*104; Council of the Russian Republic's opposition to, 149–50; imprison government officials, 162, 167, 173–75
Bolshoi Theater (Moscow), 35, 77
Bonch-Bruevich, Vladimir Dmitrievich, 170–73 and *n*22

Boris, Tsar, 14
Bramson, Lev Moissevich, 135 and
  *n*113, 171, 174, 175, 177
"Brigand" of Tushino, 14
Browder, Robert Paul: evaluates memoir,
  1–2, 8–11; on Nabokov's life and
  political career, 2–8
Brusilov, Aleksei Alekseevich, General,
  112 and *n*98
Buchanan, George, Sir, 163–64 and *n*17
Bukhara, 42*n*15
Bulgaria, 177 and *n*29

Cachin, Marcel, 117*n*101
Catherine II, 22*n*21
Chaikovskii, Nikolai Vasil'evich, 151
  and *n*8, 157*n*12
Charnolusskii, V. I., 99 and *n*79
Chernov, Viktor Mikhailovich, 79 and
  *n*59, 121, 126, 150*n*4
Chkheidze, Nikolai Semenovich, 125
  and *n*107, 128–30 passim
Collected Statutes, 29
Commission for Drafting the Electoral
  Law for the Constituent Assembly. *See*
  Constituent Assembly
Commission of Inquiry, 175
Commission of the Front, 174*
Committee for the Salvation of the Father-
  land and the Revolution, 163, 165–69
Committee of Ministers, 22*n*21
Constituent Assembly, 65; delegates,
  18*n*13; purpose of, 18*n*13, 27–28; and
  Bolsheviks, 18*n*13, 136–37; opening
  session of, 21; Commission for Draft-
  ing the Electoral Law for, 28–30; All-
  Russian Electoral Commission and
  electoral law issue, 30, 135–36,
  166–77
Constitutional Democratic party. *See*
  Kadet party
Contact Commission. *See* Soviet of
  Workers' and Soldiers' Deputies
Cooperativists, 157, and *n*12
Cossacks. *See* Army

Council of Elders. *See* Dumas; Provi-
  sional Council of the Russian Republic
Council of Ministers under tsar, 15*n*3,
  137. *See also* Provisional Government
Council of the Russian Republic. *See*
  Provisional Council of the Russian
  Republic
Crimea, 6, 35, 177
Criminal Code, 146
Crosses, The. *See* Kresty

Dan, Fedor Il'ich, 24–25 and *n*23, 149,
  150 and *n*4, 158*n*13
Danzas, Katia, 148
Davletshin, Abdel-Azis Aziovich,
  Major-General, 42 and *n*15
Declaration of London (*1914*), 92*n*70
Defensism, 30 and *n*32
Delo, 125*n*106; *Narodnoe, Narodov,*
  Narodnye, 125*n*106
Delo Naroda (*The People's Cause*), 125
  and *n*106
DeMan, Henri, 117*n*101
Dem'ianov, Aleksandr Alekseevich,
  133*, 167, 169
Demidov, I. P., 101 and *n*82
Democratic Council, 80*n*60
Denikin, Anton Ivanovich, General,
  20*n*16
Detskoe Selo, 70*n*48
Directory. *See* Provisional Government
Dni (*Days*), 7
Dobranitskii, Mr., 174 and *
Dobrovol'skii, A. A., 68 and *n*43, 154
Dolgorukov, Pavel Dmitrievich, Major-
  General Prince, 176 and *n*27
Dostoevsky, F. M.: *The Dispossessed,*
  103
Dubrovin, A. I., 65*n*38
Dumas: Address to the First Family, 3;
  Kadet power in, 3, 22*n*22; First dis-
  solved, 4; Fourth promotes reforms,
  5–6; meeting place of, 15*n*24; power
  of, 17 and *n*12; and *1905* Imperial Man-
  ifesto, 34*n*2; Provisional Committee,

47–48 and n26, 121; *1914–15* tactics of, 108; Second, 130 and n108; combined meeting of, 131 and n109; Council of Elders, 151n6; Municipal in October crisis, 163–66

Dzerzhinskii, Felix Edmundovich, 151n10

East Prussia, 108
Economists, 158n13, 159n14
Eisenstein, Sergei: *October,* 52n29
Ekaterinburg, 70n49, 71*
England, 5–7 passim, 110

February crisis. *See* Revolution of *1917*
Ferdinand, Tsar (Bulgaria), 177n29
Filippovskii, Vasilii Nikolaevich, Lieutenant, 125 and n107, 128
Fomin. *See* Krokhmal', Viktor
Free Georgia, 79n59
Freigang, Mr., 60
Fundamental Laws, 49; Article 87, 17, 18, 55

Gainash, 37
Galicia, 108
Gal'pern, A. Ia., 25, 132
Gardenin. *See* Chernov, Viktor Mikhailovich
Gaspre, 177
Gerasimov, Peter Vasil'evich, 100 and n81
Germany, 110, 113, 177 and n29; invades Crimea, 6; Soviet treaty with, 7; aids Lenin, 119, 143. *See also* Berlin
Gessen, Iosif Vladimirovich, 4, 7, 10, 36n7, 38 and n9, 39, 110
Gessen, V. M., 174 and n24
Glebov, Iu. N., 138 and n114
Glinka, Ia. N., 59
Glinka, S. V., 171
Godnev, Ivan Vasil'evich, 17 and n11, 72, 74; Nabokov on, 89–90, 93
Godunov. *See* Boris, Tsar
Goikhbart, Mr., 66

Golitsyn, Nikolai Dmitrievich, Prince, 39 and n11
Goremykin, I. L., 3
Gorky, Maxim, 66n41
Gosudarstvenny Sovet. See State Council
Gots (Gotz), Abram Rafailovich, 24–25 and n23, 150
Gredeskul', Nikolai Andreevich, 103 and n83
Grey, Edward, Sir, 106 and n86
Gribunin, S. F., 70 and n47
Gronskii, Pavel Pavlovich, 174 and n24
Guber, P., 39 and n10
Guchkov, Aleksandr Ivanovich, 44, 45, 56, 74, 94, 122, 140, 141, 145; resigns from government, 34, 48, 58, 79 and n58, 88–89; biographical note on, 34n5; and abdication issue, 48, 50; Nabokov on, 85–89; favors government withdrawal, 124
Gurvich. *See* Dan, Fedor Il'ich
Gvozdev, Kuzma (Koz'ma) Antonovich, 167–69 and n21

Helsingfors massacre, 56 and n30
Henderson, Arthur, 117n101
Hertling, Georg von, Count, 177n29
Hessen. *See* Gessen, Iosif Vladimirovich
Holstein Gottorp, 42n16
Hotel Astoria, 40 and n13, 41
Hotel Militaire. *See* Hotel Astoria

Ignat'ev, N. N., Count, 140–41
Ignat'ev, Pavel Nikolaevich, Count, 107 and n88
Imperial Council, 22n21
Imperial Manifesto. *See* Nicholas II
Imperial School of Jurisprudence, 2
International Criminology Association, 5
Internationalists, 150–51 and n4
Italy, 93, 111
Izvestiia (News), 21 and n19

July offensive. *See* Army
Junkers. *See* Army
Juridical Conference. *See* Provisional
 Government
Juridical Council. *See* Provisional Gov-
 ernment

Kadet party, 52, 118, 166; and Nabokov,
 1, 3, 4, 6–8, 10, 25–26, 29, 149; power
 of, 3–4, 22*n*22, 165; and Miliukov, 4,
 6–8, 16*n*8, 26, 101; publications of, 4,
 22*n*22, 36*n*7; policy split in, 6–8,
 25–26; and Progressive bloc, 22*n*22,
 174*n*24; and Shingarev, 101; Congress
 of, 116; Central Committee's October
 crisis actions, 146, 147, 155–57; and
 Verkhovskii, 152–55 passim; considers war's outcome, 153–54
Kalashnikov Exchange, 167
Kalinin, S. A., 70 and *n*47
Kaminka, Avgust Isaakovich, 4, 7, 8,
 36*n*7, 108 and *n*90
Kartashev, Anton Vladimirovich, 92 and
 *n*68, 155
Kasso, Lev Aristidovich, 99 and *n*78
Kaufman, M. P., 46 and *n*24
Kerensky, Alexander Fedorovich, 1, 7,
 29, 45*n*18, 52*n*29, 72, 97, 100,
 117–18, 133, 146; his governmental
 power, 6, 22, 25, 35, 44, 45*n*20, 85,
 94, 131, 149 and *n*3; and Nabokov, 9,
 36, 38, 45, 57, 69–70, 74–81, 112,
 114, 121–25, 127, 156; and abdication
 issue, 20; biographical note on, 20*n*16;
 his socialism, 45*n*20, 75*n*54, 106, 117;
 and Bolsheviks, 78, 143–45, 156; and
 July war offensive, 78*n*57; and Soviet
 Deputies, 78–79; and Prince L'vov,
 85; and Kornilov affair, 101; and October crisis, 143–45 passim, 158, 159,
 162, 164 and *n*18
Khabalov, Sergei Semenovich, General,
 39 and *n*11
Khiva, 42*n*15

Khrushchev, Aleksandr Grigor'evich,
 92 and *n*69, 155
Khvostov, A. A., 109*n*94
Khvostov, Aleksei N., 109 and *n*94
Kiev, 4, 6, 171, 177
Kirshbaum, Mr., 60
Kishinev pogrom (*1903*), 3, 9
Kishkin, Nikolai Mikhailovich, 131 and
 *n*110, 149, 155, 161–62
Kliachko-L'vov, L. M., 162
Kobozev, Peter Alekseevich, 165
Kokoshkin, Fedor Fedorovich, 69,
 89–90, 92, 109, 152; and Constituent
 Assembly, 21; biographical note on,
 21*n*17; government role of, 28, 124;
 arrested, 176
Kokovtsov, V. N., Count, 66 and *n*39
Kolomeitsov, Nikolai Nikolaevich, Ad-
 miral, 41 and *n*14
Koni, Anatolii Fedorovich, 64 and *n*37,
 65
Konovalov, Aleksandr Ivanovich, 27,
 74, 131, 149, 171; biographical note
 on, 27*n*30; Nabokov on, 96–98; in
 October crisis, 153–56 passim, 161,
 162, 168
Korff, Ferdinand Nichlaus Viktor von,
 Baron, 2
Kornilov, Lavr Georgievich, General,
 80–81 and *n*62, 90, 95 and *n*75, 101,
 149 and *n*3
Krasikov, Peter Anan'evich, 175 and *n*26
Krasnov, Piotr Nikolaevich, 164 and
 *n*18
Kresty, 175 and *n*25
Krimov, A. M., General, 95 and *n*75
Krokhmal', Viktor Nikolaevich, 151 and
 *n*10
Kronstadt, 16, 72 and *n*50
Kshesinskaia, Mathilda, 66 and *n*40, 119,
 121, 144–45
Kukol'nik, Nestor Vasil'evich, 62 and
 *n*36
Kuskova, Ekaterina Dmitrievna, 159–60
 and *n*14

Kutler, Nikolai Nikolaevich, 162–63 and *n*15

Kuzmin-Karavaev, V. D., 4

Lafont, Ernest, 117*n*101
Landau, Grigory, 10
Land Committees. *See* Provisional Government
Lazarevskii, N. I., 68, 104
Leftists, 29
Lenin, V. I., 139*n*115, 149, 170*n*22; economic policy of, 7; and electoral commissioners, 30, 173; overthrows government, 35; as Zimmerwaldist, 75*n*55; return of, 119 and *n*103, 143–44; "Letters from Afar," 144*n*1
Leningrad, 15*n*6
Liaison Commission. *See* Soviet of Workers' and Soldiers' Deputies
Liberalists, 34*n*4
Liberation movement, 3
Liberation of Labor party, 158*n*13
Liberty Loan. *See* Provisional Government
Lipskii, Deputy, 67–68
Lodyzhenskii, I. N., 60, 61
Lunacharskii, Anatoli Vasil'evich, 99 and *n*79
L'vov, George Evgen'evich, Prince, 19–20, 44, 53, 55, 57, 72, 74, 135; biographical note on, 20*n*16; and abdication issue, 48–49; and retirement issue, 62–63; criticism of, 78–79, 127–28; Nabokov on, 81–85, 89, 114
L'vov, L., 121, 126
L'vov, Vladimir Nikolaevich, Ober-Procurator of the Holy Synod, 17 and *n*11, 43, 74, 90–93

Makalov, Vasilii Alekseevich, 6, 44 and *n*17, 75, 97, 102, 108, 153, 154
Malachite Hall. *See* Winter Palace

Maliantovich, Pavel Nikolaevich, 131 and *n*110, 133, 167
Manakin, General, 42, 47
Manuilov, Aleksandr Apollonovich, 69, 72, 74, 121, 124, 147*; biographical note on, 69*n*44; Nabokov on 98–100
Mariinskii Palace: government sessions in, 21, 57, 60, 69, 72, 86, 112; army deputies at, 137–39 passim; demonstration at, 145; guards at, 148; Council of the Russian Republic at, 158; reception at, 164; All-Russian Electoral Commission at, 169, 170, 173
Martov, L., (Iulii Osipovich Tserbaum; Egorov) 150*n*4
Marxism, 158*n*13
Maslov, Semon Leontevich, 131 and *n*110
Matveev, A. S., 48, 53
Max, Prince (Baden), 177*n*29
Mel'gunov, S. P., 157*n*12
Mensheviks, 79*n*59, 158*n*13
Miakotin, V. A., 157*n*12
Miatlev, Colonel, 39
Michael, Tsar, 42*n*16
Mikhail Aleksandrovich, Grand Duke: abdication of, 6, 16–20, 27–28, 46–55, 120, 137; death of, 16*n*9
Mikhailovskii Theater, 116
Mikhnevich, General, 45
Military Affairs Commission. *See* Provisional Council of the Russian Republic
Miliukov, Anna Sergeevna, 44, 56
Miliukov, Paul Nikolaevich, 10, 38, 45*n*20, 53, 59, 74, 75, 92, 97*n*77, 99*n*78, 139; on Nabokov's memoir, 1–2; Kadet activity of, 4, 6–8, 16*n*8, 26, 36*n*7, 101; and abdication issue, 16, 48; biographical note on, 16*n*8; his resignation issue, 22, 48, 55–56, 79 and *n*58, 121–23; his concept of the revolution, 24, 56–57; and the April crisis, 34*n*4, 145; yields to Soviet demands, 35; supports monarchy, 44; appoints Nabokov, 57–58; Nabokov

Miliukov, Paul Nikolaevich (*cont.*)
   on, 76, 102, 105–07, 110–11, 115–23;
   appoints Prince L'vov, 85; on the war,
   87, 106; "Stupidity or Treason?" 110;
   and the October crisis, 143, 152, 155,
   160–61; and Verkhovskii, 154; *Istoriia
   vtoroirusskoi revoliutsii,* 121 and *n*105
Monarchist movement, 7–8, 10
Morozov, Mme., 61
Moscow, 61 and *n*35; growth of anarchy
   in, 83–84
Moscow State Conference (*1917*), 77 and
   *n*56, 78, 131, 149, 151
Moutet, Marius, 117*n*101
Murza, Nabok, Prince, 2

Nabokov, Elena (wife), 2, 39, 47, 161
Nabokov, Konstantin D. (brother), 2
Nabokov, Vladimir Dmitrievich: Kadet
   activities of, 1, 3–4, 6–8, 25–26, 29,
   149; positions held by 1, 5, 6, 28–30
   passim, 146, 151; as Head of Chancellery, 1, 15, 20–22, 35–36, 58–74
   passim, 79–80; his memoir evaluated,
   1–2, 8–11; background and early
   career of, 2–3; in liberation movement,
   3; imprisoned, 4, 173–75; as journalist,
   4–7 passim, 9, 22–24; *Iz voiuiushchei
   Anglii (A Report from England at
   War*), 5; his military service, 5, 15,
   37–38, 60; collaboration efforts of, 6;
   and abdication issue, 6, 10, 16–20
   passim, 27–28, 46–55, 120, 137; in
   Crimea, 6, 35, 177; assassinated, 8;
   and Kerensky, 9, 36, 38, 45, 57,
   69–70, 74–81, 112, 114, 121–25, 127,
   156; his antisemitism, 9–10; his intellectual and moral personality, 13–14;
   his political philosophy, 14–15;
   "Practical Lessons," 22–24; his
   qualifications as diplomat, 27; on
   foreign policy, 33, 34, 95; on *1917*
   revolution, 33, 86–87, 108, 113, 118,
   140; on overthrow of government,

34–35; on February crisis, 39–46, 146;
   stresses need for discipline, 42, 47; on
   Miliukov, 55–56, 76, 102, 105–07,
   110–11, 115–23; on government sessions, 59, 72–73, 84, 86; on retirement
   issue, 61–86; on Bolsheviks, 64, 84,
   119; on fate of Nicholas, 70–72; on
   Tereshchenko, 74, 93–96; on Prince
   L'vov, 81–85, 89, 114; on growth of
   anarchy, 83–84, 113, 120; on Guchkov, 85–89; writes government's appeal, 86; on April declaration, 88; on
   Godnev, 89–90, 93; on V. N. L'vov,
   90–93; on Konovalov, 96–98; on Manuilov, 98–100; on Nekrasov, 100–01;
   on Shingarev, 101–05; on Steklov,
   125–28; on Skobelev, 128–29; on
   Chkheidze, 129, 130; on Tseretelli,
   130–33; and electoral laws issue,
   135–37, 146, 166–77; on army deputations, 137–41; on October crisis,
   143–77; on July crisis, 145–49; Council of the Russian Republic, 149–63; on
   Municipal Duma, 163–65; and Committee for the Salvation of the Fatherland and the Revolution, 165–66
Nabokov, Vladimir V. (son), 8–10;
   Speak, Memory, 8
Nakhamkes. *See* Steklov-Nakhamkes,
   Iurii Mikhailovich
Narodnyi sotsialist. See Popular
   Socialists
Nasha Rech' (Our Speech), 36*n*7
Nash Vek (Our Century), 36*n*7
Nekrasov, Nikolai Vissarionovich, 17,
   24, 44, 68, 74, 89, 94; biographical
   note on, 17*n*11; and abdication issue,
   19, 48–49, 53; resigns, 95; and
   Kerensky, 100–01
Nepenin, A. I., Vice-Admiral, 56*n*30
Neratov, A. A., 97 and *n*77, 153
New Economic Policy, 7
New Russia, The, 6
Nicholas II, 16*n*9, 17 and *n*12, 66*n*40,

109, 110; abdicates, 19, 46–47, 49–50, 54; *1905* Imperial October manifesto of, 34 and *n*2, 61, 65*n*38, 174; fate of, 70–72

Nikitin, Aleksei Maksimovich, 167 and *n*21, 168

Nikolai Mikhailovich, Grand Duke, 45 *n*18

Nol'de, Baroness, 174

Nol'de, Boris Emmanuilovich, Baron, 55, 97; positions held by, viii; on Nabokov, 13–31; and abdication issue, 16–19, 53; Kadet policies of, 25–27 passim; on the revolution, 30; on the war, 153–54; imprisoned, 174

Novaia Rech', *(New Speech)* 36*n*7

Novaia Zhizn' (New Life), 66 and *n*41, 94, 171

Novoe Vremia (New Times), 107 and *n*87

Obolenskii, Vladimir Andreevich, Prince, 165 and *n*19

October manifesto. *See* Nicholas II

Octobrist party, 22*n*22, 97*n*77, 174 and *n*24

Office of Petitions, 137

O'Grady, James, 117*n*101

Okopnaia Pravda (Trench Truth), 119 and *n*104

Ol'denburg, S. F., 92 and *n*68, 100

Onu, A. M., 60

Oral Oblast' Soviet, 71*

Orlov-Davydov, Aleksei A., Count, 45 and *n*18

Otrep'ev, Grishka, 14

Palace Square, 130

Panina, Sofia Vladimirovna, Countess, 162, 163*n*15, 165, 167, 176, 177

Paris: Kadet politics in, 6, 7, 22*n*22, 25–26

Party of People's Freedom. *See* Kadet party

Peasants' Union, 163 and *n*16

Peshekhonov, Aleksei Vasil'evich, 39*n*10, 79 and *n*59, 151, 157*n*2

Peter and Paul Fortress, 162, 167

Peterhof, 167

Petersburg, 15*n*6; garrison in, 15, 113, 119, 120, 140; February crisis turmoil in, 39–44, 47, 52; growth of anarchy in, 83–84; army deputations in 137, 140; response to April crisis in, 145; July crisis atmosphere in, 146–49; October crisis atmosphere in, 159–61, 176

Peter the Great, 22*n*21

Peter II, 42*n*16, 90*n*67

Peter III, 42*n*16

Petrograd, 15*n*6

Petrunkevich, Ivan Il'ich, 36 and *n*8, 62

Philharmonia Hall (Berlin), 8

Polivanov, Aleksei, A., 109 and *n*93

Polkovnikov, Georgii Petrovich, Colonel, 156 and *n*11, 158

Popular Socialists, 157 and *n*12

Pravda (Truth), 119*n*104, 144 and *n*1

Pravo (Law), 4, 5, 66

Preobrazhenskii Regiment. *See* Army

Pre-parliament. *See* Provisional Council of the Russian Republic

Procurator-Generalship, 22*n*21

Progressive bloc, 5, 22*n*22, 174*n*22

Progressive Nationalists, 174*n*24

Protopopov, Aleksandr Dmitrievich, 39 and *n*11

Protopopov, D. D., 82 and *n*63

Provisional Council of the Russian Republic: establishment of and membership in, 26 and *n*28, 80*n*60, 131–33, 151–52; Bolsheviks withdraw from, 80*n*60, 150–51; Military Affairs Commission, 96, 155; aim of, 149–50; Council of Elders (*Sen'oren konvent*), 151 and *n*6, 159; and Verkhovskii, 152, 155; and Kerensky, 156; weakness of, 157; disorganization of, 158–62 passim

Provisional Government, 6, 15n4 and n5; Juridical Conference and Council, 1, 28 and n31, 138; Council of Ministers, 15 and n3, 16, 20; and abdication issue, 17–20, 27–28, 47–49, 54–55; power crisis in, 22; reactions to, 23–24; end of, 30, 94, 98; given ultimatum, 33; foreign policy of, 33, 34, 95; threat to, 34; and April crisis, 34 and n4, 123*, 124, 145; martyrdom of, 34–35; army's relations with, 42, 86, 137–41; Turkestan Committee, 42n15; Provisional Committee, 48n26; sessions of, 59, 72–73, 84, 86; and retirement issue, 61–86; provincial governments, 63; and police issue, 63, 83; power manifesto of, 68–69; and Nicholas, 70–72; triumvirate in, 94; Liberty Loan, 94 and n72; Land Committees, 104 and n85; split in, 113; declares on aims of war, 115–16; impotent, 119; and electoral laws issue, 135–37, 166–77; and July crisis, 145–49; Directory, 149 and n3; Third Coalition, 149 and n3. *See also* Provisional Council of the Russian Republic; Socialism; Soviet Workers' and Soldiers' Deputies

Pulkovo, 164n18

Purishkevich, Vladimir Mitrofanovich, 65n38

Pushkin, 70n48

Putiatin, M. S., Prince, 18n14

Putiatin, Princess, 18, 47, 53

Putilov, A. S., 60–61

Rappallo treaty (*1922*), 7

Rasputin, Grigorii Efimovich, 52 and n28, 109 and n95

Rech' (*Speech*), 4, 5, 36 and n7, 38, 69, 107, 113

Rennenkampf, Pavel Karlovich, General, 107 and n89

Revolution of *1905*, 3, 17n12, 34 and n3

Revolution of *1917*, 23, 27; February crisis, 6, 10, 29, 30, 39–46; Miliukov's concept of, 24, 56–57; Nol'de on, 30; Nabokov on, 33, 86–87, 113, 118, 140

Riga, 119n104

Rodichev, Fedor Izmailovich, 38 and n9, 75, 102, 109

Rodzianko, Mikhail Vladimirovich, 19–20 and n16, 53–54, 85, 94, 97, 112, 153, 154

Rolland, Romain, 111 and n97

Romanovs: branches of, 42 and n16; emblem of, 47n25

Rosenberg, Alfred, 8

Rukavishnikova, Elena Ivanova. *See* Nabokov, Elena

Rul' (*Rudder*), 7

Rumania, 111

Russian Academic Group, 108n90

Russian Orthodox Church, 90n67

St. Petersburg. *See* Petersburg

Salamander Society, 167

Sanders, William S., 117n101

Savich, Nikanor Vasil'evich, 97 and n77, 153, 154

"Sealed car" theme, 119

Second Congress of Soviets. *See* Soviet of Workers' and Soldiers' Deputies

Second International Workingmen's Association, 25 and n24

Semirichensk province, 42n15

Senate: First Department, 22, 67, 133; power of, 22n21; and Bolsheviks, 64

Sen'oren konvent. See Provisional Council of the Russian Republic

Shcheglovitov, Ivan Grigor'evich, 108 and n92

Shchepkin, D. M., 83 and n64

Shcherbatov, N. B., Prince, 109 and n93

Shingarev, Andrei Ivanovich, 17, 38, 44, 74, 75, 86, 100, 121; biographical note

on, 17*n*11; Nabokov on, 101–05; in
October crisis, 147, 155, 165, 166,
176; resigns, 147*; and Verkhovskii,
154
Shnitnikov, N. N., 69–70
Shreider, Grigorii Il'ich, 163 and *n*17,
164, 176, 177
Shul'gin, Vasilli Vital'evich, 45; bio-
graphical note on, 18*n*15; and abdica-
tion issue, 18–19, 48, 50, 53, 54
Shuvaev, D. S., General, 109 and *n*94
Simferopol, 6, 177
Skobelev, Matvei Ivanovich, 24–25 and
*n*23, 125, 128–29, 132, 150
Smirnov, Sergei A., 131 and *n*110, 149
Smol'nyi, 30 and *n*33, 173–74
Social Democrat Internationalists, 66*n*41
Social Democratic Workers party, 158
and *n*13
Socialism: in Provisional Government,
6–7, 24–25, 34*n*4, 123–29, 149 and
*n*3; and Kerensky, 45*n*20, 75*n*54, 106,
117; Trudovik (Toilers) faction,
75*n*54; Zimmerwaldism, 75*n*55, 106,
112, 149, 150*n*4; and Tereshchenko,
94; and Kornilov, 95; Swamp, 104
and *n*84, 151 and *n*5; French and
English, 117*n*101; and Miliukov, 121;
in Council of the Russian Republic,
149–51. *See also* Soviet of Workers'
and Soldiers' Deputies
Socialist Revolutionary party, 125*n*106,
158 and *n*13
Sokolov, Nicholai Dmitrievich, 26 and
*n*27, 133–34, 152
Soviet of *1905,* 16*n*7
Soviet of People's Commissars, 170–73
passim and *n*22
Soviet of Workers' and Soldiers' Deputies, 15*n*4, 21 and *n*19, 30*n*33; in
Provisional Government, 16, 118, 139
and *n*115; organized, 16*n*7; Executive
Committee's relations with govern-

ment, 35, 45, 71, 78, 113, 121,
128–30, 135, 144; Presidium of Executive Committee, 45 and *n*19; and
Kerensky, 45*n*20, 78; Contact or
Liaison Commission's relations with
government, 73 and *n*52, 78, 115,
125–27; and July war offensive,
78*n*57; and Liberty Loan, 94*n*72;
Soviet of People's Commissars established by Second Congress of, 170*n*22
Soviet Union: domestic and foreign
policies of, 7; executive branch of,
170*n*22
Sovnarkom, 171 and *
Spelling Reform, 100 and *n*80
Stakhovich, Mikhail Aleksandrovich, 46
and *n*23, 58, 97, 153
Stalin, Joseph V., 52*n*29, 144*n*1
Staraia Russa, 37, 108
State Council, 137; power of, 17; mem-
bership of, 17*n*12; established, 22*n*21;
and retirement issue, 64–67
Stavka, 70 and *n*46, 71
Steklov-Nakhamkes, Iurii Mikhailovich,
21 and *n*18, 22, 78–79, 115, 125–28,
144, 171
Stepanov, Vasilii Aleksandrovich, 162,
163*n*15
Struve, Peter Bernardovich, 46 and *n*22,
97, 153
Stürmer, Boris Vladimirovich, 86 and
*n*66, 109, 110
Sukhanov-Gimmer, Nikolai Nikolae-
vich, 94 and *n*73, 125, 128
Sukhomlinov, Vladimir Aleksandrovich,
108 and *n*92
Supreme Court of Appeals, 22*n*21
Suvorin, A. S., 107*n*87
Sveaborg, 16
Svobodnaia Rech' (*Free Speech*), 36*n*7

Taganstev, Nikolai Stepanovich, 64 and
*n*37, 65, 67

Taneev, A. S., 66
Tauride Palace, 21; sessions held in, 15 and n4, 48n26, 57, 82, 139, 173; in February crisis, 43–44; in October crisis, 176
Teachers' Congress, 99
Teliakovskii, Mr., 74
Tenishev School, 166–67
Tereshchenko, Mikhail Ivanovich, 16, 27, 44, 57, 153; biographical note on, 16n10; Nabokov on, 74, 93–96; and Socialists, 95; and Verkhovskii, 96, 155; Miliukov on, 121; in October crisis, 162, 168
Terroristic Organization, 158n13
Third Coalition. See Provisional Government
Thomas, Albert, 22 and n20, 117n101, 121, 123
Thorne, Will, 117n101
Tobol'sk, 72 and n51
Toilers. See Socialism
Transcaspian province, 42n15
Treaties of 1917, secret, 92 and n70, 114
Trepov, D. F., General, 4
Tret'iakov, Sergei Nikolaevich, 97 and n77, 131, 149, 153, 155, 162
Trotsky, Leon, 1, 35, 52n29, 80n60
Trubetskoi, Grigorii Nikolaevich, Prince, 26 and n29, 97, 153
Tsarskoe Selo, 18n14, 70–72 passim and n47, 48
Tseretelli, Irakli Georgievich, 79, 115, 125, 126, 149, 150; "Reminiscences of the February Revolution," 34n4 biographical note on, 79n59; Nabokov on, 130–33
Turkestan Committee. See Provisional Government
Turkestan Krai, 42n15

Union of Liberation, 22n22, 159n14
Union of Michael the Archangel, 65n38
Union of October 17. See Octobrist party

Union of Russian People, 65n38
United States. See America
University of Berlin, 108n90
University of Moscow, 99n78
University of St. Petersburg, 2
Uritskii, Moisei Solomonovich, 176–77 and n28
Urusov, S. D., Prince, 83 and n64

Vandervelde, Emile, 117n101
Vek (The Century), 36n7
Verkhovskii, Aleksandr Ivanovich, General, 96 and n76, 152–55
Vershinin, V. M., 70 and n47
Vestnik Partii Narodnoi Svobody (Herald of the Party of People's Freedom), 22n22
Vestnik Vremmenago Pravitel'stva (Herald of the Provisional Government), 15 and n5, 86
Vinaver, Maksim Moiseevich, 25–26 and n25, 56, 69, 155, 165; "To the Jewish People," 69
Vishniak, Mark Veniaminovich, 151 and n9, 174
Voinov. See Lunacharskii, Anatoli Vasil'evich
Volunteer Army. See Army
Vraskii, Mr., 134
Vyborg, 4, 15, 37, 81–82

War Industries Committees, 22n22, 93 and n71
Wilson, Woodrow, 116
Winter Palace, 69n45, 78, 132; Malachite Hall sessions, 35, 69, 161

Zemskii sobor. See All-Russian Council of the Land
Zemstvo and Municipal Officials Congress (1904–05), 3, 61 and n35
Zemstvo Constitutionalists, 22n22
Zemstvos, 61n35, 63
Zimmerwaldism. See Socialism